Bernard Fitzwalter's
Astro-Compatibility Guide

Bernard Fitzwalter's
Astro-Compatibility Guide

ZAMBEZI PUBLISHING LTD

Published in 2010 by
Zambezi Publishing Ltd
P.O. Box 221 Plymouth, Devon PL2 2YJ (UK)
web: www.zampub.com email: info@zampub.com

British Library Cataloguing-in-Publication Data:
A catalogue record for this book is available from
the British Library

Typeset by Zambezi Publishing Ltd, Plymouth UK
Printed and bound in the UK by Lightning Source (UK) Ltd
ISBN-13: 978-1-903065-71-6

About the Author

Bernard Fitzwalter's interest in astrology was sparked at the tender age of six, when he played King Herod's astrologer in his primary school nativity play. He has taught astrology for over twenty-five years, both in adult education classes, and at many astrological organisations.

He has twice been President of the Astrological Lodge of London, and for the past ten years, he has been a tutor for the Faculty of Astrological Studies. His horoscope columns are published worldwide.

Contents

Zodiac Relationships

You might think that relationships between two people, described in terms of their zodiac signs, come in 144 varieties; that is, twelve possible partners for each of the twelve signs. Not so. The whole business is a lot simpler than that, because there are only seven varieties of relationship; of course, each of those has two people in it, and the role you play depends on which end of the relationship you're at.

You may well have read before about how you're supposed to be suited to one particular sign or another. The truth is usually different. Librans are supposed to get on with Geminis and Aquarians, and they do for the most part, but it's no use reading that if you're a Libran who has always found yourself attracted to Taurus, is it? There has to be a reason why you keep finding Taureans attractive, and it's not always to do with your Sun sign, because other factors in your horoscope will have a lot to do with it. You prefer people of certain signs as friends or partners because the relationship between your two signs produces the sort of qualities you're looking for, and the sort of behavior you find satisfactory. When you've identified the seven types of basic relationship, and discovered the one that you'd most like to have, you'll soon be able to see which signs will produce that for you. Once you've found the sign that fits your current mood best, read about it in the individual compatibility sections.

Look at the following diagram; use your own sign as a starting point and see how far away your partner's Sun sign is. For instance, if you're a Leo and your lover is a Capricorn, your partner's sign is five signs in front of you. You're five signs behind your partner, which is also important, as you'll see in a little while.

ARIES	Outgoing	Physical	Fire	Cardinal	♈
TAURUS	Collecting	Physical	Earth	Fixed	♉
GEMINI	Outgoing	Mental	Air	Mutable	♊
CANCER	Collecting	Mental	Water	Cardinal	♋
LEO	Outgoing	Physical	Fire	Fixed	♌
VIRGO	Collecting	Physical	Earth	Mutable	♍
LIBRA	Outgoing	Mental	Air	Cardinal	♎
SCORPIO	Collecting	Mental	Water	Fixed	♏
SAGITTARIUS	Outgoing	Physical	Fire	Mutable	♐
CAPRICORN	Collecting	Physical	Earth	Cardinal	♑
AQUARIUS	Outgoing	Mental	Air	Fixed	♒
PISCES	Collecting	Mental	Water	Mutable	♓

If Both Partners Share the Same Sign

Somebody who is of the same sign as you is similar to you, and he or she tries to achieve the same results. If your goals permit two winners, this is fine, but if only one of you can be on top, you'll argue. No matter how temperamental, stubborn, devious or critical you can be, your partner can be the same, and it may not be possible for you to take the same kind of punishment you hand out to others. In addition, he or she will display every quality that really annoys you about yourself, so that you're constantly reminded of it in yourself as well as in your lover. Essentially, you're fighting for the same space, so the amount of tolerance you have is the determining factor in the survival of this relationship.

One Sign Apart

Someone who is one sign forward from you acts as an environment for you to grow in. In time, you'll take on those qualities yourself. When you have new ideas, your partner can often provide the encouragement to put them into practice, and he or she seems to have all your requirements easily available. Often, you feel that your partner already knows about the pitfalls that you're struggling to deal with, and this can be annoying, because your lover always seems to be one step ahead of you. He or she seems to be able to do those things that you sweat to achieve, without apparently having to make any effort. If the relationship works well, the partner is helpful to you, but there can be bitterness and jealousy if it doesn't.

Someone one sign back from you can act as a retreat from the pressures of the world. They seem to understand your particular needs for rest and recovery, whatever they may be, and they can usually provide them. They can hold and understand your innermost secrets and fears. Indeed, their mind works best with the things you fear most, and the fact that they can handle these so easily is a great help to you. If the relationship is going through a bad patch, their role as controller of your fears becomes worrying, and you'll feel unnerved in their presence, as though they were in control of you. When things are good, you feel secure with them behind you.

Two Signs Apart

Someone two signs forward from you acts like a brother or sister. They are great friends, and you feel like equals in each other's company. There's no hint of the parent-child or master-servant relationship. They encourage you to talk, even if you're reticent in most other company, and the most frequently heard description of these relationships is "We make each other laugh". Such a partner can always help you put into words the things that you want to say, and is there to help you say them. This is the relationship that teenagers enjoy with their best friend. There is love, but it may not take a sexual form, because both partners know that it would spoil the relationship by adding an element of unnecessary depth and weight.

Someone two signs behind you makes a good friend and companion, but not as intimate as somebody two signs forward. This is the sort of person you love to meet socially, because they are reliable and honest, but not so close to you that life becomes suffocating or intense. They prevent you from getting too serious about life, and they turn your thoughts outwards instead of inwards, involving you with other people. They stop you from being too selfish, and help you give the best of yourself to others. This relationship has a cool and a warm end; the leading sign feels much closer to his partner than the trailing sign does, but they are both satisfied by the relationship. They particularly value its chatty quality, the fact that it works even better when in a group, and its tone of affection and endearment rather than passion and obsession.

Three Signs Apart

Someone three signs in front of you represents a challenge of some kind or another. The energies of the pair of you can never run parallel, and so must meet at some time or another. Not head on, but across each other, and out of this you can both make something strong and well established which will serve the two of you as a firm base for the future. You'll be surprised to find how fiercely this person will fight on your behalf or for your protection. You may not think you need it, and you'll be surprised that anybody would think of doing it, but it is so nonetheless.

Someone three signs behind you is also a challenge, and for the same reasons as stated above. From this end of the relationship, the person will help you achieve the very best you're capable of in a material sense. They will see to it that you receive all the credit that's due to you for your efforts, and that everyone thinks well of you. Your reputation is their business, and they will do things with it that you could never manage yourself. It's like having your own public relations team. This relationship works hard, gets results and makes sure the world knows it. It also looks after itself, but it does require effort on both your parts.

Four Signs Apart

Someone four signs forward from you is compatible with you. They represent all the things you wanted to be, however daring, witty, sexy or whatever they already are, and you can watch them doing it. They can help you to be these things. They do things that you think are risky and they seem to get away with them. These people represent the things you aim towards, or they seem to have a way of life that you'd like to have, and it doesn't seem to worry them that things might go wrong. There are things that they do that would make you lie awake at night worrying, but they accept these things with a child's trust, and those things never go wrong for them. You wish you could be like that.

Someone four signs behind you becomes an inspiration to you. All the things you wish you knew, they know already. They seem so wise and experienced, and you feel such an amateur. Luckily, they are kind and caring teachers. They are convincing, too. When they speak, you listen and believe. It's nice to know there's somebody there with all the answers. This extraordinary relationship often functions as a mutual admiration society, with each end wishing it could be more like the other. Sadly, it's far less productive than the three-sign separation, and much of its promise remains unfulfilled. Laziness is one of the inherent qualities of a four-sign separation, because all its needs are fulfilled, and it rarely looks outside itself for something new to do.

Five Signs Apart

Someone five signs ahead of you is your technique. You know what you want to do and this person knows how to do it. He can find ways for you to do what you want to be involved in, and he can watch you while you learn and correct your mistakes. This partner knows the right way to go about things, and he or she has the clarity of thought and analytical approach necessary if you're to get things clear in your mind before you get started.

Someone five signs behind you is your resource. Whenever you run out of impetus or energy, they step forward and support you. When you're broke, this lover lends you money, and he or she seldom wants it returned. When you need a steadying hand because you think you've over-reached yourself, they provide it. They do this because they know that it's in their best interest as well as yours to help you do things, and to provide the material for you to work with. You can always rely on this lover for help, and it's nice to know that he or she will always be there. They can't use all their talent on their own; they need you to show them how it should be done. Between you, you'll fully and effectively use all that you both have to offer, but it's a relationship of cooperation and giving, though not all the zodiac signs can make it work well enough.

Six Signs Apart

Someone six signs apart from you, either forwards or backwards, is both opponent and partner at the same time. You're both essentially concerned with the same area of life and you share the same priorities. Yet, you both approach your common interests from opposite directions and hope to use them in opposite ways. Where one is private, the other is public, and where one is self-centered, the other shares himself cheerfully. The failings in your own make-up are complemented by the strengths in the other. It's as if, between you, you make one whole person with a complete set of talents and capabilities. The problem with this partnership is that your complementary talents focus the pair of you on a single area of life, and this makes for a narrow outlook and a lack of flexibility in your response to changes. If the two of you are seeing everything in terms of career or property or personal freedom or whatever, then you'll have no way to deal effectively with a situation which can't be dealt with in those terms. Life becomes like a seesaw, so it alternates as to which end is up or down, and can sometimes stay in balance, but it can't swing round to face another way, and it's fixed to the ground so that it does not move.

****

These seven types are the only combinations available, and all partnerships can be described as one of the seven types. However, some of the roles are almost impossible to fulfil, due to the essential energies or natures of the signs involved, which derive from the planets that underpin them. As you go through this book, you will discover how the signs and their associated planets interact. These effects can make relationships heaven or hell.

****

Something else to remember when reading this book is that we live in changing times; besides the discovery of Chiron, many new dwarf planets (or planettes) have recently been discovered, and even Pluto has now been downgraded to "planette" status. It will take some time to assimilate properly and accurately all this new data into the various systems of astrology currently in use. Therefore, this book uses only the traditional seven visible planets for purposes of interpretation; they have proved very accurate ever since the birth of astrology, and for the general viewpoint of sun sign astrology, you can see for yourself how accurate these interpretations are.

The Approach to Relationships: Aries

Symbol:	The Ram	♈	Element:	Fire
Planet:	Mars	♂	Quality:	Cardinal

An Arian is wholly motivated by his need to experience things first-hand, as a result of his own actions and decisions. He's entirely self-motivating, self-sustaining, and self-centered. Most people read the words self-centered as if they mean "selfish", but that's not the case here. In this case, self-centered means centered on the self rather than being centered on any ambition, possession, political persuasion, religion, friend, relative, or circumstance, Just on the self. It will seem obvious to you, as an Arian reading this, that your self matters most, and it's very difficult for you to imagine anybody thinking any other way. However, only Arians and people of other signs born with Mars in important positions on the birth chart think this way, and the vast majority of humanity does not.

When you enter a relationship, therefore, you're seeking to express yourself physically to the other person, and to experience their response to you. You want to experience the excitement of being in love or of having a new partner, and you want them to excite you with their response.

Aries - Aries

Like most of the relationships formed by two people of the same sign, this will tend to show just how similar you are, but it also brings the sides of yourself that you dislike into view. Mars is the guiding principle here, and it's not in his nature to give ground or assimilate another point of view. An Arian has to push forward the whole time, and the problem will be making sure that the two of you are in fact pushing in the same direction, because otherwise there will inevitably be stress that will lead to friction and arguments. As long as you're interested in the same things, there will be no problems. Progress will be rapid because you have twice the motive power available, and because you'll fuel each other's enthusiasm while your interests are the same.

The weak point in all this is that neither of you is interested in the relationship itself, so you won't do anything for the sake of the relationship alone. You never do anything that's of no actual interest or profit to you personally, and in this case, this applies to both of you. Another problem area is that an Arian gets frustrated at lack of progress. He has no patience at all, and he will be particularly annoyed if he sees his partner doing just what he wants to do, and doing it first. When someone thwarts him by being impatient, headstrong, imprudent or just downright selfish, then that doubles his displeasure. Another Arian displaying the usual Aries "me first" attitude right in front of his face does nothing for an Arian's temper. Luckily, both of you will forget the incident and move on to something else very quickly, so you may take comfort from the thought that disagreements between Arians are of short duration, with neither side holding grudges for long.

This double helping of Martian energy, with its tendency to extremes of enthusiasm and dislike, makes for a lively friendship that's likely to be punctuated by frequent arguments. As a basis for a love affair, the same thing applies: the passions will be intense, and to some extent feed off each other to give an even greater intensity; quarrels will be violent and quick to flare, but quick to cool again also. As time progresses with such a pairing, the intensity does not diminish, but the time scale extends somewhat; arguments take longer to arrive and to fade away, but the passion and intensity of both the arguments and the good times in between remain undiminished.

As a business partnership, Aries - Aries needs careful channelling; for best effect, indeed for any progress to be made at all, you must split the tasks between you, and each devote his full attention to his own tasks. Authority within your own appointed areas must be absolute, and on no account should you attempt to interfere in any way with your partner's side of things. If this partitioning is not adhered to, your energies will hinder and oppose each other, and the resulting arguments are wasteful of time and energy for the business, which sadly, neither of you can actually see as an entity in itself.

Aries - Taurus

On the face of it, this is probably the hardest of all the zodiacal partnerships to envisage. Your intensity and eagerness is completely at odds with the patient qualities of the Taurean. Venus looks after Taurus, which means that the underlying quality is one of stability and comfort; the Arian's Mars qualities demand new experiences and sometimes danger and hardship, and these energies have nothing in common with those of Venus. This seems hard enough, but the animosity is deeper still, because the signs follow on from one another in the zodiacal sequence.

You're always striving to make something of yourself. You want to be the one to discover, develop, and use something first so that you can truly say that it's your very own thing, and that nobody else thought of it before you. What you do when this is achieved? You fear that you may be forced to settle down and look to your responsibilities, and to endure that your projects become mature and established. Although this is the right way for things to develop, you're afraid that you'll become boring, and never know the thrill of starting something new again. The eternally forward-looking, childlike Aries doesn't like growing up any faster than he has to, and he will avoid the whole process if he possibly can.

The same process applies to Taurus in reverse. It's part of Taurus to value the ground he stands on. Think of a bull in a field continually defining and guarding his territory. A Taurus considers that he must conserve all that he owns and that it's his duty to look after it. This means that a Taurus's "territory" keeps getting bigger throughout his life, and he becomes less and less inclined to give any of it up. The idea of an Arian trampling all over it, changing it, trying to do something new and original with it or worst of all, throwing it away to concentrate on something completely new, horrifies him. The Taurean has already been through the energetic process of acquisition, and he prefers the steady state of being in possession. Because Arian energies are part of his past, he finds them irritating and clichéd, which in turn enrages the Arian, to whom they are new and vivid, and who would like them appreciated as such.

If the friendship between these two is not intellectual, then the relationship must eventually become a series of battles, where the Aries temper and desire to win cause the Taurean to dig his hooves in even deeper, refusing to move. Eventually the Taurean's anger will explode, and the force of it will flatten even the Arian for a while. This sort of thing is dangerous for both of them. The Taurean's flat refusal to change will frustrate the Arian even more, and the partnership is unlikely to develop.

With a little thought though, a working agreement can be found, which will work well both in business and on a personal level. What needs to be achieved first is an understanding of each other's needs. After that, things are best arranged so that the Arian does the active work and deals with anything new and energetic, while the Taurean does the maintenance and the support duties for the team as a unit. In this way, the Arian is spared the repetition and the inactive periods that he so hates, and the Taurean has plenty to look after and consider his own.

You must remember that the Taurean is possessive of you as well, and he will be extremely jealous if you show any interest in another person. The Taurean must remember that Arians need to move around a bit to be at their best.

Aries - Gemini

Aries and Gemini were made for each other, because your need for action is matched by the Gemini need for novelty and stimulus. You'll find that the Gemini is much faster mentally than you are, and that he's ready to move on to new challenges and new concepts almost as soon he has arrived at them. You find all this stimulating, and relish being forced to keep up. You hope that it's all as honest as it seems to be, because you have a sneaking suspicion that the Gemini might be presenting things to you the wrong way round just for the fun of it, and you might not be quick enough to see through the deception. The trouble here is that Aries is a straightforward sort of sign, and it lacks the subtlety of intellect required to play with words and ideas, to conjure fantasies from nowhere, and to make clever lies that live alongside the truth, unable to be distinguished from it. Gemini, on the other hand, is almost pure intellect. Everything is examined for its mental rather than physical qualities. Gemini turns everything this way and that to see if it has anything interesting to offer when looked at from a different point of view. Duplicity is easy for them. A Gemini is not fundamentally dishonest, but he loves arguments for their own sake, and he loves all forms of trickery. You won't tire him out, nor he you. You have much greater physical capabilities than he does and much more sheer strength, but his speed of reaction is phenomenal, and he uses himself much more sparingly. He does with reflexes what you do with muscle.

As a friendship, there's little to fault the pairing of these two signs, but love might not work for you. There's no lack of sexual compatibility. Both of you enjoy physical activity, and you'll get extra pleasure from the laughter that the Gemini will bring. The trouble starts when the Arian falls in love; your simple and direct passion, when honestly and earnestly expressed, will amuse the Gemini, and he will lose interest and start to turn to something else. This isn't rejection, it's just that earnestness is too serious for the Gemini mind, and the fun is taken out of anything for him when seriousness starts to creep in. He needs variety, and by the time you start to get serious about things, the relationship will have been going for a while and he will be bored and looking for a change. If you can put up with his lightweight response and his refusal to be committed, then things can continue almost indefinitely. He can provide you with a seemingly endless series of ideas and new projects and you can explore them together. Just keep it light, and keep it moving.

In many ways, this one works best if kept at the level of two very close friends. You'll never really understand or appreciate what goes on inside the Gemini's head, and he will never believe what deep satisfaction you get out of using yourself physically, testing your own limits, doing something that nobody else has ever done, and experiencing it for yourself at first-hand. He would think such a notion absurdly over-dramatic and inflated, and he prefers not to think of you, his best friend, in such terms. Therefore, you must stay side by side, moving in parallel, enjoying each other's company, and taking individual pleasures in different ways from the experiences you share. Kept like that, and kept light and active, the relationship is nearly perfect.

Aries - Cancer

This one seems the most unlikely partnership possible, but it can be surprisingly productive if approached in the right way, and the feature that surprises most of all is its strength. Both of you have the Sun in

Cardinal signs, and this means that you both think that if you don't do things for yourself, then they won't happen. You share the ability to get things done, and you recognize and respect it in each other. You realize that you're both directing your energies in very different directions, but that these directions are not necessarily opposite. The Arian is keen to find things out for himself by direct action, while the Cancerian does not feel the need for this, but he's very concerned that he's in control of all the things around him.

Cancerians don't just put down roots; they actively dig foundations. They want to look after things, but that means looking after them their way, and making sure that the creative and directing energy to achieve that comes from them and them alone. As an Aries, you appreciate this directing energy, while your Cancer partner appreciates the personal drive, energy and confidence that you have in your own abilities. This simple mutual appreciation of forcefulness is probably enough to turn an acquaintance into an affair. After all, the Arian can only show his admiration for the other's energies by physical demonstration, because he doesn't work any other way, and the Cancerian can't but be flattered that someone as certain in his opinions as an Aries directs his energies in a way that recognizes the similar qualities that you share.

The problem then becomes one of timing. Cancer has a much longer view than Aries, and is likely to be considering the affair as the preliminary groundwork for a much more lasting partnership. Marriage is always a possibility, if not a necessary condition, in a Cancerian relationship. There's an element of protection and security built in to the notion of marriage, and a Cancer feels that this will help to fight any future events that involve change and the unexpected, which would stop things being the way he wanted them. As an Aries, you feel that this over-reliance on security is a silly idea, and fail to give it the importance that it has to your partner. You may also feel that marriage is not a goal worth aiming for in your case. That doesn't mean that it isn't what other people go into relationships for, though.

What you'll realize is that Cancer will look after all those areas of your life that you can't be bothered with, and this can keep you on a firm footing, without making you feel restricted. Your Cancerian lover will look after your home and guard your interests in exactly the manner that you like, and you appreciate the energy and confidence in his approach to domestic matters. In return, you can give him the appreciation he deserves, and you can be his public representative, using your personality and flair to do the jobs that your partner's natural reserve prevents him from doing. You can be his public face and he will be right behind you, making sure that everything is under control and looked after.

The nature of this relationship is that you fight on each other's behalf, and do the work for each other that you can't do yourselves. There are bound to be arguments, since you both like doing things in your own way, but they will pass quickly. As a marriage, it won't be easy, but it will be strong, and it will be very productive.

Aries - Leo

The union of two signs of similar element, such as the two Fire signs in this case, is usually taken to be a good thing. This is no exception, though there are one or two problems caused by your being too similar. Both of you need to be number one. For you as an Arian, the emphasis is on doing things for yourself and excelling at what you do, but the Leo sees things a different way. For him, the emphasis is on being seen as leader, being recognized as the natural center of things, to whom people turn for reassurance and warmth. You're not likely to give a Leo the sort of respect he thinks he deserves when you think that you can do something better, as this will undermine his position. If, on the other hand, there's something that you know you can't do better, you should therefore look to Leo for advice. Sadly, then you'll view him as a rival and you'll be forced to compete with him until you eventually surpass him. You see yourself as a natural leader, and you think your place is in front.

If you can see that you're essentially similar in outlook, you can get along very well indeed. You're both active, in that you prefer to do things yourselves rather than be passive and wait for things to happen. You're both essentially outward looking and optimistic, believing that things can and probably will improve. You both have a lively sense of humor, with the Arian probably the sharper of the two, and you're both capable of giving out enough energy to inspire and help others who aren't able to make it on their own.

Where you differ most is that you need to create your own territory, to go where others haven't been before and claim it for yourself, whereas the Leo is much happier to find himself in an existing situation and put his energies into it from the inside. Eventually he becomes the central figure wherever he is, and becomes responsible for the general morale and social life of the group. It isn't important for the Leo to be seen doing the impossible or proving that he's the best; what is important is that he be recognized as such, and given the respect due to his position.

Provided that neither of you trespass on the other's territory, your bright and radiant personalities will attract each other without much effort, and an affair could easily grow. This will be conducted with all the heat that Fire signs usually generate, and the warmth of the affection will be visible to outsiders, though it won't seem especially passionate to you, since you do everything with that sort of intensity. Emotions will be easily expressed in a simple manner, because both of you are surprisingly unsophisticated in your emotional requirements. You're both easily hurt, and you'll show that you're hurt. Hurts come because you both want your own way at once, and one of you has been forced to take second place.

If you can learn to take second place occasionally, perhaps by taking turns, then a warm and lasting marriage is possible. You can be very good for each other, with the Arian learning the pleasure of giving to others, and the Leo learning that responding to challenges doesn't necessarily mean loss of prestige.

Aries - Virgo

In all relationships where the two Sun signs are five signs separated, there's an element of adjustment that's needed, so for the two people to work at all well together, they must be prepared to modify their usual point of view, because in this case, there's little if any common ground between them.

You're too forceful and immediate for Virgo. As an Arian, you'll find that Virgo's willingness (or preference) to do the same things repeatedly until familiarity is exceeded will drive you to distraction. It's enough for you to do something and get it right, it's often sufficient just to do it and get some sort of a successful outcome. Not so the Virgo. He likes to master the manner of doing things as much as he likes getting a result. Technique is important to him. Each time a Virgo does something, it's not the same as before. He modifies his way of doing it, learns from it, understands more about the processes involved, and analyses all this in a way that's quite alien to the Arian way of thought.

If you have common interests, then you can approach them from your separate directions, and progress through each other's talents. You can be the driving force and he can be the technique. You use his knowledge and skill, while you supply the enthusiasm and motivation. Seen from the other point of view, the Virgo finds that he's saved from getting bogged down in small detail, and rescued from those times when he can't provide the impetus to move forwards, by your eagerness to get things moving, and your general vitality. There's always power and stamina on hand in the Aries character, and the Virgoan is grateful for it.

A Virgoan is careful, and he needs time to analyze a new idea before he commits himself to it, while your way of throwing yourself into something just because you feel good about it will meet with a less than equal response. You must be ready for this if you find yourself emotionally involved with Virgo. It's not that they don't respond, just that they need convincing that the affair is going to be the sort of thing that they'd like. They can take quite a bit of convincing at times, and are not to be won over by five minutes of impassioned protestation.

As business partners, they can be wonderful, provided that both of you adapt your working style to take the other's strengths into account. Virgoans can think of all the possibilities inherent in a business stratagem and utilize your energies to make them work. If you accuse the Virgo of being too meticulous, then you're throwing away his analytical talents, and exposing the pair of you to the sort of oversights that you yourself make through haste and over-eagerness. He must learn to make decisions in a once-and-for-all manner, and be prepared to take a few risks. If he doesn't, he loses all the advantages of your speed and talent for effective action. You must both be prepared to do things the other's way some of the time, as then things will go very well.

As marriage partners, Virgoans are very careful about the family's diet and general state of health, whereas you tend to eat anything you can find when you're hungry. There will be times when Virgo seems to do things very slowly, but you must just accept this, just as Virgo has to accept your rapid changes of mind and impassioned outbursts when things don't turn out just the way you want. To the Virgo, this looks like sheer carelessness and lack of planning, but he will forgive you.

Aries - Libra

This pairing is based on the attraction of opposites. Briefly, everything you do or feel is done in the opposite way by the Libran, because his motivation is so opposite to yours. Librans are far less active than you are, and less decisive too. Where you want to do things for yourself and rarely consider what anybody else might want to do, the Libran is always ready to listen to alternative points of view, and is quite likely to be swayed by any of them. He would much rather do something in company than on his own, which means that he's likely to find himself doing what his friends suggest, rather than to be left out.

Your decisiveness will guide him easily. You decide what you want to do and the Libran will agree. The benefit to you is that you have a companion, and the benefit to him is that somebody is taking the decisions for him, so that he doesn't have to think too hard. Librans can become inactive and ineffective because they have an infinite capacity for putting things off, so having an Arian partner will cure this. Of course, you have to be prepared to push them into action some of the time, and if you don't want any of that, then perhaps this relationship is not for you.

The problem in this particular coupling of zodiacal types is that you're both concerned with personal issues. If that sounds strange, think how much the Taurean is concerned with what he owns or the Capricorn with his status, so that neither of them are bothered too much about themselves as people. You and the Libran are much more concerned with yourselves as people. You're concerned with your individuality and the Libran with being a partner to somebody. Therefore the relationship between you has to be built on your personal relationship, and can't rely on common interests such as children, shared careers, shared possessions and activities. You have to actually like each other. If the Libran feels that he isn't close enough to you, he will become remote and dejected. If you feel that he's a weight round your neck, then you get angry and feel that you can't be yourself on your own any more. As you can see, it's a tightrope existence, and you must both be very careful. All "opposite sign" relationships are like this, but yours is the only one that works at such a personal level.

In any relationship with a Libran, you'll feel that their heart isn't in it. How else, you reason, could they account for being so slow to respond? You see it from your own point of view, which is reasonable enough. The Libran wants to know how little things will be disrupted if he does something new, and how he can keep things as they have always been. He's willing to try things, especially if you think it's a good idea, but he needs time to think about it. He will try, but he will also want to ensure that there's very little disturbance of his usual routines. Once you realize that you will always be the one to make the moves, and who wants things to happen at once, all will be well. Once the Libran realizes that being active isn't likely to throw him off balance, and that when he's finished being active, he can sit down again in his favorite chair, things will be better yet.

Any long-term relationship such as a marriage or going into business together is bound to be something of a seesaw arrangement, alternating between furious activity and periods of quiet. More than anything else, you have to like each other if the undertaking is to be a success.

Aries - Scorpio

This is the sort of relationship you always promised yourself - somebody with the strength, drive, and pure sex appeal to give you a run for your money, test your strength and stamina, and completely fulfill you. The trouble is that it's not like that in real life. It can be, but there's always more than you see at first glance, and it's the "more" part that makes things difficult. The plain truth is that a Scorpio will give you more than you want.

You're both ruled by the planet Mars, and that's what gives both of you your limitless reserves of energy. All this energy needs physical expression, if not sexual expression, and for the Arian it seems as though everyone else in the Zodiac is a little dull and lifeless compared to the powerful pulse of Mars he himself enjoys. Scorpio is the other, indeed the only other zodiacal sign with Mars as the driving force. The difference between you is that while you're motivated by being Mars, expressing it as a physical force, the Scorpio is motivated by controlling Mars and using it as a powerful tool.

The Scorpio has none of your instinctive belief that nothing can go wrong because you can somehow be able to blaze your way through your difficulties with a touch of luck and some applied enthusiasm. For him, nothing goes wrong because he stays in control, and everything runs in the paths he chooses. The Martian energy is used to direct and control. He needs to know how things work, and what goes on in the background while nobody else is looking, and how he can stay on top of it all by pulling a few strings here and there. He's very emotional and his emotions run very deep, so most of them are below the surface, but he never stops thinking and never stops feeling things either, which most people forget. All the intensity of emotional response that's on your surface is also within him, but it's hidden. A chastening thought, isn't it?

Consequently, a love affair between you will be a very powerful thing, stronger than you can imagine. You can only imagine things on one level at a time, but the Scorpio has no limits. When a little trust has grown between you, some of his depths will become visible, but not all of them. You'll offer him your physical self. That is all you have to offer, and it's the part that means most to you, while he will match your strength. If you're very strong, he may withdraw a little, because to lose to you would entail loss of control, which he can't risk. There must always be a little bit left in reserve. He will control you (or try to) and he will be possessive, for to be otherwise would involve losing control. You may resent this, and fight him more fiercely than is good for either of you.

A Scorpio makes an admirable business partner, but you may not like the way he withholds information when it suits him, and the way in which things seem to be going on over your head. An open sort of business relationship where there are no secrets, is easier for you to grasp, and you feel happier there too, but you're unlikely to get this with a Scorpio. Still, Scorpios are very good indeed when it comes to making money grow.

Perhaps the passions and jealousies make this one a poor idea as a marriage partnership, and it will certainly be up and down for most of the time, but it can work well as an affair, I think.

Aries - Sagittarius

This is the last of the Fire-to-Fire groupings, and like the Leo partnership, you have a lot in common. This is the Fire sign with the greatest mental capabilities, and probably the greatest mental capabilities of all the twelve signs. Sagittarius is even brighter than the Gemini, and honest as well. The honesty of the Sagittarian, which shows itself to you as a bright kind of openness and optimism in speech, appeals to you. You can't help but like a person who says what he thinks, no sooner does he think it. He seems to have the same immediacy and delight in thought and speech as you have in action and movement, and he seems to get the same kind of pleasure from expressing it. All of this strikes you as very appealing, and you'll be pleased to know that you're right to find it so.

Sagittarians are very much a matter of "what you see is what you get" and they are almost incapable of deception. So much so that they are tactless, because they can't help telling it as they see it, and the honest truth spoken to someone's face often gives offence. Both you and the

Sagittarian find this funny, and the two of you will be more convinced than ever that you're perfectly suited.

Basically, you find Sagittarians inspirational. You'll wish, when you've got to know them for a little while, that you could have just a little of their intellect, and you'd gladly trade some of your ease of movement and strength for that. This is because they dazzle you to some extent with their brilliant wit, their capacity for learning and remembering things and their fantastic imagination. They show you all this with such confidence and ease that you're over-impressed. Truth to tell, they show all these things to anybody, but it's the confidence and energy that appeals to you, because they seem to be speaking in your own language. They are. It's the language of the Fire signs. Their tales sound terrifyingly risky to Cancerians and woefully unplanned to Virgoans, but to you they sound like high adventure.

Sagittarians are changeable creatures, so an idea only lasts as long as it takes for another to replace it. This is not so for you. Once you have an idea, you make it work and make a success of it and they find this very impressive. They appreciate your forcefulness, because they can never be anything for long. They love your self-assertive outlook, because it matches theirs, and they don't like dull company.

This changeable nature extends to their love affairs. It's not that they deliberately cheat, but if somebody else seems attractive and available, their curiosity means that they have to try it. They will be genuinely apologetic afterwards, and would never willingly cause you any anguish, but they just can't resist the lure of something new, and they are going to do it again, too, so be warned. You're likely to find this upsetting, not because you can't stand the competition, but because you can't stand the idea of being moved from the number one slot! They won't be able to see why you're so upset, which won't help at all. Whatever you do though, don't demand loyalty, because your lover will treat this as a serious attempt at curbing his freedom, and he will do anything to stay free. The more you insist, the more he will try to escape, and probably succeed.

A business venture between the pair of you will rise quickly, but you need to employ somebody else to look after the background work which neither of you enjoy, or you'll have nothing to ground you. You're both eager to develop new areas of business without doing much to maintain the old ones. As a marriage, provided you recognize that you give your partner a bit of space from time to time, you'll have a friend for life who will be almost everything you ever wanted, and who will never fail to impress and amuse you.

Aries - Capricorn

The essential thing to remember about a Capricorn is that he's concerned first with what people think of him. If this doesn't meet with any understanding from you, then forget about any kind of relationship. Capricorns are devoted to getting on in life, so that they can be seen to be doing well. Status symbols were invented for (and perhaps by) Capricorns. They all have high ambitions from an early age, and spend most of their lives working extremely hard so that these are achieved in one form or another. You can understand the idea of being number one, but you'll find it hard to understand the desire to promote yourself at the expense of everything else. A Capricorn doesn't mind hardship as long as he gets what he wants, and he thinks that hard work is much too serious a thing to be enjoyed. The sheer pleasure of being you that runs through every vein of the Arian is not there in the Capricorn. To your eyes, this makes them unimaginative, unfriendly and dull.

If a Capricorn is interested in you, then you must ask yourself what he wants out of it, because his ambitions will still be in the forefront of his mind. He's likely to want to tap into your energy and ability to succeed, because he lacks some ability to attack problems and he knows it. He recognizes your drive, because it's similar to the drive of his own ambition, and he appreciates that. From your point of view, of course, you appreciate the things he has accomplished. You can admire a person who decides what he wants to do, then goes out and does it. You admire each other, but neither can understand why the other does things the way you do. Most Aries - Capricorn relationships start from mutual admiration.

You're likely to be the one who makes the running in the relationship. If you really want to find someone who can't compete with your lively approach, then all is well, but most of you will find a Capricorn careful and emotionally reserved, which is not the way you work at all. In some cases, you may not be ambitious enough for them, especially if you're the sort of Arian who has a great time just being yourself and the type who doesn't really make any plans for the future. In this case, the Capricorn will push you into doing things that you don't much like. He will feel that you're holding up his plans and not making best use of your energies for your joint future.

As a business partnership, this has much to recommend it, especially if you let the Capricorn do the organizing, and just address yourself to specific tasks that need your kind of approach. Your partner will ensure that you get the status you both deserve, and you'll make sure the business has the energy and drive it needs to bring your joint plans to fruition.

Aries - Aquarius

This is the sort of relationship that you like. It's similar in some ways to the Gemini link, in that the rapport is light and fast moving, and that your freedom to go your own way is not hindered in any way. An Aquarian needs to form friendships. He works best in groups of people, and would much rather give his energies to the group than concentrate on his own ambitions. When you first meet an Aquarian, it's likely to be in a group, and in those surroundings, he will appear bright and attractive, somehow representing the best qualities of all the people present. That is exactly what he is doing, because he will have put himself into the group's identity, and taken on its coloring. On their own, Aquarians are shy, rather distant and not particularly impressive. They need the warmth of friendship to make them work properly, and when that friend is someone as naturally fiery as you are, their needs are met perfectly.

You need a friend who is there whenever you want them, but is never so close that they try to tell you what to do. You also need a friend who is essentially kind and honest, because your own straightforward approach to life makes you easy meat for those whose outlook is less than scrupulous. As far as you're concerned, the Aquarian is just the job. They are by nature quite straight and fair in their dealings, and are unlikely to deceive you on purpose, though genuine misunderstandings can still occur, as in all relationships. Their relatively unemotional approach to life means that you're unlikely to meet strong opposition to your ideas, and this means that you don't have to waste time and energy convincing your partner how right you are.

On the other hand, you may find that they lack deep feelings or passion about anything, and this may be a drawback. Perhaps you'd like them to be a little more forceful. Try being boorish, unrefined, rude or cruel and see where that gets you. An Aquarian can't stand to see any of these qualities displayed, and will make quite sure that they are not displayed again, usually by getting other friends and associates to chastise you on their behalf. You won't be able to spot the way in which the

Aquarian works, because he does this through people he knows, rather than directly. It never occurs to you that anybody could achieve anything in any other way than by himself or herself, but that's exactly how the Aquarian does things. He will change your tastes, moderate your excesses and turn your physical grace into social grace, your childishness into charm and your will to win into inspired leadership.

What they get out of it is your warmth; the never-failing enthusiasm and passion for things that take your fancy captivate them, and if these are the things that you fancy, then they feel warmed, loved, and rewarded. An Aquarian can't love himself, and he needs others to love him before he can feel content.

As a partnership for business, this has everything to recommend it. The Aquarian will be full of new schemes, and he has a talent for the unusual that will surprise you. His capacity for making contacts is unparalleled. Make sure that you don't rush in and destroy the delicate networks of communication and cooperation that he has set up just because you want something done immediately.

Marriage is unlikely, because you like to go your own way, and an Aquarian isn't going to try to tie you down. Aquarians are also solitary creatures and there are times when they want their own company, because constant emotional interchange is tiring for them. Marriage seems too restricting for the pure Arian and too tiring for the pure Aquarian, so other factors would have to make you tie the knot. Once married though, you can be sure of a light and bright partnership, full of affection, if not very passionate. There will be plenty of variety, and challenges will be taken up and met, rather than avoided. You could do worse.

Aries - Pisces

This is an odd partnership, which, like the Aries - Taurus combination, brings two adjacent signs in the zodiac into confrontation, each seeing what he is, plus what he could be and what he fears. This time, the other sign is behind you in the zodiacal circle, and thus it represents all the things you secretly fear. Do you want a relationship with somebody whose motivation is to exhibit and promote those qualities that worry you? I know you think that there's nothing that really worries you, but there is. You're quite sure that in a definite situation, you can apply your directness of mind and physical approach to get things going the way you want, but what about a situation that's indefinite? How can you cope with a situation where nothing is certain, where there's nothing you can be sure of and nothing static or dependable? Now you begin to see what I mean. You represent a focus of energy, a point where things happen and take form. Pisces represents defocusing and a "nowhere-in-particular point" that's everywhere at once, where everything is possible but nothing is definite.

Pisceans are people of infinite flexibility, who can take up any cause or put on any appearance according to the circumstances in which they find themselves. If you're playing strong and sexy, they will too. If you're playing active and sporty, they will change to suit. They will reflect and complement you, which you'll find attractive. Pisceans long for a definite situation, and they wish that they could be as firm and effective as you are. Consequently, they see in you a desirable state, and they can temporarily be as you are, in order to amuse themselves and to please you. You'll notice the differences. The Piscean will never learn to concentrate on the moment, his whole being given to the immediate present, because he exists in a sort of no-time, where everything is immediate, but the future has the same immediacy as the past. You don't have much of a sense of future time at all.

You'll notice how the Piscean reacts to obstacles. Challenges are something to meet as far as you're concerned, but to him they are to be avoided. Whenever difficulties arise, the Piscean melts away, makes himself scarce and flows round them, only reappearing once the problem has been removed. If you try to pin a Piscean down to a commitment, he will agree that it's a good idea and then find something very important to do that takes him elsewhere. He may even become argumentative and unpleasant in an effort to remove whatever happens to be irritating him and preventing him from flowing ever onwards.

As business partners, it's very difficult to make this one work, unless you're in something connected with the media or the arts, where you make the impact and the Piscean supplies the sensitivity and imagination. As a marriage, the only answer is the understanding and tolerance that comes with time, because you're very un-alike. You might learn to enjoy uncertainty of mind, and your partner might learn to appreciate the practical advantages of decisive action. It would be an interesting experience for both of you to become lovers, but possibly no more than that. Your lover may take you on flights of fantasy where nothing seems real, and they will be invited to play games where strength and passion are the preferred currency. You may be happier meeting on occasion to play Dungeons and Dragons!

The Approach to Relationships: Taurus

SYMBOL:	THE BULL	♉	ELEMENT:	EARTH
PLANET:	VENUS	♀	QUALITY:	FIXED

Stability is absolutely essential for your happiness. As the first Earth sign of the zodiac, your roots and where you live are of prime importance to you. You can reassure yourself about the rightness of your existence if you know where you are; familiar surroundings enable you to orientate yourself properly. If you're in strange surroundings, or for some reason your usual routines are disrupted, then you start to worry, and the old uncertainties about where your next meal is coming from start to surface. You define yourself in relation to your surroundings, so if the surroundings are unfamiliar to you, then you don't know who you are. It's as simple as that.

You are very possessive of your loved ones, and will be deeply wounded by any separation. If someone in whom you have placed a lot of trust and affection goes out of your life, you feel insecure because things have become unstable again, and your emotional stability and nourishment have been interrupted. As you no doubt know, this can grow into jealousy and a suffocating possessiveness; on the other hand, your loyalty, devotion and unwavering constancy are the envy of anyone who wishes that love was, for them at least, for keeps. It certainly is for you.

Taurus - Aries

All zodiacal partnerships involving adjacent signs are difficult, but this combination is possibly the most difficult of them all. The simple fact is that Arians annoy you. They worry you and they move much too quickly for you to be able to keep a proper eye on them. You like to know where things are, and where they are going to stay, but Arians don't stay anywhere for any length of time, and this is disturbing to you. Perhaps it was the Arian's forcefulness that attracted you, but soon you will have discovered that it's not directed towards the defense of their position as yours is, but towards personal movement. Their energy moves them for movement's sake, while you only let yourself be moved when threatened.

They are highly active people who need to keep busy doing things, whereas you're quite happy to keep things the way they are. This means that while you're at your best staying in one place doing one thing, they are likely to be changing from one thing to another and you find this disconcerting. They would like you to be active as well, and they will try to make you move faster than you would really like. Moving too quickly means that you can't feel the earth under your feet, and this removes you from your natural element of Earth. You're frightened to do this, so you refuse to move as quickly as the Arian would like. He sees this as lack of spirit, but he does not hold this against you in any way. He must go his own way and he has no time to spend cajoling you into joining him. The fact that you're unwilling or unable to join him is a great pity, but can't be helped. It's important for you to understand that the Arian thinks no worse of you because you won't join in his activities; he simply thinks that it's your loss, and can't be helped. He doesn't feel betrayed, injured or thwarted in any way. You feel all of those things when relationships go wrong because that's how you are, but he doesn't work like you at all, and that doesn't mean that either of you are wrong, but just that you're not like each other.

Physically, you're well matched, because you both use your bodies as a prime expression of your energies. You'll find Arian energy attractive, and would dearly like to be able to keep some of it for later, or to have it for your own. The Arian finds your strength an invigorating test for his sexual capabilities, and on that level, you should have a lot of excitement and satisfaction. The problems arise when you try to convert the relationship into something more than a momentary passion. The Arian gets bored, and you become possessive. The level of energy in the liaison drops, and the sexual excitement fades. You become increasingly determined to hang on to what you see as yours, but which you think is mysteriously being taken away from you. The Arian senses the lack of excitement, the lack of development and novelty as the situation becomes static, and immediately looks for a more interesting project. The result is bound to be disappointment for both of you. There will inevitably be one of those thankfully rare occasions where the Taurean loses his temper in a big way, because he feels that he has somehow been deprived of what was rightfully his.

As a long-term relationship, such as a business or a marriage, this coupling can only work if roles are strictly defined and understood. If that's done, the pressure that you can both bring to bear on problems that beset you can make for a very successful team. The Arian must be allowed to do all the development work, and to do it as his own pace. New things and those that have to be done quickly with no time for preparation must be left to the Arian. The Taurean must do all the backup work, and he or she must be allowed his or her own territory. Taurus must also convince the Arian that all this effort is worthwhile by being patient, which is a quality that the Arian lacks. In return, you'll be shown that new beginnings are far from impossible, even when your position really seems hopeless.

Taurus - Taurus

Two bulls in the same field: quite an entertaining proposition for a spectator, but rather uncomfortable for anyone in the field, and necessarily painful for both of the bulls. The relationship is likely to start with the realization that you have something in common. Perhaps you like the same sort of food and enjoy working your way round all the restaurants of that type in your area. Perhaps it's music or gardening. Whatever it is, you'll be pleased that someone else has the same high opinion as you have, of the things that you enjoy. For a Taurean, to have someone give you credit for your tastes is an irresistible compliment to your ego. Needless to say, the same thing is also happening to the other Taurean.

It's easy to get yourself into a race in this situation, where both of you are in competition with the other to have more of whatever it is that you both admire and enjoy possessing. This will last until one of you runs out of money or time, and that's fine as far as it goes, and as long as neither of you take it seriously. Both of you will strenuously deny that it's at all serious, but it will be so nonetheless, because you hate losing, hence the denials that there's any kind of contest. Both of you like to have just that bit more than the other does. The person who first came up with the phrase "I'll have the big half" was undoubtedly Taurean, and he may not even have seen anything funny in what he'd just said.

It's difficult for you to understand the give and take of a relationship at times, because as far as you're concerned, you're in the right. This means that if your partner does something that you disagree with, or far worse, tries to get you to change your ways, you feel criticized and under attack. There's no reason for you to feel this, but you do nonetheless. If the matter is a small one, you'll take no notice, confident that your partner will soon see things your way. If it's a request for you to do things differently, you simply take no notice, because they are wrong and that's that. If it's something important, or the requests for unaccustomed action are persistent, then you'll wait patiently, and only when the situation becomes intolerable will you move. When you move, you move to re-establish your way of doing things.

As a marriage, the best thing to do is to find an area in which you both agree very strongly, such as money or the acquisition of property, and make everything else subordinate to it. Working together, your natural tendencies to keep a good thing going if possible will motivate you to settle minor differences for the sake of your greater possessions.

Taurus - Gemini

This partnership is as difficult for you to understand as the Taurus - Aries one is, but it's nothing like as threatening, so you can afford to let your differences go by without worrying or being forced to make changes. You like peace and quiet and letting the world go by in its own way without interference, which is simply not comprehensible to a Gemini. Their need to think, read, receive information and voice an opinion on it will occasionally make you wish you could switch them off like a radio. You can't, so you'll have to live with the noise. What you find strangest of all with the Gemini is their apparent disregard for material things. If there's a meal put in front of them, they will eat it, but it isn't anything like as important as it is to you. They like a well-appointed house, but who doesn't? However, they don't see that as a reflection of themselves and their tastes in the way that you do. What really interests them is a new idea, new information and new developments, so the sort of thing you turn your back on in case it heralds change, is the stuff of life to them.

Geminis are the sort of people who think that they are always right, because they have thought about things and come to a definite conclusion. You can appreciate this because you know that you're right too; not from thinking about things, but from feeling them, and taking things in slowly. What will surprise and upset you is that a Gemini can change his mind completely every five minutes, and each time he's convinced that he's right. The same mental evaluation has taken place and the same force of conviction is there, and yet he has changed viewpoint completely. This is very unsettling to you. You come to the conclusion that he's making it all up, which is potentially threatening to your stability because you may be taken in, or he's right each time, which is worrying because you can't react that fast. If you don't panic, it may dawn on you that this mental evaluation process is actually what he likes doing best, so he does it as often as he can, continually fascinating himself with the varieties of argument he turns up. As you will realize, all this happens in the world of the imagination and does not affect your position, your territory or your possessions one bit. You're quite safe, and can let him exercise his imagination to his heart's content. This is why he's less of a threat to your stability than the Arian is. Relax and listen to the chatter. He can be very entertaining indeed once you realize that very little of it is for real.

As lovers, you're a strange mixture. You'd like to have his lightness of touch and his way with words; he makes you feel clumsy and slow, but you find his conversation flattering and he makes you feel good. From the other side of the relationship, he needs your stabilizing influence, especially when things aren't going the way he'd like them to, which will be a lot more frequently than you would imagine. It's because he never believes that effort is a necessary component of success. You'll have to take the role of an understanding parent, while he takes that of the child.

Unless you have strong common interests, it will be difficult to make a lasting partnership from these two signs, because you're not concerned with ideas any more than he is with material things, and he will lose interest in you unless there's something you both enjoy. You must expect arguments from time to time, especially when he changes his ideas and denies having thought differently before. He must remember that to make his dreams come true requires patience and application, and you're his best source of both those qualities.

Taurus - Cancer

This is a splendid partnership. You're both concerned with the same things in life, but approach them from different directions. Both of you are determined to hang on to what is yours and not to lose things, but you're not in competition with each other. The important thing from a Cancerian point of view is to have a firm base, to look after what you care about and make sure that you know about all that goes on in your territory, and then worry about your responsibilities and your safety. As a Taurean, you ensure that your territory stays secure, and being recognized as the owner is a welcome bonus.

The Cancerian worries too much about things, whereas the Taurus trusts his own abilities and is of the opinion that if nothing is done to upset the general arrangement of things, nothing drastic will happen. The Cancerian comes to the Taurean for advice and reassurance about worries, knowing that he isn't going to sound silly. In return, the Taurean wants somebody to share his possessions and his taste for the good life without getting into a game of one-upmanship or a situation that threatens his position. He can see that the sensitive Cancerian is just the right person for this. In a way, the Cancerian is like a younger brother or sister, who is mildly envious of all that the Taurean has managed to collect, but appreciates being allowed to use some of it. The Cancer partner may not agree with the Taurean's taste, but he or she is too reserved and too aware of what's good in the long run to voice criticism.

Cancerians are quite capable of expanding their responsibilities in those areas under their control, and they often do. They are happy to do something completely new if they feel that it's in their best interest. It's not usual to call them adventurous, but this contrasts with the Taurean, who will always take the tried and tested method rather than risk anything unfamiliar. A Cancerian is motivated to advance his ideas into new fields, but having got there, he feels responsible for all the people under him and is unable to simply to pass the job over to them. It's not a territorial urge so much as a caring and almost parenting feeling, but it's one that a Taurean understands.

Home is important to a Cancerian, because it's his personal caring environment. It needs to be secure and it needs to be comfortable. Taureans are fond of lavishly appointed homes, so any home that you share together will be of great importance, and you'll both work hard to make it as comfortable and welcoming as possible, if for slightly different reasons.

As lovers, you'll be very affectionate, very caring and very understanding, although the physical electricity that the Fire signs like Aries and Sagittarius bring to a relationship will be missing. Earth and Fire are a lightning strike, whereas what we have here is Earth and Water, and that produces a fertile environment. That works in all ways. Earth and Water people often have large and happy families.

As a marriage, the arrangement seems perfect. If there's a flaw, it may be that you become so set in your ways and so home-centered that you feel a need for something else to do. However, taken as a whole, the marriage is unlikely to develop any more serious problems than obesity as the two of you indulge your liking for food and the security it represents.

Taurus - Leo

This is an interesting pairing, and it's almost interesting enough to sell tickets for. Two powerful animals, a bull and a lion, who are both used to being their own masters and who are both unaccustomed to giving way on anything, attempting to make an equal relationship. If it succeeds, and there will be a few broken plates before it settles down, then it will be very strong indeed, and it could be a union that will bring great material wealth and prestige to its partners.

The essential conflict is something similar to ignoring a "do not walk on the grass" notice, right under the park-keeper's nose. A Taurus person has a very acute sense of his own territory, and will have things done according to his wishes within that territory. Trespassers or people refusing to recognize his authority within the boundary are seen as threats. So far, so good. A Leo sees himself as the natural authority figure and center of the world, wherever he happens to be, and will behave in the firm belief this is indeed so. He also feels free to go wherever the wind takes him, so long as he has an opportunity to display his warmth and radiance to a suitable audience. When he wanders into the Taurean's territory, he will expect appreciation and respect, and be hurt not to receive it. Almost as hurt as the Taurean is by the lack of recognition he is afforded by the Leo. Neither of them is of the sort likely to smile and forget. They insist on recognition, and because they are both Fixed signs of the zodiac, they won't bend an inch away from what they think is right. Such arguments can lead to separations lasting years, and family members who refuse to speak to each other for generations are typical of this Fixed sign behavior.

The only way for a Taurean to achieve some measure of success with a Leo is for Leo to handle the theory and Taurus to handle the practicalities. If they agree on the same program, then Leo can provide a way for the Taurean to display it without seeming offensive (everybody likes Leos, and expects them to be rich, but not everybody likes a wealthy Taurean). The Taurean generates more wealth from the opportunities that Leo provides. If this is done, a partnership is capable of making very large amounts of money, provided you find yourself doing what you know best and don't branch out into the new and unfamiliar.

As lovers, you'll enjoy taking your territorial struggles to the bedroom. You'll both be strong, but a little conventional, in your approaches to sex. You'll have to be ready to listen to a few tall stories from your Leo lover, but don't be surprised if he continues to tell them in the pub. Leos are the best in the world; they know it, and they tell everybody so when they get an audience. Everybody loves them for it, and nobody cares whether any of it is true or not.

As partners, you'll be loyal to each other, and you'll fight on each other's behalf when necessary. You'll build a fine home and family life that becomes richer and more plentiful as the years go by. Leos are easily hurt if they think that you don't care much for some of their ideas, so you'll have to develop a way of letting them down gently, using that Taurean patience. You'll be needlessly possessive, but they are as loyal as you are. They will have to learn that you're the boss in the home, and as you're unlikely to teach them or spell it out for them, they must learn it on their own. Sometimes they are as slow to accept the unpalatable as you are, so give them time to get used to the idea.

Taurus - Virgo

This partnership can work very well. You're both Earth signs, so you're both interested in using your energy in the same general way. You may find the Virgoan fussy, though, and they will almost certainly find you rather hefty and careless in your approach to many things.

The essential thing about a Virgo's approach to life is getting the details right. It matters to them that they have the right way of going about things. They can find enjoyment and satisfaction in a repetitive job, because they are continually learning and refining their technique. "Practice" is a very Virgoan word. They like things to feel good, and they are much happier when they can feel and touch things for themselves.

They modify whatever they own, changing little bits of it here and there to make it that little bit neater or a closer fit or whatever.

To you, this obsession with detail is strange. You can understand the care and attention that's lavished on belongings, because you feel strongly about that too, but the constant search for perfection baffles you. You don't like to change your way of doing something. You only learn it once, and however sloppy you become after that, you still believe that you're doing it in the same way, and you'll not be persuaded otherwise. The Virgoan is never sloppy. His technique is always up to the mark and constantly in practice, because he analyses what he does as he does it. He analyses what he's about to do before he does it. He thinks about how he would analyze it before he has to, and he makes the best possible use of all the material at hand. You care for what you have and you preserve it rather than trying to improve it all the time, and you need others to recognize this. The area in which you're closest to each other is in that of selection, where you'll pick the best you can, and reject the rest – perhaps selecting one on the grounds of flavor, and the other on the grounds of excellent quality.

In many ways, you wish you could be as careful and as perceptive as the Virgo; you feel that your life could be incredibly enriched by Virgoan knowledge and insight. His knowledge of correct techniques would save you from making an ass yourself on numerous occasions. For his part, he wishes he could command as much respect as you do, as then he wouldn't have to spend his time working on small jobs. He can imagine having the confidence and wealth to be a success, but even with all his skills and insight, he can't be bothered to strive to become rich.

As lovers, you'll have to be gentle and easy in your approach. Virgos are delicate creatures, and are easy to trample. You must be considerate and careful and take time over details. In the long run, he will have to realize that your big gestures of affection are not at all clumsy or uncaring, but genuine declarations of love on a rather bigger scale than he thinks is proper. He must restrain himself from telling you how to do things better, which is only a mask for his insecurity. A Taurean in love is a bit too forceful for him to deal with in small sections, as he would like to.

As a marriage prospect, these signs are better than most of the same element pairings. The constantly active nature of the Virgoan will stop things from becoming to familiar, and he will work hard to make all as good as it can possibly be. Let him use you as a protector and defender against his enemies and fears, whilst you use him to help you get the very best use out of whatever it is that you've achieved. Not only will you have your own bit of land, but you'll then also have the neatest, prettiest and most fruitful garden you've ever seen!

Taurus - Libra

A very happy partnership, this, because both of you are motivated and directed by the planet Venus, which looks for points of common interest, and tries to promote friendship and harmony. So not only are you pleased to meet somebody else who has a similar motivation to you, but you actually like them as well. What's more, they like you in return, and that's always a good sign in a relationship.

Librans have a distinctive talent for saying the right thing at the right time, and for adding little touches here and there which make things easy on the eye. They can see what needs doing to make a room beautiful, and they will do it without fuss, just to please themselves. A Libran home is always refined and beautiful, but pleasant to be in as well, which might not always be the case with other home-building signs. They have the same simple elegance in their clothes, so whatever they wear looks just right. Even their speech is pleasant. There's always something about the way a Libran does things that makes others think, "I wish I could be like that!"

As a Taurean, you appreciate beautiful things and you like to have them around you. The attraction to others who are themselves beautiful and graceful, is not hard to see. From the other side, they see you as offering the sort of appreciation they like, and feel that they could form a close and rewarding relationship with someone who shares their view of life. A Libran is always trying to form relationships, make friends and gather people close to him. The problem is that many people don't share his aesthetic view of things, or are unreliable, discourteous or disloyal. All these things upset the exact balance of the Libran existence and cause disharmony, which he feels strongly. He knows that he can always rely on the Taurean to be constant, and unchanging. That, coupled with the Taurean appreciation for all things that are beautiful to look at, makes for a good friendship that's especially valuable to the Libran. He can go to the Taurean when the world seems to be over-demanding, harsh or threatening. Through you, he knows that his essential values and desire for a quiet co-existence are worth pursuing, and while he needs no training in artistic sensibilities, he does need strength and he has to look for it outside himself. You can offer that in abundance, and he will give you in return the grace and charm that you sometimes feel you lack.

You may feel in the initial stages of your friendship that the Libran is too cool. Librans are certainly light in their approach to things, and the airy delicacy of their way of conducting an affair may seem insubstantial to you. From their point of view, you'll seem heavy and a little lacking in subtlety. They will also find you short of originality, and a slow talker. Librans are from an Air sign, remember, so they need to circulate ideas. They also need to circulate amongst people, so don't keep them indoors, and don't get upset if they like talking to everybody else at a party. They'll come back. Remember that social circulation is as important to them as eating is to you. Do you want them to starve to death? Take things on a light level if you can, and keep the relationship mobile.

As lovers, you might have to be very understanding with each other. The Libran will find your passion and strength a little overwhelming, and lacking in refinement. You'll find his preference for love and romance rather than sex delightful to begin with, but frustrating later. Don't get upset if he runs away; just make sure that he realizes that continuity means a lot to you. As marriage partners, you should be amusing to watch. Both of you are very particular about your home environment, and you'll furnish it beautifully, but neither of you will want to do much about its upkeep, because you're both quite lazy. You'll eat the most exquisite meals in the greatest style, but neither of you will want to wash up afterwards. You'll have not only to take responsibility for the house, but some of the actual work involved too, and the Libran will have to accept his share as well.

Taurus - Scorpio

The meeting of two signs opposed to each other in the circle of the zodiac is a powerful thing, especially when they are both Fixed signs. You can expect the Scorpio to be just as determined to have his own way as you are, and just as obstinate if he feels something isn't right for him. You can expect the Scorpio to have talents that you don't have, but you also have some that he doesn't have. You have quite a lot in common, and you can be happy together, as long as you don't pose a threat to each other.

You like to be in control of your physical environment, which means that you like to know what's yours, and what comes into or goes out of, or goes on in your little bit of space. It's your field, and you're the bull in that field. A Scorpio likes to be in control of his emotional environment. This means that he likes to know how he feels, and how everybody else's actions and feelings are likely to affect his own. He has to look into things to see how they work and what's going on, because unless he's fully up to date with all the possibilities, he may not be able to maintain his control over how he feels. You have an easier job of it, really because possessions don't change as fast as feelings. You may feel that you have more than a little of the Scorpio in you, now that you've read about what he's trying to do, and many Scorpios will feel that they have more than a little of the Taurean in them too. They usually like having things, such as motorbikes and powerful cars that remind them of how powerful and in control they are.

The difference between the two of you is the difference between maintenance and control. A Scorpio isn't trying to maintain his feelings in the same state; he's trying to control them so that they do what he wants. You're not trying to control your territory, but merely to maintain it, so that it stays pretty much as it is, while improving it where you can. If the two of you are placed too close to each other, you could both feel threatened. So powerful and strongly controlled an individual on your territory is obviously unsettling to you, especially as you're unable to see what he's thinking, and are afraid that he might take something from you. On his side, he's bothered by your immovability and apparent imperturbability, which could make you difficult to control, and have a possibly upsetting influence on his feelings. Given a little distance, you'll both be able to see that your areas of concern may overlap but they don't intersect, so you need have nothing to fear from each other.

As friends and partners, you could make a great deal of money because you represent the signs that are concerned with the effective use of all kinds of resources, including financial ones. Provided you have one person to do the organizing and the other to look after the stock, you'll make an effective team. This might suffer from being a little on the dull side, since neither of you're originators of new ideas, but the Scorpio's assiduous research capabilities should ensure that you keep up with new developments in business as soon as they have been tested and found to work.

As lovers, you express yourselves very powerfully indeed, but you will find that the emotional intensity with which the Scorpio conducts his love affairs will make your Taurean head dizzy. You like things to be powerful for sure, but you like them relaxed and easy-going, too. The constant atmosphere of almost possessive passion will leave you gasping for air. Still, if you can stand that sort of thing, you won't feel that it isn't strong enough for you, as you might have done with the Libran, for example.

As marriage partners, the same thing applies. You both want success and security, and as a couple you should have no problems in achieving these goals. When you've got all that, though, you want to sit back in relative tranquility and enjoy it all, whereas the Scorpio is driven to do more or look for something to add to the situation. Basically, they never stop, where you feel that resting after your labors is important as the work itself. If you can live with his constant determination to achieve more, without feeling irritated or that he's criticizing you, it will be fine.

Taurus - Sagittarius

These two signs are very different. They seem to get in each other's way more often than not when they act together, but when they stand back and look at the other in action, they can each see what the other is trying to achieve. The Fire of the Sagittarian seems to scorch and wither all that the Taurean has worked so hard to achieve, while the Taurean seems too much of a plodder to appreciate the brilliance and verve of the Archer. There are other ways to look at it though. The Taurean can provide a solid home base for the Sagittarian to come back to when he's in one of his crestfallen phases, and the Sagittarian can provide the optimism and insight that Taurean folk often can't find in themselves. It takes effort from both sides to achieve this, so there must be some very good reason for the couple to stay together long enough for that kind of rapport to grow.

Think of the bull and the horse. The bull lives in his own field and doesn't move far from it, while the horse leaps over the fence and is soon away into the far distance, running with the wind for its own sake. It's important to understand that Sagittarians need to be free, and to have the joy of doing things for their own sake, out of curiosity. The horse is more beautiful when in motion, while the bull is more majestic when standing still. Horses are essentially a luxury item, whereas cattle are useful in terms of what they produce. You can perhaps begin to see that the signs don't have a great deal to offer one another.

Having a Sagittarian friend is a disturbing experience for a Taurean. They seem to move so quickly; you take life at a steady pace where you can, and you dislike being rushed. The Sagittarian focuses on intellectual things, ideas and concepts that have no real foundation or practical application, and they can be captivated by something that they read in a book. One minute they are on about one thing, as if it were the only thing in the world, and the next minute its something else altogether. If you think about it for a moment, you'll see that your Sagittarian friend can answer the deepest questions for you, even before you ever thought of asking them. You might ask yourself, as you go through life looking after and assimilating your belongings, whether there was more, and where it might come from. The Sagittarian shows you endless realms, shows new things coming into being as ideas, and being translated into action and form. He's a creator and you're a collector. The relationship can be a deep one.

Sagittarius sees you as a route for making his ideas concrete. If this works for him, the planetary energy will be collected into one place and become Earth where it was once Fire. Besides, without the wealth of material that you offer, not only in terms of money, but also in terms of effort, loyalty and patience, he can achieve nothing. On a personal level, he sees you as slow and rather predictable, but he's more than a little envious of your patience and the steadiness you seem to bring to life. He would not really wish to trade the roller coaster of emotional ups and downs he thrives on, but a little of the opposite always seems attractive.

As lovers, you'd be a lot more successful physically than you might have thought, but the rest of the relationship would take a lot of work. The trouble is that you need to feel that a person belongs to you and you to them, while a Sagittarian belongs to himself and to nobody else, and if you start to get possessive, he will gallop off and find somebody else. Even when he's pledged to you, he will still entertain himself with new acquaintances of the opposite sex. Variety and games are very important and restorative to him.

Doing the same things day after day makes him depressed. If he leaves, he will choose to come back to you quite freely, but he can never be compelled to do so. Being loyal to him doesn't really count, as he then sees your loyalty as a millstone. A Sagittarian really does need to be allowed to go his own way. Trap him and his fire dies, which is useless if what you were trying to do was keep his warmth for your own private use.

As marriage partners, you'll have to make allowances for the Sagittarian's need to move around, and make sure that you give him both the space and the opportunity to use it. He will need to realize that you need a base that's permanently and unchangeably yours. If you're living with a Sagittarian, you must already have found some shared interest that's strong enough to hold you both together. Without that joint interest and goal, you'll need to put in what is probably more effort than you'd like to make the relationship really work.

Taurus - Capricorn

This is the relationship that's built to last. Two Earth signs, one Fixed and one Cardinal, both interested in making things firm, secure and unchanging; and both with a fondness for things of enduring value, so here is the recipe for a life partnership. The relationship might take a while to get off the ground, because you're both secure in your own areas, and see no reason to interrupt things. Allowing the entry of someone new into your life may feel threatening, but when you see how similar you are to each other, you start to like each other, and things grow from there.

This is the four-signs-apart relationship, so it's the mutual admiration society where each partner wishes he were more like the other one. In this particular case, the Taurean is probably impressed by the way that the Capricorn seems to get recognition and respect for all that he has achieved, and is seen as a natural and obvious winner in life. Taurus would like to have acclaim and recognition for his or her efforts, and it's the hope of this that motivates them anew when they are despondent. They also appreciate and approve of the way a Capricorn measures his success in material terms, or in the way that the world in general values Capricorn for showing that he's made it in life. Sometimes Taureans get a little confused by people from the other elements who don't seem to value bricks and mortar to the same extent as they do; but then along comes a Capricorn who both reassures and encourages the Taureans, so confidence is renewed. This is an important process. Fixed signs don't like to be insecure in any way, and need reassurance from time to time, so to a Taurean, a Capricorn is the answer.

From the other point of view, the Capricorn finds the Taurean solidity and determination the perfect expression of the work ethic, which is so central to his way of seeing things. In point of fact, Capricorns are just the faintest bit lazy. It's a very faint bit, but, although they will work to achieve something they have set their hearts on, when faced with determined and repeated opposition, they give up and then aim themselves towards something else. You can see why this is with just a moment's thought. Capricorns need to feel a sense of achievement, and if things look like being unattainable then an alternative target may give them that sense of achievement. A Taurean takes opposition as a personal affront, and stays where he is until he has worn the opposition down. The Capricorn thinks this is admirable, as he can understand working hard for just rewards, while working patiently and unceasingly with no guarantee of having the work recognized, as the Taurean often does, strikes the Capricorn as an almost saintly devotion to the cause, and he's lost in admiration.

As a friendship or business partnership, this pairing has a lot to offer; the Taurean can share in the Capricorn's achievements as reward for his efforts, and the Capricorn can aim even higher, in the knowledge that the Taurean will never deviate from the job in hand, no matter how difficult progress becomes. You'll need to have somebody else around to provide both of you with new directions and ideas from time to time, or you'll become rather dull and unimaginative, but otherwise there's a lot to recommend this as a business partnership.

As lovers, there will be many power games for the two of you to amuse yourselves with, but the cool Capricorn does not understand the nature of real passion, and his response to your Taurean physical needs may not be enough. You'll have to show him that physical contact and being touched are important to you, and invite him to express himself in a similar way, He'll never quite get it right, but he can be persuaded to join in to a certain extent.

As a marriage, this partnership looks good. Your tastes are different though. You like things to be soft, pretty and luxurious, with plenty of food available, while the Capricorn often doesn't care what or when he eats. Some Taureans and Capricorns are very flashy dressers though, so this could provide a further point of contact through your love of color and texture, and this will help you build a comfortable home together.

Taurus - Aquarius

This match isn't easy at all. To put it simply, Aquarians feel safest in a crowd, whereas you feel safest at home. They are better with lots of people at once, and you're better in a one-to-one relationship. Any pairing that's three signs apart is a difficult one.

You're dedicated to the maintenance of what's yours. You've worked for it, you're going to keep it and you want everybody to respect you for the efforts you've put into its acquisition. An Aquarian is dedicated to the breakdown of all structures that imply that anybody is better than or higher than anybody else is. Difficult to imagine, isn't it? Why were you attracted to him in the first place? It may well have been the fact that he always has so many friends and is so popular. You become part of the audience, find that the group is a generally happy one and enjoy the companionship that you get from other members of the group. Then you project yourself towards the group's center, or charge straight for it as Taureans do, and acquire him. Now you can become possessive with him, as he's yours, but unfortunately, he's not going to see it your way. He's not going to understand the depth of your feelings or your need to hold on to what you have, or your need feel appreciated. You're not going to understand why he still wants to have a hundred friends when he has you.

Aquarians like to be different, and more than that, they need to be different. Whenever they see something that has been established for some considerable time and is doing quite nicely thank you, they feel that it's time for a change, so they disturb, rearrange and sometimes destroy things. It's not from a sense of malice or even one of mischievous glee: it's simply the way they are built. They represent the idea that everything has its time, and at the end of that time, it must change. Change is then a natural state for them, and the movement and conversation that flows is an environment as natural and healthy for them as the home is for you. Being static is an unhealthy thing for them, and the idea that things are set to last seems absurd, because they are dedicated to the concept of change.

It would seem that there could be no contact between you, but in fact, there's a genuine attraction of opposites. He's interested in the nature of constancy simply because it's alien to him, and you represent that, while you're interested in the nature of change. You'll be strong in each other's defense, and yet equally strong in maintaining your differences within the relationship.

As lovers, you're bound to have difficulties because of the differences between Taurean possessiveness and Aquarian freedom. Physically, he will be inventive and adventurous which will excite you, yet emotionally rather uninvolved, which could make you feel betrayed. In turn, he will find your passion and devotion rewarding, though its persistence and occasionally demanding nature will make him want to slip out from under from time to time, to see other people and feel refreshed in their company.

If a marriage is to be built out of this relationship, you'll both have to compromise to a large extent, so that his more revolutionary and far-ranging ideas will have to be shelved. You must offer him some sort of willingness to cope with changes from time to time. Shared interests will help. Both of you like music as a rule, though it may not be the same kind.

Taurus - Pisces

Here is the relationship you've been waiting for, where you hardly ever have to show your horns, and you can give yourself almost completely to a life of relaxation and softness, self-indulgence for both you and your partner. You're both just what the other one needs. The softer side of you, which, given a chance, would spend its time in pursuit of elegance, artistry, and gracious living, finds the romantic and impressionistic approach of the Piscean very easy to accommodate.

Pisceans are supremely sensitive individuals, and they will adapt themselves to anything that comes their way. They are refined and fond of luxury if they can get it. Your strong point of view and determined way of doing things are more than enough guidance for them, while your own tastes lie along the same lines as their own. There should be very few disagreements.

You often feel yourself to be a little dull mentally and wish that you could be as intellectual as some of the other signs are. At the same time, you're wary of the harsh brilliance of the Gemini's wit or the simply overwhelming erudition of the Sagittarian mind. Perhaps there's a softer mind, a gentler imagination, to which you might aspire? The Piscean has exactly that, so he will help you develop your own imagination in the best possible way. The softness of the Piscean is no threat to you, and you'll seldom have to fight to get your own way. Most of the time, you won't notice that they have any opinion that's different from yours. You'll also enjoy looking after them and loving them, because they are so delicate where you are strong, and so very appreciative of any kindness shown to them.

From the Piscean point of view, you're the sort of firm, no nonsense individual that he needs to put some sort of shape and organization into his life, without being bossy. He recognizes that he's not able to take assertive action by himself and needs guidance, but he's afraid that any such guide might be negative to his feelings, and unappreciative of what he has to offer. In the Taurean, he knows that he has the perfect answer, as he's strong, determined and purposeful, but very caring and also very sensitive at the same time. In return for putting his life into manageable order, the Piscean offers heightened sensitivity and understanding on all matters to do with the emotional response to life, and he has an unmatched imagination - plus the ability to escape into fantasy and self-comforting whenever life becomes too depressing!

As friends, you should be constant, forgiving of each other's excesses, and very fond of each other. It's not a great partnership with which to go out and achieve things; it's much more like a restorative retreat for two people who can get easily bruised in the outside world, and need a little care and attention in their private life to redress the balance.

As lovers, your relationship should be very romantic indeed, but you may be surprised and confused from time to time, because the Piscean is not as direct as you, and he or she does things in rather vague and difficult-to-grasp ways. Be patient: they are not being devious, just vague. Try not to be heavy-handed in your demands. They love you dearly, but they just don't have the physical needs that you do.

As a marriage, this pairing should work very well, provided that somebody takes responsibility for something. In this case, it's probably best if you make the decisions and they abide by them, because you're the more sensible of the two.

The Approach to Relationships: Gemini

SYMBOL:	THE TWINS	Ⅱ	ELEMENT:	AIR
PLANET:	MERCURY	☿	QUALITY:	MUTABLE

Gemini is a double sign. There are two twins in the picture, and I've lost count of the number of Geminis who have said to me, 'I'm a Gemini; I must be schizophrenic!' This well-worn quip brings out two facets of the Gemini mind. Firstly, that Geminis do have more than one way of seeing things the whole time, and secondly, that they don't think much of astrology. Astrology can seem to suggest a world where everything is known beforehand. A Gemini wouldn't want that, because it would remove the possibility of novelty, and seriously disrupt the way he performs his thinking. If he couldn't think, he couldn't live.

The idea of communication, especially argument, where the same idea is modified as it goes back and forth, is ideal for the Gemini mind. So is anything that works as a communication on more than one level, and even more so if the second level reverses the direction of the transaction.

The Gemini makes sure that he is in circulation. He likes to be with young people rather than old, and with people who talk readily, rather than quiet types. What he is doing is to ensure that he gets plenty of new material to think about, and which he can change into his own opinions for later communication.

Gemini - Aries

This is one of the best friendships in the whole zodiac, because you genuinely like each other. There are many qualities that you both have in common, and the areas in which one of you is deficient are filled by the other. There's a sort of joy in doing things together, so richly enjoyable that it's almost gleeful, except that there's no malice present, nor any sort of triumph at the expense of others. Here is the pure fun of two boys playing together and miraculously maintaining their enthusiasm and innocence right through adult life.

From your point of view, you see the Arian as the sort of friend you always wanted and are thrilled to have found. You always want to do things at once, and novelty is important to you. The Arian works on a slightly different principle, that of getting started and seeing what it turns out like, rather than waiting and thinking, but you'll understand straightaway that the two approaches are closely parallel. What excites you both is the idea of immediacy. You enjoy it because you need a constant flow of new things to occupy your mind, and the Arian needs a constant flow of new things to use up his physical energy.

You're faster than Aries is, so if the task at hand does take a little time to complete, you'll find yourself thinking of other things that seem more interesting to you, while the Arian is still enjoying himself slogging away at the current project. He's a marvel to behold, but to you he seems to be slogging because you can never see the point of physical exertion for its own sake. You have the ability to see the thing in its finished state in your mind's eye, and that satisfies you. You like his determination, though, because you aren't as good as you'd like to think you are at getting things finished. There are likely to be several half-finished jobs around the house, not to mention things that you've started at work and then left pending or handed on to somebody else when something new came along. The satisfaction of seeing a project through to its actual completion is as real to you as it is to everyone else, provided that you don't have to do too much to bring it about; this is where the Arian has the most to offer you, and you're not slow to realize this.

What he has is the power to make things take physical shape, as he's an achiever, while you like to plan things and to consider ideas and suggestions. He's nothing like as flexible mentally as you are, though he's quick thinking and decisive, which are qualities that you share and like in others. The relative balance of power suits you perfectly; and you appreciate his quick mind. You'd find him intolerable if he was dull witted, but you like being his mental superior. He feels the same way; he appreciates your brilliance, because he values any sort of confident energy, but he feels that you can't match his ability to bring things about by his own efforts. He needs some of your good ideas, and to be presented with the variety of different approaches to a problem that your imagination throws up, while you need his energy and capacity for effective action to make your dreams come true.

You don't get in his way or cling to him when he needs space for his work, and he doesn't restrict your freedom to think and talk to anyone about anything; you're never in conflict at a level that's deep enough to cause a problem. Besides, you're both the sort of people who would rather get on with the next thing than examine the failure of the last one. As a friendship, the relationship is perfect. As lovers, you'll be surprised by his passion, and he will be surprised by your lightness and facility for teasing and playing. You'll have to build up your strength. Neither of you have feelings that are easily crushed, so you won't have to tread carefully round each other.

As business partners, there will be no stopping you, provided you employ somebody else to do the routine work, which both of you will try to avoid if you possibly can. As a marriage, this combination has a lot going for it. You work well with each other, you don't get in each other's way and you keep the whole thing light and flexible, so that nothing gets on top of you. Above all, you amuse each other, and laugh in each other's company a great deal. You could hardly ask for more.

Gemini - Taurus

There are enormous problems built into this partnership. You're essentially as different as it's possible for two signs to be, and yet there's a sort of fascination between you. Your flexibility of attitude is the only saving grace here, because the Taurean can't change his ways, but you can - provided it amuses you to do so, and if the Taurean can hold your interest.

There are two areas of contention, which are stability and reality. The Taurean is dedicated to the idea of stability. For him, the less anything changes and the longer it stays in the same state, the better. If he can have any control over it at all, he will make sure that everything is kept exactly as it is, without changing. Anything that moves or is unstable disturbs him and he will turn away from it. Anything that puts him as an individual in a state of change or instability, is very upsetting, and will be resisted to the very end. You can see how different this is from your viewpoint. If your surroundings don't change, you feel trapped. Not being actively involved in the exchange of new ideas, making new plans and examining new problems makes you feel trapped, and then you feel as though you're dying. The two of you are bound to come into conflict sooner rather than later. Even if you have a common interest, the mere fact that you'll want to go further and faster with it, while the Taurean will want to enjoy it as it is, is going to lead to arguments. Arguments to you are a part of life, and you enjoy the heat, the challenge of making up counter-arguments and effective phrases on the spot. Arguments to the Taurean are a deeply wounding process, an occasional necessity from which there can be no real victory.

Taurus is slow! You could have written the book by the time a Taurean has read the blurb on the back, or so it seems to you. Can you slow down enough to make friends with the Taurean? To make matters worse, there's the business of reality. For the Taurean, a thing is good if you can touch it, and if it doesn't have a price tag on it, it isn't real. For you, a thing is good if it's a new idea and different from others you've seen, and it doesn't matter whether it's real or not. As a consequence of this, the Taurean will tell you that your brilliance and mental agility isn't concerned with anything real, and therefore it can't be important. This extraordinary response, combining head-in-the-sand ignorance with matronly condescension, will enrage you. The more you rage, the more you'll be ignored. You can probably appreciate that it's a defensive mechanism on the part of the Taurean, but you'll never forgive it, because it appears to value your essential self at nothing, and nobody likes that.

What does the relationship offer? It offers you a sense of security. If you're under pressure at work, to the point where your schemes are about to collapse around you, or if you're being forced to prove that your ideas actually work, then you'll feel insecure. At that point, you'd appreciate having a partner who doesn't want you to do anything, and who will care for you anyway. The Taurean will do that. On their part, you offer them a tantalizing glimpse of a world of ideas. They don't really want to be in that world, but they like to have a look at it now and again because it seems glamorous to them. Being able to see it, and then return to their own habits and well-worn ways, is something that they like.

As lovers, you're miles apart. Taureans have a slow and possessive passion that will shock you with its intensity and stifle you with its clinging embrace. The Taurean will see your light and flippant attitude as evidence of lack of commitment. As business partners, you could do quite well, provided that you looked after the sales and marketing, while they manage the finances.

You could make something of a marriage. The Taurean would stay loyal to you, and if you were to appreciate the benefits of having a comfortable and secure home to return to, there would be quite a lot in it for you. However, how would you occupy your mind? They are still too slow for you, and you're always going to be stifled by too stable an environment. Truth to tell, there are better pairings than this one.

Gemini - Gemini

As with all pairings of two people from the same sign, this friendship works quite well on the surface, but not too well lower down. The reasons for this are quite straightforward - since the planet Mercury makes the pair of you enjoy differences rather than similarities, you'll find yourself disagreeing for the sake of it. In addition, neither of you brings sufficient emotional weight to your relationships to ensure that the affair will last.

Geminis love talking, so the two of you will talk to each other endlessly. You never seem to run out of things to say, and each day has more than enough in it to keep you discussing it for hours. You'll both take in huge amounts of information from the television or newspapers, and then proceed to tell each other all about it, even when the other partner has already seen it! Geminis frequently alter the truth of what they say, because they enjoy playing with the elements of a story in their heads, and sometimes rearrange them for fun. Are you sure that you can see how another Gemini has altered his story? If it matters, this could be a major problem for you, but if you don't care anyway, then you'll both be quite happy.

A problem for the pair of you together is that you're both concerned with ideas and explaining these ideas to other people, but neither of you is very gifted at putting them into action, nor do you possess the necessary organizational talent or physical stamina to do the work yourself. This means that joint schemes could remain at the theoretical stage for a long time, and you'd have to make a special effort to ensure that things actually were finished and put into action; you'd feel your shortcomings particularly keenly in this respect, and would see it in the other, too. Disappointment could follow.

Mercury, your ruling planet, makes you quite cool emotionally. You don't really feel at home with heavy declarations of undying love or deeply sentimental scenes of arrival and departure. You're happy enough if somebody you like is around when you are, so that you can see and talk to your partner, but if he or she is not, then you'll soon find something else to occupy your time. In a relationship, this means that you're both unlikely to develop close ties to a partner, or to care much if they don't feel particularly devoted to you. There probably isn't going to be enough dedication and commitment to keep this partnership going. You'll both find yourselves much more interested in the next new and interesting person who happens along.

As lovers, you'll spend a lot of time on the opening games, so you'll enjoy the meals out, the letters and phone calls and the arrangements for meetings. When that stage is past, and it's time to build trust and friendship, you both lose interest. Emotional exploration isn't as rewarding to you as the preliminary courtship. You're more than likely to start the whole game over again with somebody else. Physically, you'll spend more time talking than making love.

As business partners, you should be very successful, provided that you don't spend all day talking to each other. If you both spend your day separately, talking to non-Geminis, then you will do well. You should be in a job that involves words and communication, such as a public relations or promotional agency.

As marriage partners, you'll both have to learn to finish the housework. There will be no shortage of chatter and laughter in the house, but there will also be piles of unfinished housework to mark where the pair of you stopped to talk about something else!

Gemini - Cancer

This is another difficult match that, in its way, is as hard as the Taurus partnership, but it's considerably more fluid, so you can at least move the difficulties around a bit and put them out of your way. Gemini is concerned with mental output while Cancer is equally obviously concerned with emotional response. This means that the Cancerian will listen carefully and take in all that you say for as long as you care to speak, but you won't get anything like so ready a reply to your questions.

You're being very open and they are being very receptive, but the reverse is not true at all.

The real difference between these two signs is that between thinking and feeling. You don't consider the way that you feel about something to be important. In fact, you'd rather that you weren't drawn into that side of things at all. As long as you can examine something, turn it this way and that, have an opinion about it, assess it and know it, you're happy. Your way of thought is rather clinical, and you don't see why it has to affect your feelings. If you do have feelings about things, you look at yourself from a distance, mentally, and examine yourself having these feelings. When you've noted all there is to note, you think of something else. How different the Cancerian is! They only know something because of how they feel about it. They are more concerned about their response than the facts of the matter, and they hardly ever analyze why they feel the way they do. Imagine it. It must be like finding your way by radar.

Both of you are concerned with a world of the mind rather than with physical things, and that's a point of contact worth developing. You could go to see plays, films and concerts together. One of you would analyze the form and content of the presentation, and the other would respond to it emotionally. Two very different points of view, but you'd both be enjoying yourselves. As the Gemini, you could tell the Cancerian all that you noticed or thought about it afterwards. You could probably find the very different-ness of the Cancerian response interesting in itself.

You both like variety and change, but you don't mind what changes, while the Cancerian wants the changes to suit him, and he's quite prepared to put some effort into ensuring that they do. There's a static element in Cancerian thought, one that wants to put things in order and then keep them that way, and you'll not appreciate that. Cancer is Cardinal, and you're Mutable, and if you're not careful, the Cancerian will try to make you conform to his or her idea of how things ought to be!

There's also a need to provide a secure emotional base, like a home or family life, which the Cancer always works towards establishing, and this is just the sort of thing you can't understand. It seems to embody the two things you dislike most, which are a lack of movement and emotional involvement. Do you dislike these things because you feel attracted to them in a peculiar sort of way? Is it that Mercury, representing the eternal young man, is unwilling to surrender his youth to become a parent (the Moon, ruling Cancer), but feels that he must eventually do it? The lure of the next sign on from your own is strangely powerful, no matter which sign you are.

Sentimental Cancerians would love you as a lover; because of all the sweet words that you'd say to them, and the little teasing games of courtship in which you're so skilled. However, they would want to make you settle down, and you wouldn't want that. You'd find their powerful emotional response fascinating, but ultimately frightening. It's so strong, so uncontrolled, and so lacking in analysis. You'd prefer to keep things at a lighter level, but this isn't going to be possible.

As business partners, you would do well if the Cancerian made all the decisions, as they would be best at looking after the business. You're quite likely to launch off into an unconsidered project that would bankrupt you. You should handle the creative side and the publicity, not to mention the selling, at which you're very good.

As marriage partners? You'd have to be patient, and they would have to learn not to be too surprised by your bright new schemes or your desire to sell the house and buy a mobile home every summer. If they look after the house and you look after everything else, including playing with the children, then all will be well, if you really think you could handle such a long-term project.

Gemini - Leo

This one works very well indeed. Leos are like the Sun, which is warm and radiant; while you behave like a planet, running rings around the Leo, but warmed and given your motion by his energy. What you like best about the Leo is his outgoing nature. He seems to have an unending generosity of spirit, which can produce enthusiasm for anything at any time, not only in himself, but also in others. You appreciate this because it gives you energy and puts you in contact with other enthusiastic people who surround the Leo, and this provides you with opportunities for the exchange of ideas and conversation. All your need for variety, company, conversation, mental stimulation, enthusiasm and outgoing energy are met and provided for by the Leo almost as a by-product of his existence. He would do all this whether you were there or not, and therein lies another important attraction from your point of view. You would not be under any sort of obligation to him for providing you with the things you need, so you need not to be bound to stay with him, to provide for him or have any emotional duty to him. Paradoxically, this binds you closer to him than ever, simply because you stay there through choice rather than obligation.

To say that the Leo requires nothing from you is not strictly true, but he's not likely to ask for it, and you provide what he wants as a by-product of your existence anyway, which is handy. What it means in real life is that neither of you feel that you have to put any effort into the relationship, but it's very rewarding for both of you just the same. It all looks very promising. Perhaps it would spoil things if you knew the mechanics of the relationship, but to appease your enquiring mind, here they are.

Quite simply, the Leo requires an audience. He needs to feel that he's the center of his world, that everything revolves around him and that he is accepted as its central figure. In return, he puts out a steady flow of creative energy to influence his surroundings, and to attract the attention of those around him. The two things that a Leo can't stand are being ignored, either because he's not dominating the action or because he is made to feel unimportant and to look foolish. You don't threaten him with either of these things. You can hardly ignore him, because he's so central to whatever's going on, and you're never involved in status games anyway, so you're not trying to undermine him. You're an ideal audience because you'll respond to everything he says, so in this way, you'll feed his need for attention in the same way that he feeds your need for communication. In addition, your mental energies and his physical ones complement each other. He will seize one or two of your ideas and put them into practice in the way that an Aries would, and that process convinces the pair of you that you're good for each other.

A downside is that the Leo doesn't always think sharply enough for you. He likes to take a very broad view of things, trusting in his own luck and intelligence to make things turn out right in the end. You'd prefer it if he took a more detailed look at things. The way round this is for you to do the detail work, and then advise him privately, so as to preserve his public image. Once again, you're both serving your best interests by acting in this way, and the result should benefit both of you. The Leo also likes to stay with a situation that he likes, whereas you like to move on to new things, and once again, the answer for you is to keep moving, but to refer back to him when you need his support. This way, you can turn the differences into advantages.

As lovers, you should have a great time and an extravagant one, because you'll acquire the Leo's taste for expensive amusements. As business partners, you'd have to keep an eye on the finances, because both of you think it's just for spending. As a marriage, the only problem is that Leo wants his own way all the time.

Gemini - Virgo

This is one of two relationships in the zodiac where two signs are of the same quality (Mutable), but different polarity (one outgoing, the other collecting), and yet they are governed by the same planet, which is Mercury. You represent the different sides of Mercury, you'll each find your astrological alter ego fascinating, and recognize much of yourself in the other.

Because you're three signs separated from each other, you represent each other's basis and reputation. Let me explain. From a Gemini point of view, the careful analysis of all material and all structures to see what they contain is the basis of all investigative thought, and it's also the essence of Virgo. From a Virgo point of view, the ability to understand and retain new ideas instantaneously, to be able to make up any sort of argument or phrase in no time by drawing on a powerful and imaginative memory, is the height of ambition. To be recognized for that ability is real status in a Virgo's eyes. That ability is also the essence of Gemini, the sort of thing a Gemini does all the time, because he can't imagine doing things any other way.

You both admire the other's way of working, the more so since you work in different universes. The Virgo works in a physical world and he enjoys the feeling of things. He's concerned with quality, whereas your prime concern is the concept behind the article. You work in a mental world, where ideas and words are the main currency. Although Virgos are good with words, they treat them as though they were precious, and they feel that such things are not to be wasted. This makes them careful writers and speakers, so they don't necessarily have the speed in communication that you do, or the brilliance that comes from spontaneous thoughts.

Their careful attitude will infuriate you at times, because you turn a thing this way and that in your mind, seeing if it looks as interesting another way up, while they turn a thing physically this way and that, to see if it can be made any better, tidied up, polished and improved. You may see this as a critical attitude, and it is, but you must bear in mind that this is simply a physical expression of your mental curiosity. Mercury is at work behind both of you, looking for things that are different, things that can be changed.

If you let them get a word in edgeways, and you can manage not to lose your temper when they tidy everything away after you, you can build a productive friendship for yourselves. The world won't think so, though, because two Mercury ruled people let loose together will have great fun criticizing everything in sight, and the sharpness of your tongues will lose you many friends. You'll enjoy yourselves immensely, though.

As lovers, you'll need to work quite hard at growing any sort of emotional bond between you. Mercury is not a very emotional planet and you're both a little cool; besides, you both enjoy pulling things apart, and any sign of un-analytical sentimentality would soon be demolished by the other with much sharp humor. You like each other, but you don't love each other much, and perhaps you don't need this as much as the other signs. Virgos are perfectionists, and they can always think of something to stop you from sweeping them off their feet.

As business partners, you need to be a little more sincere and generous if you're not to lose trade; make sure the Virgo doesn't become too obsessive about things, and spend uneconomic amounts of time on small details.

There are no real objections to a marriage, but other people would find your home a little clinical, and perhaps the softer, more emotional moments of family life would be missing. Nevertheless, it would suit the pair of you and you could be very happy to work together for a joint future, so why not?

Gemini - Libra

This is a union within your own airy element, so you feel much more at home here. The currency of the transactions between you is always going to be in ideas and words, and it's always going to be essentially light in tone. You'll feel relaxed with a Libran. The heavy emotional loads that the Earth and Water signs can put on you are simply not present in this relationship. Both of you are eager to please the other, and willing to contribute to the relationship without wanting first to get something out of it. In many ways, the Libran is everything you ever wanted to be, and he seems to embody all the best bits of you, so it's difficult for you not to admire him, and even harder for you to find fault... at first. You like talking to people, but he seems to be friendliness personified. He seems to get the response that you always wish you would get, which is that everybody seems to like talking to him, and he seems to have the ability to make friends with everybody. He makes friends with you, too. He's a delight to talk to, and very amenable to your every suggestion. When you're with him, the world is a friendlier place, and everything seems to turn out better.

From his point of view, you're everything he needs to inspire him to better things. There are times when he can't seem to form a definite opinion about something, but a short chat with you will soon have the matter analyzed, stripped down to its component parts and as like as not, have fun made of its obvious faults. How decisive you are! How you seem to know what you want and exactly what you're doing! This is the sort of behavior that the Libran finds exciting, and which makes him strive to keep up with you. Whenever he dithers, you have the ability to take him back to the beginnings of things and to show him where it started. This is a most useful approach, and one that he simply can't do for himself. The way he sees it is as follows: if he knew more about everything, and could see what was going on, then he could make things even nicer. You can give him this insight, or even better, show him how it's done, so that he can do it for himself. In practice, though, he gets far more out of having you around to help than he would from doing it himself, so he never quite manages to train himself this way.

There are two areas of possible disagreement between you. The first is that you're concerned with finding out what's new and different while he's concerned with finding out what's easiest and nicest. "Nice" is a very Libran word in all its senses, so the ideas of being neat, pretty, rather bland, generally pleasant and inoffensive are all Libran. You'll see after a while that the Libran has none of your cutting edge, and he would rather not criticize. You can easily assimilate this in a relationship, but he's not quite the soul mate you imagined. You'll also notice after some considerable while that he's much less fond of change and novelty than you are; although he's not greatly disturbed when it occurs, he won't actively seek change in the way that you do.

The second major area disagreement is that, although you enjoy company, you're happy to be on your own if you have enough to occupy you. The Libran must have company if he is to function properly, and eventually you'd find this wearisome.

As lovers, you should have an enjoyable time. Librans are happy enough just to be liked, let alone loved, and their need is for daily reminders of fondness in preference to the heavy declarations of devotion that the Fixed signs require. Keep the cards and the little presents coming, and your Libran will be enchanted. The watchword is romance rather than anything heavy, as the Libran is an Air sign, as you yourself are.

As business partners, you'll do well as long as your business is not involved with anything that takes too long to produce, because neither of you has the stamina for that. You must take care that you both get on with business rather than spend the day chatting to clients and employees. You may also need help with major decision-making, but apart from that, all looks well.

As marriage partners, there should be few problems. You'll try to make your partner more active, and he or she will try to make you less frantic, but there are no irreconcilable differences, at least not in your view.

Gemini - Scorpio

This is an odd pairing. You're as different astrologically as it's possible to be. You don't share an element, quality or ruling planet, but you have a complementary mental approach, which is that you both like finding things out. You're a surface reader, so you take in enormous amounts of information from all sources, and use it to understand the nature of whatever it is that holds your interest. What you don't do is look for information, because it's usually there when you want it, and you don't have the sort of dedication that's required for research. The Scorpio, on the other hand, does just that. He's the sort who will dig deeper and deeper until he has uncovered all there is to know about whatever it is that holds his attention. He can't use things that he reads or hears in the same way that you can, nor can he think as quickly. He needs to experience things, find out for himself and check things out to see if all the pieces of the puzzle fit. He's never dissuaded from his goal, and he always gets there in the end. What you have in common is curiosity and an interest in seeing what there is about things that makes them how they are, but you approach things from very different ends. A relationship between you will work in a similar way. You may have similar interests but for different reasons, and you'll approach them in very different ways.

From your point of view, you can use the Scorpio's determination and thoroughness as a way of getting things done, where previously you'd let them slide. It's quite reassuring to have somebody there to lend you firmness and muscle when you need it. In addition, you know very well that you have a tendency to let things go half-finished, or move on to something else when you haven't thoroughly understood the previous thing. Although you're a quick learner, this surface-skimming technique has its drawbacks, although you've become adept at getting round them. In a Scorpio relationship, you have the chance to explore an equally well-informed way of working, but one that offers you thoroughness and stamina above all else. It sounds attractive, because you can imagine adding Scorpio depth to the breadth of your knowledge.

From the Scorpio's point of view, you're the edge he sometimes feels he needs. If a knife is to cut, it needs more than just pressure on the blade, because it also needs an edge. A Scorpio likes to know what's going on, but he also knows that he has a rather heavy and over-serious approach to things. He needs somebody to provide him with the information he needs to stay in control (control is what he's ultimately aiming for) and to show him different avenues of approach. He also needs somebody with a sense of humor to lighten things a little, and your slightly waspish idea of humor appeals greatly to the hint of cruelty in the Scorpio. He needs someone to help him communicate, because he knows he can be a little reticent when left to himself. You're the provider of, and vehicle for, all these things.

Difficulties in the relationship will arise because he will attempt to control you, but your Mutable nature will enable you to sidestep him with ease. He's only doing it so that he can keep the relationship the same and under control, but you see this as unnecessary and undesirable. He will tire himself out by trying to pin you down, and you can make it very hard for him if you wish, especially when he annoys you. The relationship may well break at this point. In addition, he will insist on everything being true and verifiable, so your occasional tall tales will be examined, and you'll be called to account for your deliberately misleading behavior. You don't like this sort of thing, and it may be enough to drive you away to somewhere where life is taken less seriously. As lovers, you're not terribly well matched. You can't tease a Scorpio, and they are both passionate and possessive, while you're not. You may find that your interest wanes, because there's nothing to amuse you.

As business partners, you're better suited than you might think. Scorpios are naturally successful in business and that might keep you interested. You'll have to be the one who adapts to change, because he just can't do that. A marriage will work in the same way, which is quite successful as long as you do the adapting and the Scorpio allows you some freedom of movement.

Gemini - Sagittarius

Like all of the pairings between two signs on opposite sides of the zodiac from each other, you represent different ends of the same stick, and the name of the stick in this case is knowledge. You're both very much concerned with mental activity. The difference is that you're concerned with short-term knowledge, as per the here and now and what's in today's newspaper, while the Sagittarian is concerned with deep knowledge, the eternal, and what's in the serious literature on the subject.

From your point of view, Sagittarians are an exciting but exasperating mixture of enviable talents and irritating viewpoints. They have the deep knowledge that comes from study, whereas you have the immediate knowledge that comes from having seen it this morning in the paper. Somehow, no matter how hard you try, you can't seem to get your knowledge to spread out and take shape as a thing in itself that can be applied to life as a problem-solving technique. The Sagittarian can do this, and frequently does. This is one of the differences between you. You're both Mutable, but he's Fire and you are Air. He can apply knowledge through his will to make things happen the way he wants them to and you can't, because Air is related to ideas rather than reality. The Fire signs are all good at making things happen, and you find this quality fascinating and exciting in all of them. The Sagittarian is the best of them all for doing this, because he changes this approach according to the circumstances in which he finds himself. He takes other people's energy and changes it into something all his own. This is a Mutable sign in action, and you have this quality in common, but what exasperates you is that he can turn it into reality and you can't. You communicate things, but you don't make them happen.

All this would be well if you think he uses his talents properly, but he doesn't – not according to you, anyway. Sagittarians are so straight, so honest and so naive, that you simply can't believe it. You can think of a million and one things that you could do if you had their vision and knowledge to add to your own opportunist talents, but the Sagittarian won't do them, because some of them are a little less than legal, or are unfair to somebody else or might inconvenience a third party. Sagittarians are so honest that it's embarrassing. You find yourself being careful in their company, because the slightest deviation from the truth on your part makes you look like a confidence trickster. They never lie, not ever. Not even white lies. There's honesty and there's tact; and the difference lies in the choice of words, as you well know. Sagittarians only have honesty. At the end of the day, you love Sagittarians for their wisdom, their universal knowledge, their clear insight into any situation, and their eternal optimism, but you just wish they could be a little less noble about things, and a little more useful in the situations of real life.

What do they see in you, you wonder. Detail, mainly. They always see the big picture, and miss the details. They love your ability with words and your conjuror's skill in story telling, and they find your sheer knavery very exciting. Partly, this is because they are honest and gullible, so they wish that they had your lightness of touch. Their planet is Jupiter, the largest of all the planets, while yours is Mercury, which is one of the smallest, so they don't have your maneuverability and deftness. In one sentence: you know something because you've just heard it, and they know something because they believe in it. Your knowledge comes from outside, and theirs from inside, and that's the essence of the relationship.

As lovers, you can have a lot of fun. They will teach you things and they will enjoy your teasing them. They are a lot more physically demanding than you'd think, because the Horse rules your sign. This is the case with all animal signs to some extent.

As business partners, you'll do very well indeed when things are expanding, because you both welcome challenges. The low periods would need careful management, though, as neither of you is terribly good at maintaining what you have and staying static.

As marriage partners, you should get on very well. You'll buy a very big house with room for all the books, magazines, newspapers, TVs, IT equipment and other information sources that you both love so much.

Gemini - Capricorn

This is a strange partnership, in which you can use your talent for buying and selling. Capricorns think in terms of money, and you think in terms of deals, so there's considerable scope here. In addition, Capricorns have a very slow, but rather sardonic sense of humor, which you find great fun. In terms of a business partnership, you could be just what the other one needs, but a personal relationship would need a lot of work.

The Capricorn is the original business person: ambitious if unimaginative, very hardworking and a measurable success, when you consider the state of his bank account. He's a little on the serious side when it comes to having a good time, though. Everything for him has to have weight before he can appreciate it. Something that makes an impression on its surroundings is acting in a Capricorn way, and he will try always to work this way himself. The ripple of interest and respect that runs through a factory when the Managing Director decides to pay a little visit, or the way little cars give way to limousines at traffic junctions, and the effortless way limousines overtake slower traffic. The satisfying sound of expensive shoes on a wooden floor compared to the apologetic squeak of synthetic soles... all these things are symptomatic of Capricorn, because they speak of power, authority, respect, success, weightiness and influence. It's difficult for you to understand this.

To you, everything is light and constantly renewed in your imagination. Capricorn, like the other Earth signs, prefers the solidity of matter. He needs to feel that he's doing the right thing, and he needs to be recognized for the things that he has done. In addition, he wants to control the way things are done, and do that by his own effort. Your enthusiasm for trivia and novelty strikes him as a waste of productive time, and your constant chatter seems to have no purpose to him. The idea of modifying his opinions and of exchanging ideas for their own sake is one that he will never understand.

It so happens that you're a born salesman, because you need the ability to tell stories to the customer in the way he wants to hear them, to keep thinking of your next move and to calculate discounts, and percentages as you go along This is quite some mental exercise, and it amuses you greatly. The fact that you don't really take any of this very seriously is probably the reason for your success. This obvious talent will be noticed by a Capricorn, who is a little short on the skills necessary to deal with people successfully. He can provide the organizational weight that you lack, and you can provide the communications facilities that he lacks. You'll see that the relationship has much to recommend it, as he will bring the success that you need and you can provide the flexibility and fun.

Transfer this relationship into your private life, and the problems begin at once. You enjoy varied company, but Capricorn prefers the company of a selected group of friends. You enjoy doing several things at once (and finishing none of them), but the Capricorn can only concentrate on one thing at a time, and he makes sure that it's done properly and well. That seems tedious to you, and if there are a few cross words about your preference for doing things in quick bursts while the interest holds you, you'll misbehave even more. They seem to have no sense of adventure, and they wonder if a suggested activity is worth the time or money, whether it might not be a better idea to do something else. To you, things don't need consideration, because either you feel like doing them, or you don't.

If you want to become lovers, you should have no problems. Capricorns find light-hearted speech so difficult that your chatter fascinates them. It never occurs to him or her that you talk to everyone this way, and that you can't really talk any other way. As a marriage, this pairing could be very productive and successful, in the same way as a business partnership would. It really depends on how much you recognize and use each other's real strengths. It's unlikely to be a particularly loving or devoted loving match, but neither of you really wants an emotional response at that level anyway.

Gemini - Aquarius

This is another pairing where the planets involved are Mercury and Saturn, but one with a very different flavor to it. This one is one of the easiest friendships for you to form, and one of the longest lasting. It isn't particularly warm or emotional as friendships go, but you both like each other a great deal, and neither of you is the sort to restrict the movements of the other. Neither of you is jealous or possessive. You understand that the other, like yourself, needs the contact of many other people besides just you if he's to be happy and healthy. Neither of you makes emotional demands on the other, as both of you prefer to contribute to a situation rather than take from it. Both of you thrive on change and novelty. It seems strange to outsiders that a friendship can be so firm when you're so cool and dispassionate towards each other, but as far as you're concerned, that's their problem. You just plain like each other, and you like things the way they are, which is relaxed, flexible and uncommitted. You'll have enormous numbers of friends whose company gives you both immense pleasure, and you may be so satisfied with the intellectual stimulation you get from each other and your friends that you may not feel the need to form a physical relationship at all. What is the essence of this extraordinary friendship, then? It's simply this. You're both expressive of Air element energy, but you each greatly admire the way the other uses this energy and would like to copy it yourself. You're each fans of each other's technique.

To you, Aquarius is just what you've always thought you ought to be. They seem to be able to bring out the best in people and they seem always to be in a crowd of the most interesting and lively company. More importantly, they seem to be able to generate good ideas from inside themselves, without having to get the ideas from somewhere else first, as you do. They seem to be able to work with ideas too, and to make other people believe in them. You're always ready to communicate this kind of thing, but somehow it's carried away in the general tide of conversation, and you can't make it stick the way an Aquarian can. They seem to be different from everyone else somehow, and their difference seems to go all the way through them from head to toe. The idea of being this different fascinates you, and you'd love to share it if you could. You might not like it when you got there, of course, but from your viewpoint, it seems the most tantalizing thing in the world. Essentially, you want to make solid, to make reality out of your ideas, but not to lose your mental agility or love of variety in the process. To you, only the Aquarian seems to have managed it.

To him, you seem a brighter version of himself. He recognizes that he thinks differently from others, and that he's at his best within a group, but there's a certain seriousness he has about what he says that does not show itself as dullness, but rather as earnestness, as a genuine belief in his words. He would love to be able to take things less seriously, to make use of words for their own sake and to laugh at what he hears himself saying. He loves those with a brilliant, sharp mind, and the Gemini has it. He doesn't know that the brilliance comes from the reflection of incoming images from a moving surface of a shallow mentality, and that deep thought dulls the sparkle. The Gemini's wit seems to be the most entertaining thing ever created to the Aquarian, and he loves to be in the Gemini's company because of it.

As lovers, why would you want to spoil a beautiful friendship? You probably don't need to. As a marriage, it's just an extended friendship, and that should be fine. It will certainly be different and varied, too.

As a business venture, you're superb together, as long as you don't have to become bogged down in actually producing anything. Stay on the consultative side, where people meet and talk to each other.

Gemini - Pisces

This one really isn't easy. It might seem that there can be some points of contact, as you both work more with mental images than reality, you both like change and variety, and both of you are sensitive to what is going on around you. The similarities stop there though, because you analyze and think about everything that comes your way, while the Piscean deliberately tries not to think about anything too much. At the end of the day, you're essentially unmoved by what you've seen and considered, while the Piscean is overwhelmed.

The Piscean has no analytical mind at all. Turning a thing this way and that to see how it works, exercising any sort of curiosity and putting an idea into words are all second nature to the Gemini, but strange to the Piscean. It's not that they aren't receptive to new ideas, far from it. It's just that they prefer to be influenced by the ideas themselves. They take on the qualities of whatever it is that they're interested in and become like chameleons. In the company of somebody who likes football, the Pisces likes football. At the cinema, they completely identify with the leading character. If they live in France, they are more French than the French are, and in England, they are very traditional. Small wonder that so many are in the movie business, where they get to be a star every day! There's never any sense of standing back and assessing what there is in a given situation for a Pisces. He's completely within the situation at once, part of it rather than an onlooker.

Whilst you admire this fantastic flexibility of mental stance, you have great difficulty in understanding how they could live this way. They have no sense of differentiation. They don't sort things into categories the way you do. Even words are sometimes too precise for the Piscean mind, so they prefer to let words, sights, and sounds coalesce if possible. They prefer poetry to prose, because it has so many meanings. You prefer playing with words in the form of speech, because that way you can communicate what you think. A Piscean doesn't need to communicate, because all his responses are internal ones, and he has no desire to make a precise and individual statement about anything. You have a facility with numbers and figures, while Pisceans just don't. Numbers don't have much emotional content, and therefore the Piscean can't enjoy experiencing them.

You'd have difficulty living in a world where everything was part of everything else and was seen as part of a whole, because you prefer to think of things as separated items, arranged in a sequence within space or time. Not so the Piscean!

Given these two ways of seeing things, could you ever begin to see their way without losing your identity? You'd have to forego all your love of words and wit, as well as your roguish ability with money and salesmanship. You'd have to accept that any reply you got to your questions would be entirely conditioned by the prevailing mood of the conversation, and all your powers of inquiry and analysis would be considered useless to the Pisces. However, you would be given a glimpse of a truly internal world where everything experienced was somehow assimilated into the whole and never discarded. Psychedelia was a Piscean expression of life with the inside patterns on the outside. This is not really your way of thinking, is it?

The grand irony about this partnership is that you both work by being receptive to people, and you like that in each other. You wish he would be less emotional about things, while he wishes you'd get involved in something for once, instead of being so detached. You like each other, but never understand each other.

As business partners, you'd make a poor team. As marriage partners the same applies really, because you'd become cruel and sharp when angered, and the sensitive Piscean would be much more deeply wounded than you can imagine.

Pisces needs a lot of emotional response, and it's not something you're terribly good at, nor is it important to you. You'd both enjoy writing letters to each other in the early stages, but as things grew deeper, you'd realize that he wanted more than you could give.

The Approach to Relationships: Cancer

SYMBOL:	THE CRAB	♋	ELEMENT:	WATER
PLANET:	THE MOON	☽	QUALITY:	CARDINAL

For Cancer, emotions are used to define the world. Emotional nourishment is needed and actively sought. Relationships with the immediate family are used to provide a secure base for all the emotional requirements, leading to the development of feelings of caring, nurture and belonging. All of these are the essential business of the Cancer phase of the zodiacal circle. When the emotions are secure, confidence builds, and then the individual can act as a source of sustenance in himself for those around him.

Cancerian moodiness and over-sensitivity are simply due to an instinct for self-preservation. If every outside influence is known to produce an emotional response in the Cancerian, then he stays away from those things which affect his emotions in a way that he doesn't like. It's exactly the same as not eating those things that you know will upset your stomach. One of the keys to understanding Cancerian thinking is to think of a box. Whatever is inside the box, he regards as his, and he cares for it. Everything outside the box, he will resist, protecting his own possessions and resisting any unwanted intrusions into his security and privacy.

Cancer - Aries

On the surface, this relationship would appear to have little to recommend it. The blazing energy of Aries and the careful nature of Cancer don't have a lot in common. In actual practice, this pairing is much more successful than it looks at first sight, and often becomes a very strong bond indeed.

In some ways, it's precisely because you're so different that this union works so well. Aries is the embodiment of Mars, the masculine sexual principle, and Cancer is the embodiment of the Moon, the feminine principle. There is thus a natural union here, because the masculinity of the one is the perfect partner for the femininity of the other. It does not matter if the Arian is female and the Cancerian male, nor indeed if they are both of the same sex, because the energy flow is just the same.

The Arian is very direct, very energetic and very simple in his approach to problems. In order to achieve his purposes, he throws himself at his tasks with all his energy, and usually succeeds just by the force of his attack. He's not very sophisticated in his analysis of the situation though, and if he's thwarted for any reason, he feels confused and unable to see why things should be this way. This is a rather childlike approach, and as with children, it's beneficial if someone is on hand to dry the tears. Cancerians fill this role admirably. There's something about the stunned helplessness of an Arian who has just failed to do something that appeals to the caring instinct in the Cancerian soul. The Arian can play the role of the child to the Cancerian mother, and the arrangement is emotionally satisfying to both sides. Arians understand things best if they are direct and uncomplicated. The care and sympathy generated by a Cancerian are both of these things, and what's more, they are not the sort of thing an Arian can produce on his own, so he's grateful to have his emotional needs looked after by someone who is much better at it than he is.

Both of the signs are Cardinal, which means that both partners prefer to make the decisions about what form their life takes, unlike the Fixed-sign people who prefer to fit into a pre-existing role. One of the differences between you is that the Arian really does make the decisions about the form of his life, whereas the Cancerian is often inhibited from doing so. The very effectiveness of the Arian approach thrills the Cancerian, because when in partnership with Aries, he gets the power he needs, and his ambitions start to become realities. It's really simple physics, because Water (Cancer) is a slow if steady force, but if you heat the water with fire (Aries) you get steam, and you can drive locomotives with that!

As a friendship, this is one of the most open you could wish for, because neither of you is in the slightest underhand or dishonest. Your emotions won't let you be and Aries simply can't be, because it wouldn't occur to him! Although Aries may sometimes be upset by the force of his temper when you disagree, you're grateful for his honesty, and you also know that his rage doesn't last long. You're more likely to be hurt when he asserts his independence and rushes off in pursuit of a new adventure, leaving you behind. You have to understand that this is not deliberate cruelty, just youthful boisterousness, and you must learn to live with that, just as mothers learn to live with sons who behave in a similar way.

As lovers, you have a great deal to offer one another on a very high level, so it's the meeting of the masculine and feminine principles again. You'll have to accept his occasional lack of tenderness and also realize that you sometimes want to be with him more than he wants to be with you. Fire sign people are like that, so you can't hold them down. It will break your heart before it breaks his, so you need to accept it.

As marriage or business partners, you could do very well together. Remember that you may share the same goals, but your methods and priorities in working will be wildly different, so allow for this. Aries will provide the drive, and Cancer the care and support. To Cancer, Aries will appear reckless, while to Aries, Cancer seems to be a timid worrier. You appreciate each other's efforts though, and that's the key to it.

Cancer - Taurus

One of the easiest friendships in the whole zodiac, for the Moon has a particular affinity with the sign of the Bull. The whole relationship has something of an organic quality to it, though, as intuition and the hidden pull of the tides are present in this pairing. This relationship works below the surface, where each one of you instinctively feels right with the other, without knowing why and without having to ask. You protect and nourish each other, and you never expose each other to anything that might worry or disconcert you. You feel safe in each other's presence, and while you don't stimulate or challenge each other, you comfort and reassure each other, defending each other against anyone and everyone who is harsher and less sensitive.

What is the secret of this closeness? It's to do with something called exaltation, which is one of astrology's little nooks and crannies. Each planet has a sign (not usually the one it rules) where its energies are particularly well received, and in the case of Cancer and the Moon, this sign is Taurus. Since the Moon is particularly happy in Taurus, it follows that a lunar person, a Cancerian, will be particularly happy in the presence of' a Taurean.

The key is in the feminine and nurturing side of both signs. The Moon is very receptive. It takes the energy of the other planets, especially the Sun and looks after it, modifying it and softening it as it goes. This process is connected with natural cycles of growth, and with natural processes of nourishment. All of this is very similar to the Taurean's emphasis on feeding and growth. Both signs are receptive and supportive, and both give rise to a sensitive and maternal attitude in people. True, Taurus is more concerned with purely material things and Cancer is far more able to make major changes in life, but there's much in common in their outlook. Both appreciate security, and both are essentially shy in their approach to new people. As a consequence, the relationship will be very close and emotionally satisfying for both of you, but it will be very much a closed affair as far as outsiders are concerned, because you see no need to share yourselves with anybody else and you feel quite happy in each other's company.

The lunar emphasis of this relationship will mean that you don't develop anything new out of it. This isn't the kind of friendship that produces new ideas, provides mutual encouragement for pioneering achievement, or strikes sparks from the meeting of two minds, which can be used to kindle bigger fires. This is the one that works as a closed-circuit retreat for you both. It can lead to a sort of smugness, or to fits of giggles at private jokes that no one else understands, or to a tight, defensive cliquiness, depending on other factors in the horoscopes of the two individuals.

As friends, you comfort each other and support each other. As lovers, you attempt to possess each other. The Taurean thinks that the Cancerian is his personal property, and the Cancerian feels that he has an absolute right to the Taurean's time and affections. Whilst this kind of devotion is useful in cementing a relationship, it's possible to have too much of a good thing, and there's too much of it here. Eventually you'll stifle the very real joy of the early days of the affair with feelings of obligation and suspicion, Neither of you is willing to let go, either, so perhaps this friendship is best not taken to so intense a level.

As business partners, you'll be industrious but cautious; so a third person is needed to give impetus and contribute fresh ideas. As a marriage, this will definitely have the emphasis on a secure home. You'll be very considerate of each other's needs, and as a safe base from which to raise a family, it could hardly be bettered. It will be very static, so you had better not have any secret desires to move around or make far-reaching changes, because this isn't the sort of marriage to accommodate them.

Cancer - Gemini

This is the most difficult friendship that a Cancerian can try to make. The sign before your own is always difficult to handle, because in one sense, you feel that you've grown past that sort of behavior, but in another sense you're afraid that you find it too appealing. A person from that sign seems to know all your weak points in advance, but despite that terrible thought, you find them irresistible in an odd sort of way.

The essential problem is that you don't think you can actually trust a Gemini. They are never short of things to say; indeed, they think aloud at times, but what they say isn't necessarily what they believe. Belief is an emotional addition to a logical conclusion, and as such is not part of the Gemini mind. They are also likely to change their minds as soon as another way of looking at something occurs to them, and the apparent conflict between their opinion now and their opinion yesterday doesn't bother them one bit. On the other hand, you react quite strongly to what they say, and will react just as strongly to the amended version, too. Constantly changing your reactions and beliefs is both wearying and worrying for you, and after a while, you begin to wonder whether you can believe any of it at all. You and Gemini will become irritated by your attempts to provide the right replies each time the conversation changes. Gemini will find your insistence on sticking to one thing at a time very tedious, while you find his constantly changing point of view rather devious. Neither of you is right.

You face the world in different directions. Gemini has a very low emotional level but a very high intellectual level, and you're just the opposite. It would be easier if your signs shared the same quality or element, but they don't, so there's nothing in common here. Perhaps the most difficult thing of all for you to understand is the way that the Gemini never takes anything at all seriously, and how the idea of putting others first never enters his head. In his turn, the most difficult thing for him to understand about you is that you feel rather than think, and place sentiment above almost all other values.

If your acquaintance is to develop into friendship, you need to be ready for his changes of mood and opinion. You'll also need to be ready for his complete inability to understand your values. That doesn't mean that he isn't interested in your point of view, so be ready to tell him about everything you feel (not easy for a Cancerian, I know) and you'll maintain his interest in you. In return, you'll be vastly entertained, and swept along with him as he lives his life as fast as he can. Perhaps you'll enjoy watching him get away with the things that you know you couldn't.

You need the same readiness to accept his changeable nature if you're to become lovers. He will take his freedom when it suits him, not to hurt you, but because it never occurs to him that this would worry you. He's completely blind to the devotion with which you cling to him, and can have no inkling of how deeply you're wounded when he decides to try something (or somebody) else for a while. Yet, deep down, you know that his freedom from ties, his autonomy, is just what you find so attractive.

As business partners, you would do better looking after different sides of the company, while as marriage partners a similar division of labor would be the best policy. You'll have to adopt his practice of logical appraisal rather than pure gut reaction to solve major problems together, but he must learn to express the emotion he secretly fears if you're to live together.

Cancer - Cancer

This is a cautious and considerate combination. You might think that having two lunar people together would make for a close and understanding relationship, but it isn't anything like as comfortable as the Cancer - Taurus union.

Both of you go in phases like the Moon, so you want one thing for a while, and then lose interest and want a change. You're often tired by the effort of dealing with people you don't find comfortable to spend time with, and there are times when you need a rest, some time to yourself, some time to be private. Sometimes you want somebody to warm you and share his or her successes with you, whilst shielding you from any unpleasantness. What happens if your partner is just as changeable, but the two of you happen to be out of phase?

The chances of you being in exactly the same phase are small, although having said that, two women living or working together will align their physical cycles, but the problem doesn't get better even when you're aligned, though, because when you both need someone to help you restore your energies, you're rather stuck.

In forming this relationship, as with all relationships between two people of the same sign, you must remember that you're both motivated by the same energies, and both are trying to achieve the same result. If that result comes from a one-way transaction, so that you gain something at their expense, then obviously one of you is will be disappointed. In fact you both are, if you think about it. On the other hand, the positive talents that you bring to the relationship are doubled since you're both contributing, but that may not necessarily redress the balance. After all, if you make cake with twice as much flour and only half as many eggs, you still get a cake, but it doesn't taste quite the way you expected.

Both of you like to feel that you're quite sure how the other person is likely to behave. If the other person hides his feelings a little or is uncommunicative and shy, as Cancerians often are, then you may have a little difficulty anticipating their moves. This is even more pronounced, of course, if they have changed their mood since the last time you met.

Both of you ideally need somebody to act as a Sun to your Moon, somebody who is going to be able to light up the partnership with his own cheerful personality and enthusiasm. If you have to play this role for each other, it may feel like a heavy responsibility and that you give out more than you get back, which will worry you a little. Sometimes you'll be unable to muster the energy and enthusiasm required to lift the pair of you, because you're uncertain of what to do for the best, and it's at times like this when the partnership starts to sink. The further it sinks, the more concerned you get and the more you worry, but as I hope you can see, that's precisely the wrong sort of energy needed on these occasions.

On the positive side, you sympathize with each other's misfortunes and cares, and can provide real support for each other in the way that only Cancerians can, and that's a very big plus mark for this particular pairing. If you have mutual interests and shared goals, you can use them as anchor points that help you haul yourselves out of the bad patches and therefore, help you make progress.

As lovers, you'll be supremely sensitive to each other's needs, knowing as few other signs do, that love exists on many levels at once. You hang on tightly to those you love, but if this doesn't work, you must let go.

As business partners, or as marriage partners, you'll never lack care and concern, though you may well lack flexibility and a sense of enterprise, so try to see the grand scheme rather than the immediate problem.

Cancer - Leo

Here you have all the solar energy that you could want, because Leo is the embodiment of solar power. You always say that you want somebody who can provide you with warmth, and here he is, so why is this such a difficult relationship? It's something to do with the fact that this is one of those pairings where both the element and the quality are different. The two signs represent different universes, which are Water and Fire, and two different qualities, which are Cardinal and Fixed. It certainly seems as though you're a universe apart at times.

The Leo is an energy source all to himself, generating energy and radiating it outwards. He likes to feel that he's at the center of things, and he likes things to go his way. Since he's usually the prime mover in any situation, things usually do go his way. Thus, by placing himself at the center of a small group of people, and taking on the role of their natural focus and source of inspiration, he achieves what he wants, and feels satisfied.

To you, this seems remarkably pompous. You feel that he does what he does, not because he cares for the people who surround him, but to reassure his own vanity. You're right, of course, but are you sure that you don't care for those around you because you welcome their appreciation of your efforts, or because it enables you to keep up with what's going on? It's very difficult to assign blame in the business of planetary energies, because in the end they work to everyone's benefit.

There's a mutual antipathy between you that needs to be overcome, and it springs from the fact that the two signs follow each other in the zodiacal sequence. Leo would rather enjoy the company of his friends and supporters than worry about his motives, and he sees your careful, inward-looking attitude as a criticism of his happy state. He's trying to keep things as they are, with everybody smiling. He is, after all, a Fixed sign. He knows that he benefits from everyone's admiration, but they benefit from his warmth and generosity, so why not? In addition, because he believes that things can be made to happen by applying energy to them, he does so. If he stopped believing this, stopped being generous, and started to worry about whether anybody really liked him, he would slip back down the zodiacal scale towards the sign of Cancer, which he tries always to avoid.

For your part, you see him as prodigally wasteful of his energies. He also seems to have no sensitivity to the emotional climate of the moment. Nor should he, if you think about it, because he's not reacting to the thoughts of others; he's radiating energy and enthusiasm outwards from himself. Still, you see him in your terms, and he seems brash and insensitive to you. He gives out personal information, which you keep very close to you indeed. How could he be so stupid? Simple: to him it isn't stupid. He's simply putting more of himself on display. You may not admit it to yourself, but you find this secretly wonderful. If only you could have the sort of confidence, that invulnerability to the opinions of others, the unshakable belief in your own capability, and not the least, the sheer generosity of the Leo. All this is something you can only aim for but never achieve, because this is the exclusive preserve of the next sign from your own, and you must stay where you are in the circle of the signs.

The way to form a friendship with a Leo is to surrender to his generosity. If he wants to buy you expensive presents, accept them, because there's no emotional blackmail going on, as Leos simply are generous people. All you have to do is recognize them as the central figure in your life, which is the difficult bit for you. You have to let them have their own way, and you won't like that either. Relax, because there's no malice here; you're quite safe.

Whatever your relationship with a Leo, be it as lovers, business partners or whatever, keep your worries to yourself. To express them suggests that you doubt his abilities, and annoys him. Besides, you have no need to worry - everything goes right for a Leo.

Cancer - Virgo

This is a lovely union. You're complementary to each other and each of you fills in the bits that the other doesn't have. Cancer is very emotional in its outlook, and spends most of its time dealing with the world of feelings, to which it applies care and understanding. Virgo is much more concerned with the physical world and spends most of its time dealing with methods and materials, which it does with care and understanding. You can see at once that there's great similarity of approach.

Virgos share your belief that little things matter. When a Virgo comes into contact with something new, he spends a lot of time with it, looking at it, thinking about it and getting to know it. He spends a lot of time actually holding it, feeling it, running his hands over it. A Virgo needs to get to know the shape of things. Nor is he likely to do this just once, because repeated activity is very important to the Virgoan mind. The Virgo is building up a sense of how he reacts to the physical nature of something, in the same way as you work with the emotional nature of something. You understand very well the idea of doing something more than once, because there's a kind of reassurance in being able to get things right repeatedly. Patience and practice are Virgoan words, and you have little difficulty in understanding the motivation behind them. Virgoans like to understand things fully, right down to the component parts. They do things in a methodical and patient way, always trying to see how the whole thing fits together and gaining satisfaction from that understanding. In short, they handle people's external natures and movements the same way you handle their internal natures and movements, and you recognize a mind that works in a similar fashion to your own.

To the Virgo, you seem to have the right ideas. The quality that they see as the most evident in your nature is that of caring. They care about doing things properly. Whilst this is true, it's being looked at from two very different angles. You care about details because you want the things in your care to behave in an entirely predictable way, while they care about details because they can only understand the whole by noting all the parts and then adding them up.

As friends, you should be able to appreciate both the similarities and the differences of your points of view. Remember that the Virgo's way of looking at things starts with the details and works outwards, so when they remark on some small point about you it isn't the criticism that it would be coming from anybody else, it simply denotes interest and an attempt to communicate. As lovers, you'll take some time to get going. This is because of the Virgo's inability to see things on the grand scale. He's never going to be swept off his feet by mad passion, and your grand emotional overtures may not be recognized as such, simply because of their scale. Affection and care, yes: helpless love, no.

As business partners you should get on very well. Virgo has the ability to make you talk, which the other signs can't do very well, and you can help him develop a feel for things that's intuitive rather than analytical. The strength of the one is the weakness of the other, and there's a genuine desire to help each other along. Both work hard and long when necessary, though you're both prone to overwork unless reminded that you sometimes need a holiday. You're both "collector" signs, and have a tendency to think that working hard solves problems, which is not always true.

As marriage partners you'd be very well suited, since you can both understand, and be sympathetic to the other's approach, but you must to look outwards and upwards from time to time.

Cancer - Libra

This is an easy relationship at the start. The pair of you get along passably well on the surface, and your opening behavior, the kind that you use to form an acquaintanceship with anybody new, suits the Libran well enough. As the relationship deepens, you'll see the fundamental differences between you at the same time as you discover how much you genuinely like each other. If you manage to accept those differences and work with them rather than against them, you'll make a very strong partnership indeed.

Librans are almost too nice to be true on the surface. They are ruled by Venus, which means that they will always see the best in someone rather than criticize them. There's always something about you that the Libran can find to like, and this is very flattering to you. There's no trickery here, because Venus is looking for something to identify with and relate to, and it has to start on the outside, because that's what it meets first. Librans like liking things. This is an outgoing sign, remember, so they are not gathering things into themselves. When they say they like you, it's real. You find this captivating; you can hardly believe your ears.

Librans are very refined people. They like anything that's beautiful, symmetrical, pretty, pleasing, or harmonious. This is because Venus draws them away from anything that's unbalanced or inelegant, and as a result, they are all natural aesthetes. Since your behavior pattern on meeting somebody new is unfailingly polite, partly to prevent strangers from trying to penetrate your outer shell, the Libran will find you attractive. After all, to him, anybody with such good manners and restraint must be a balanced and refined person, and he likes that.

The trouble with this relationship is that Librans are at their best on the surface, because the murky waters of the emotions are too raw and unbalanced for him. To be fair, that's not really his fault, because he isn't a Water sign; he's an Air sign, and a Cardinal one at that, so he's therefore as determined to make his world work in airy terms as you are in watery ones. You're the different tides of mental energy. He's the outgoing, communicative tide, and you're the incoming, emotional one. Because you work in the same universe but in different directions, you find each other both amenable and infuriating at the same time.

Problems arise when you're in one of your low phases. You'll feel very possessive of him, and you'll try to tell him how much you need him and how much time you've spent with him in the past. Then you'll discover the meaning of the famous Libran balance. Hit him on one side, and his other side comes round to hit you in return with an exactly equal force. He will remind you of all the things that you've done to annoy him, which he hasn't mentioned until now. He will remind you of how much he has given in to your selfishness in the past. All of this will hurt like hell, and you'll be very shocked. Libra's picture in the heavens is not an animal, it's a machine, so what else did you expect? Realize that he deals with everybody equally and that he dislikes anything that emphasizes one person's needs above another. Show him your inner self, and let him like it. Offer him your care in return. Achieve a balance.

As lovers, you'll emphasize the softer sides of your natures and the union will have a romantic flavor to it. As marriage or business partners you'll do well if you maintain the balance, so forgive his occasional vagueness and lack of concentration, and he will forgive your worries and fussiness over little things. He's really a very good partner for you.

Cancer - Scorpio

Here the fountain meets the lake. Scorpio is the Fixed Water sign. A Scorpio somehow seems to be a stronger, more powerfully developed version of you. You're very much in awe of Scorpios, and you'd dearly love to be one. You don't find Scorpios frightening, but they seem so much more effective in their dealings with people than you are, and you admire this. In fact, the relationship between you is very much one of admiration on your part.

One of the most informative ways of looking at a Scorpio and of comparing him to a Cancerian is to look at the zodiacal animals. The Scorpion has a hard outer shell like your crabs, and he has eight legs and a pair of claws. In addition to all this weaponry, he has a lethal sting in his tail. Like the crab, the scorpion doesn't move from his position easily, and when in serious trouble he will sting himself to death rather than surrender. Scorpio people show all of these characteristics, so you're dealing with a creature of the same type as yourself. Not of the same reputation, though, because the greatest difference between you by far is how the world treats you, which is also reflected by the animals. The world thinks of a crab as touchy and snappy, and eventually someone takes a hammer to it and makes it into pâté. The world fears scorpions, and stays a respectable distance away when it meets one.

You find the Scorpio so strong and determined that you can hardly believe it. If you were so determined, you think, you'd burst from the pressure. Possibly so, but not Scorpios. You take energy in and put it out again in the form of caring, because your aim is to protect yourself and those who are around you. The Scorpio is past all that. He takes energy in and keeps it there. His main aim is to control - again mainly himself - but also those who are around him, and eventually everybody.

Scorpios work at a very intense level indeed. Since this is all emotional energy, you think you're familiar with it, but the sheer scale and scope of it frightens you, and you fear for your safety. That might annoy the Scorpio, your tendency to wonder if you'll get hurt. Scorpios don't care for their own safety. They know they will survive, and they can take enormous risks as long as all the elements of danger are under control. Control is their motivation, and power is their goal.

You'll find a relationship at this level very exciting. You must not think of the risks, only of the passion. If you feel safe with them, you could find yourself sharing in their manipulations, and enjoying the sort of power to which you've always felt attracted.

From you, the Scorpio gets a reminder of the true nature of emotional energy. You generate it freely from within yourself, whereas he doesn't. You can give emotional energy out to people in the form of care and protection, knowing that there's always going to be more where that came from. Your resource is infinite because you are the definition of emotions, the Cardinal Water sign. The Scorpio has to keep and control his emotions in tact, because he feels that he has no way of making more. Your simple maternal impulses make him feel ashamed of himself. He knows he could never show that kind of devotion. You're the shy and uncertain possessor of the most powerful gift of all. The zodiac works that way and so, of course, does life.

On all levels, this relationship is powerful and productive, good for both of you. If you can stand the pressure, you'll love the heat! When Scorpio tries to control you, you can defend yourself quite well, and in return, you can protect him from his own sting.

Cancer - Sagittarius

This is one of the two five-signs-apart relationships, and such pairings are not at all rare. There's a lot of work to be done by the two people concerned, because in almost every possible way you're different, so you'll need a lot of patience and a willingness to adapt for this one to work.

You're very sensitive to what people think about you and you're easily hurt by unkind words. Within ten minutes of meeting a Sagittarian, you'll feel that he has probed, prodded, exposed, inspected and finally beaten you up and left you to die by the roadside. Yet, the Sagittarian is so charming with it! How does he do it? In addition, why is he so cruel to you? Sagittarians are insatiably curious. They have to find out all they can about everything they meet. When they meet you, you're likely to be polite but reserved, and you'll show a genuine concern for his welfare. How interesting, he thinks. He decides to find out more. This is not cruelty. This is the Sagittarian showing you how interested he is in you. He has an alarming talent for looking into people and seeing their inner workings as though they were transparent. He also has a facility with words, and a desire to show you what he has seen. The Sagittarian has no tact. It doesn't matter where you are or whom you're with, they have to tell it as they see it, there and then. Don't even attempt to explain your embarrassment, just slip back into your shell and play with the hors d'oeuvres. There's a great deal of similarity between the Sagittarian and the puppy that keeps bringing you things he has found in the garden. You don't want them to do it, but you know that he's showing his affection. Why do you find Sagittarians so irresistible, then?

They are warm, openhearted and free with their emotions. They are romantic and they are always optimists. That's why. You need them to put some warmth into your world and to show you that life isn't as hard as you make it seem. What they need in return is somebody who really is cheered by their relentless optimism, and somebody to comfort them when their schemes collapse, and somebody to look after the serious side of life for them. They know that they have to show a sense of responsibility now and again, over such things as mortgages and taxes, but it really doesn't suit them, and they tend to shy away from it all. You can provide the home base that they need, look after the organizational side of things, and they will provide you with an exciting life in return.

You'll argue over money. Cancerians are very careful with their money, and you save it whenever you can, because it adds to your security. Sagittarians have never understood the word "security" and they can spend money quickly, but when they start to spend your money, there will be arguments.

If you're lovers, you must try to allow for the fact that the Sagittarian is often in love with more than one person at once. You can't expect his exclusive attention. Think of yourself as number one wife in a harem instead. Remember that he doesn't do any of this to hurt you, and indeed wouldn't hurt you for the world, but he just has to keep moving, and you find that upsetting.

If you want to make a marriage out of this, you'll have to be prepared to move around, and make sudden changes. It's not as hard as it sounds. A crab, like a snail, takes his house with him when he moves. You don't lose emotional ties just by changing direction, and you know that.

Cancer - Capricorn

As with most of the relationships formed by two people from opposite signs of the zodiac, this one is quite easy to handle, and in fact is concerned with the same thing, which you approach in different ways. In this case, you like organization or structure as this acts as a shield against your enemies, while Capricorns like structures so that they can use them as ladders to climb to the top.

The Capricorn is concerned with material things in the same way that you're concerned with emotional things. He uses people's reactions to material things to define his world, in other words, he gets his status from status symbols. That sounds a little hollow, but a Capricorn is more than a status symbol collector. He's the one who decides what it is that confers status in the first place. He wants to be noticed and recognized for his achievements, and he's prepared to work very hard to get what he wants. He also wants that recognition to be permanent, and to him, the best way of doing that is to make it physical. It means much more to him to have a silver trophy than to win the race. The elation of winning only lasts for a day or two or until the press has forgotten about it, but the trophy stands on the sideboard forever. He will need to invent a whole vocabulary to show his success in visible form, so that people are constantly reminded of his achievements, and see him as a success. Now we can see why he likes status symbols. It's expected of him. If Capricorn chooses to display some new and expensive object, it becomes a status symbol simply because it's the sort of thing a Capricorn would have.

Given the choice, Cancer would like to be a private individual, at home with his family. Given the choice, Capricorn would like to be on public display. Successful Capricorns who are millionaire recluses are only that way because it draws attention to their status. In earlier societies where there were no newspapers with gossip columns, Capricorns were the ones with the bands of armed guards who walked about reminding you how powerful they were.

What attracts you to a Capricorn? Determination, mostly, along with their withdrawn exterior. When you meet one, you'll perhaps think that you're looking at a similar individual to yourself, but one who keeps his feelings to himself. This isn't really so. Capricorns are serious and withdrawn it's true, but their emotional level is so low that you wouldn't recognize it. Emotions aren't the kind of things that you build firm reputations and business empires on, so they don't give them a lot of time. Perhaps you're drawn to his strong determination to have things his way, no matter how long it takes him to get there. Perhaps you like the self-control that he shows in the face of adversity. Perhaps it's simply the fact that the world looks up to him. It may even be that he recognizes the importance of the rules in life, just the same as you do. In return, you can show him that a heart of stone is capable of being warmed, and that success with people is as rewarding as success with material things.

As lovers, you'll be the warmer partner, which means that the union will be a cool one. If you want love rather than sex, don't choose a Capricorn. As business partners, you'll do very well. Both of you understand the way money works, and have the knack of acquiring it. The workplace could be humorless at times, though.

As a marriage, this one is very traditional, but none the worse for that. Home life will be rather formal, with Capricorn as the father figure and Cancer the mother figure; these roles will be adhered to.

Cancer - Aquarius

This is the second of the five-signs-apart pairings you could have; like the Sagittarian one, there are massive adjustments to be made by both of you if the relationship is to develop satisfactorily. Once again, the principal obstacle is the other person's unwillingness to stay in one place for too long. Aquarius is the second sign to be governed by Saturn, but this time, unlike Capricorn, the Saturn influence is itself of a lunar type. This is a cool, low-key and offbeat relationship, based on fascination and a certain quirky amusement rather than admiration or affection.

An Aquarian will leave you alone when you want it, and that makes him unique in the zodiac. You're very grateful for this, and a partner who does not swamp you with his presence has a lot of appeal for you. Sometimes it can be difficult to get him really involved when you want him to be close to you, but you can't have everything. Aquarians have a lot of compassion, and they do care. You recognize this and find it a sympathetic viewpoint to your own. Where you differ is that they care on a general scale, whereas you care on an individual scale. Social injustice awakens the Aquarian spirit, where personal injustice excites yours. You'll find it difficult to believe that they can't scale down their concern to match yours, but it is so. They don't lack feeling, but they do lack involvement. You're intimately involved with every action you undertake, but they are not. It will take you some time to understand this devotion to the universal, but distinct coolness towards the specific.

Aquarians are fascinated by anything unusual. In fact, the unusual is the usual for them. You're a very conventional soul, who finds comfort in the familiarity of known and trusted things. The Aquarian has to try the unknown just to see what it's like. You might try to make the Aquarian conventional or to make him give you affection. They need large numbers of people, while you're happier with a small group. These two areas of difference between the large-scale and the small personal, along with the unusual and the conventional, are going to crop up over and over again in your relationship, and you'll have to make a great effort to get round them.

As friends, you'll get along easily, especially if you're part of a larger group. You both recognize that the other one doesn't like being pressed too hard to do anything, and you maintain a discreet distance. He likes your sensitivity and your quiet exterior. If you deepen the friendship and become lovers, you'll find things more difficult. You require a personal devotion he can't provide, and his affections lack the depth you seek. He will always be looking to change the relationship, and you to give it some sort of roots, so it isn't easy.

Should you marry, you'll learn that making emotional demands leads to trouble, and will have learnt to live with their independent behavior. You'll be keen to give the Aquarian the individual care you think he needs, but he will say that you cosset or smother him. Again, it isn't easy.

As business partners, this will work if you look after everything financial and he looks after everything else. This relationship is a much better proposition than marrying each other.

Cancer - Pisces

This is a Water and Water partnership, and your animal metaphor helps you to understand how you work together. Both crabs and fishes live in the sea, surrounded by the watery element that supports them in every way. The fishes move around constantly and if they don't, they sink to the bottom. Neither of them is a threat to the other, since you don't eat each other, but occasionally the fishes get curious and come a little too close to the crab, and then they get nipped, which they don't like at all. Life between a Cancerian and a Piscean is remarkably similar.

The situation is quite similar to the Scorpio relationship, but with the roles reversed. This time the Piscean is the one lost in admiration, and you're the one who seems to have all the power and authority. Strange, isn't it? Pisces wants to be as protected as you are, and he's horribly vulnerable to almost anything you can think of. His complete inability to do anything assertive or decisive means that he could really do with something like your shell. You may be reserved, but you know what you want. Pisces is pathologically shy, and has no real course of action at all.

You may think you're sensitive, but your range of sensitivity is markedly crude in comparison to the Pisces. These people are as sensitive as an old photographic plate. They catch the mere shadow of something and hold it forever. They have a remarkable chameleon quality in that they can (and do) take on the character of their companion and his surroundings. You'll find that they share your enthusiasms, and even dress in the same style, given long enough. Such fantastic sensitivity is a revelation to you. These people can make a whole way of life from a fleeting impression, and fashion reality from fantasy as though it were made of bricks and mortar. You wouldn't really like to be a Piscean. They have no control over what makes an impression on them next, and they can't make emotions for themselves, but only react to circumstances. No self-direction, and no structure: not your sort of thing at all.

As friends, you have coincident views most of the time, since your opinions are both shaped by similar reactions to external events. The difference is that you respond to external stimuli by deciding whether or not you need to deal with them as a threat, while the Piscean just reacts, and has to see where that gets him. You don't have his amazing flexibility or his adaptability, but you do have some measure of control over your life, which he doesn't. You must be careful not to defend yourself too strongly if he threatens your privacy; just a word is enough to a Piscean, and if you hurt them with your crab's claws, you'll do more damage than you intended.

As lovers, you'll surround yourselves with every emotional indulgence, and everything that produces a response from the other. Romance is the keynote of this liaison rather than passion or power. Roses and poetry are going to feature more strongly than sexual athletics. It could get a bit too dreamy for you, because you're a Cardinal sign, and you don't lose sight of your objectives. It will certainly be a luxurious experience.

As business partners, you really lack the edge required to make any sort of mark in the commercial world. The media loves Pisceans, though, so perhaps you could aim yourselves in that direction. You're best as employees rather than employers.

As a marriage partner, you could hardly do better. Most of the time, your lover sees things the same way as you do, and when your partner becomes over-sensitive, you can protect him in your way. You can build a safe base for your family, filled with love and understanding instead of tension and defensiveness. You'll have to take the decisions, though, because a Piscean just can't.

The Approach to Relationships: Leo

SYMBOL:	THE LION	♌	ELEMENT:	FIRE
PLANET:	THE SUN	☉	QUALITY:	FIXED

Leo is concerned with being in control, but also being the instigator as well. It's the difference between being a commander and being a mere manager; words that imply a sense of action, command and being the principal person are all Leonine in their feeling. Leos are kings, rulers, generals, emperors; they are leading lights, superstars, grandmasters, conductors of the orchestra. It's an essential part of the Leo experience to be addressed in terms of respect, using a title that shows recognition of the Leo's place at the center of things.

The orchestral conductor is a particularly good example. The conductor is the one whose interpretation of the work is expressed by the musicians. He organises, leads and conducts them, but does none of the actual playing. He inspires the performance; he is its center and focus. Why? Because he takes an existing situation and makes it his own. He is the heart of the performance. Energy radiates out from him as he inspires the performers to work together in expressing the vision of the music. Leos are always the inspiration of their group, and they have confidence in their abilities and their vision.

Leo - Aries

This is one of the great friendships of the zodiac. You think that Aries are dynamic and confident, which is just the way you think people should be, but they change direction too much for your taste. You think they might settle down in a few years' time, while they think that you have the right sort of enthusiasm but you're a little unadventurous, a bit of a home-lover, and that all you need is a bit of a push to get you onto the right track. You'll enjoy trying to make these final adjustments to each other. Neither of you will succeed in making the other more like yourself, and it's better that you should not succeed anyway, because those little differences give that extra sparkle to the relationship and stop it from becoming boring.

You've a great amount in common. Both of you are Fire signs and both of you believe that action is better than inaction, that getting personally involved is the only way to be effective, and that your own ideas are naturally the best ones available. People who sit still, who worry about things, bore both of you very quickly, because you're both optimistic, forward-looking and confident that you can handle anything that comes your way. Let us examine that last phrase again. Leos are not normally confident about handling new things. You're confident with things that are familiar, but not with new ones. Where has the confidence come from? It comes from Aries. To you, he represents the source of all personal energy. You feel that you might not have the resources to cope with anything completely new and unfamiliar, in case it requires more than you've got, but Aries seems to be an inexhaustible supply of whatever it takes, and your confidence in facing the unfamiliar grows strong in his company. After all, you think, between Aries and me, we must have more than enough energy for anything, and you're right.

It works the other way round, too. Aries knows that he has the raw bravery to attack anything that comes his way, but he also knows that he doesn't have the staying power of the Leo. If a problem is likely to withstand his first onslaught and require real determination, then he knows he would be better off trying something else, and he changes direction accordingly. A partnership with Leo gives him the stamina he didn't have before, and he's the stronger and more capable for it. In terms of their element of Fire, Arians have the spark of ignition, but not the heat of combustion. Together, the two signs give a steady burning fire which can be started anywhere.

In a friendship, the thing you'll like about each other most is the fact that you're each as enthusiastic and energetic as the other. The Arian doesn't have to slow down and wait for the Leo, or limit his activity in any way, nor does the Leo find the Arian too cautious to share fully in his grandiose way of life. Both find life exciting, and you find plenty to make you smile. You're both used to things going right, and used to feeling pleased with yourselves. To have a friend who feels exactly the same way is fulfilling indeed.

In love, you both bring the heat of your Fire sign energies with you, and your physical relationship is likely to be hot and strong. It's not that you're not romantic, but beneath the sentiment, you're both essentially interested in expressing your energy through physical activity. Neither takes from the other, as you're both givers, and with such generous contributions from both sides, you're going to have a fine time. Enthusiasm and confidence make for more of the same, so you can't lose. The only way that you're different is that the Arian is likely to tire of the relationship before you. He's not necessarily exhausted, but he needs fresh challenges to be at his best. Too much that is too familiar makes him restless.

In a marriage or as business partners, you should work very well together. If you try to dominate the Arian, he will direct his energies elsewhere, which would be detrimental to the partnership. Try not to organize him overmuch, either. The only problem is that you both like spending money more than you like to save it, and somebody has to keep an eye on the finances.

Leo - Taurus

This is what you could call a steady relationship. If you're the sort of Leo whose energies are best directed into material things, who dines well and has a sumptuously decorated house, then this is the relationship for you.

This is an "accumulating" partnership, so almost from the word go, you'll find yourselves buying things together that somehow express the pleasure you get from each other's company. Most of these things will be expensive, luxury items that appeal to you both. Perhaps you'll be surprised at how your tastes coincide. In fact, they don't, but they do overlap quite substantially in the realms of the opulent and ostentatious. As the relationship goes on, you'll find that you've collected a large number of things together and the relationship is taking visible form through these objects.

It's a relationship where the essential principle is strength and position. The maintenance of your position is vital to both of you, and in many ways this partnership over-emphasizes the heavier facets of your personalities at the expense of the others. The Taurean's gentleness and feeling for the land won't be in evidence when in your company, and your generosity towards others will be diminished in the same way.

What the Taurean is after is material security. He measures his existence by his surroundings, and the more things he can touch and keep, the better he feels. Your way of life usually involves any number of nice objects as a matter of course, and the Taurean finds these very attractive. You're naturally generous and will probably take your Taurean to a restaurant soon after your initial meeting or give him or her a small present. They will be highly appreciative, because material things are important to them and they keep them forever. You enjoy being appreciated and you enjoy being generous, because it expresses your confidence and your liking for yourself. They enjoy being taken out and love receiving presents, because it increases their liking for themselves. You've found the perfect receptacle for your generosity, and it will all be converted into material form.

What you want is someone to appreciate you and you'll certainly have that in the Taurean. The problems arise when you find that the Taurean isn't necessarily going to give you what you want. You want someone who will do things your way, and you don't want someone who is going to stand his ground when you're trying to move him. Taureans do exactly this, giving you two alternatives, which is that you can both stand your ground and shout at each other, or you can take your partner's point of view and bring your own special radiance to it, which is a better result. You can now see why you're accumulating so many expensive things: they are "Leo-ized" Taurean acquisitions.

As friends, you'll enjoy the good things of life together. Provided that you live essentially separate lives, you're unlikely to quarrel, and the biggest problem that faces you is that of obesity, as you'll encourage each other's over-consumption in all senses. As lovers, you'll be powerful but rather ponderous in your behavior. Taurus gives no sparkle to the union, and it could be a bit of a wrestling match. You're both possessive, and this will slow things down further.

Provided that you don't spend too much time fighting each other from entrenched positions, either marriage or a business partnership would work well. Money is an essential lubricant in this relationship though, and if there isn't enough of it, things will soon come to a grinding halt.

Leo - Gemini

This relationship is bright, alive and fun all the way. Gemini doesn't care how much money you have or how generous you are. What he cares about most of all is how much you get out of being yourself. He has a similar feeling about himself, and he can't wait to share it with you, and to find out about your feelings at the same time.

You see him as the sort of friend you always wanted, because he's bright, pleased to see you, actively seeking your company, and making you part of whatever he's doing. You love a chance to show yourself off, and there's always some way to do that in a Gemini's company. You don't like dull surroundings, and there's always something lively happening wherever a Gemini is. He always regards it as a bit of a game, something diverting and not to be taken too seriously. How could you not shine in an atmosphere like this? All the ponderous and static parts of your nature are miraculously converted into good-humored boisterousness by the Mercurial talents of the Gemini. You can't stand still for too long when he's around, but he has taken away your fear of having to try unfamiliar things by doing them for you. You can stay where you are in the midst of all the fun while he presents new amusements to you in a constant stream. In many ways, the relationship is like that between a king and his jester. He's a willing satellite, racing around you at a giddy rate while you stay beaming in the center, and you find the arrangement very satisfying.

He sees you as somebody he can rely on. You're always going to be constant in your reactions to him, and he finds this useful. He may change his tune from one minute to the next and he knows it full well, but to have a friend who finds him fascinating no matter which side out he is, and who will always be there, is something worth looking after. He's also well aware that he needs shelter and support from time to time, when one or another scheme collapses. Geminis are very good talkers, but their lives seldom match their plans. In such cases, it's most reassuring to have a friend who will stick up for you and not betray you, and to lend you a few quid when you're broke; in short, a sort of ersatz elder brother. Leo fulfils this role for Gemini admirably and the Gemini loves it. It's not all take and no give, though, because the Gemini renders the Leo worthwhile service. It works like this; A Leo likes to know what's going on in the world and to be up to date, so that he can stay in command. If he's overtaken by new developments, then he could be made to look silly, and this he is anxious to avoid. Finding out about things from ground level is a bit undignified for a regal Lion, so he gets his information from the Gemini, who picks up information like the rest of us breathe. It looks like the king and his jester again.

As a friendship, this has everything to recommend it. You have to accept that the Gemini will tell you different tales on different days, and you mustn't expect him to give you much in the way of respect. He does like you a lot, though and he relies on you – as much as a Gemini relies on anybody.

As lovers, you're more likely to break ribs from laughter than from the fierceness of your embrace. The light, playful, essentially un-serious way a Gemini leads his public life extends to his private life as well. The Leo must remember that the Gemini has no real notion of loyalty or commitment, but provided he can live with that, the two of you can have a wonderful time playing expensive and intimate charades with each other.

For business, the combination could hardly be bettered. Your unity of purpose but difference of approach will have your competitors absolutely baffled. In a marriage, and especially for family life, these two signs have a lot to offer each other. Leo gives the warmth to sustain a relationship, and Gemini stops it from becoming too set in its ways.

Leo - Cancer

Relationships formed with the sign immediately before or after your own are the most difficult of all. To give you your due though, you manage this difficult task better than the other eleven signs, but you're still unlikely to choose a partner from a sign adjacent to your own, unless other factors in your horoscope predispose you to do so. The reason is simple. The sign before your own represents you looking over your own shoulder, as they embody all the things you'd rather not think about.

You see a Cancerian as an impossibly worried person, because you don't understand how anyone could be as afraid of life as he is. How do they manage to get up in the morning? The answer is through familiar and safe routines, and with care, not at all like your confident stride through life, trusting in Fortune to smile on you. You each have very different views on life from the other. You give them everything, and they seem to offer you nothing in return. You wear your heart on your sleeve, but you know next to nothing about how they feel. Worse still, they don't tell you how much they appreciate you.

It's not as bad as it seems, although you'll have to try very hard to see it the way it really is. They are actually in awe of your energy and generosity. A Cancer assimilates things a bit at a time, making sure they are thoroughly familiar before moving on, so the scope and power of your way of doing things, in great open gestures, is too much for them to handle all at once. You're forthcoming and open when you speak, while they are shy. If they could manage to answer you in the way you expect, you'd probably do something else large and dramatic by way of response, and that would be altogether too much for them to manage. Quite simply, you overwhelm them.

Cancer would like to show you how much you're appreciated, and they do this by caring for you when you're not feeling as brilliant as usual. There's no such time, you cry, and there may well not be. Even if there were, your solar, solitary nature would prevent you from either taking or seeking comfort from another person, so the Cancerian's prime function is denied. You really aren't a great deal of use to each other, as one is too much for the other to handle, the other offers a response that the first one doesn't want.

There's a more subtle way in which the Cancerian gives you all the things you don't want. You feel confident because you've mastered your fears fairly early on in life, and they only come to the surface again when you're presented with something completely new. Changing circumstances worry you, because you must make yourself master of them before you can settle back into the role of the relaxed, unflappable, serene, ruling figure. For this reason, you're none too fond of practical jokes. You laugh because you feel you have to, but you seethe inside because somebody has tried to unsettle your confidence. There's a worried person inside every Leo, but he's a very long way down, and he need not be considered most of the time. A Cancerian brings him to you in the form of another individual who is just as worried, just as defensive and just as easily upset. In fact, a Cancerian is much more than these attributes, and he works on a different wavelength altogether. You only see the parts of yourself you'd rather not consider.

It's difficult to make this friendship work. You really can't function with someone who worries every time you get interested in something, and the Cancerian just can't stand the tension, as he thinks your luck has to give out sometime. It's unlikely that you'll be lovers, at least on the level of your Sun-sign energies. If you do become lovers, though, you'll find that the major obstacle is the Cancerian's inability to really give himself. Keep the relationship light if you really want to keep it going. You both enjoy the surface of courtship, with the flowers and candle-lit dinners, so leave it there.

As a marriage, you can only make this partnership work if you both stick to the traditional roles, with Leo as the father and Cancer as the mother. A modern or loosely structured relationship will probably not work.

Leo - Leo

Forming a partnership of any kind with a person of the same sign as you may not be good, but on the other hand, it's nowhere near the disaster that it's sometimes made out to be. At least you know what you're getting!

Here, the relationship is made from two people who both like to be the center of attention, and both like having a good time. The easiest way to make this work is to avoid any sort of situation where either of you have to make a decision, because each of you would like to be the one to do it, and neither of you will be particularly happy to do what the other has decided. If you're simply enjoying each other's company in an environment where the social rules are well known and familiar, then you'll have no problems at all. Everybody else in the immediate area will find themselves being naturally drawn to the crackle of energy between you, and soon there will be an instant party starting up.

What you like about another Leo is his openness and optimism. There's nothing secretive about a Leo, for he has no reason to be. When one Leo meets another, both feel very relaxed, because they each know that the other is not trying to out-maneuver him in some sort of personal chess game, the way the Scorpio does, or use your leonine energy to meet his own needs, as a Taurean might. A Leo puts out solar energy and likes to see some of it redirected back to him by appreciative friends. This energy usually returns in a much weaker form. When the appreciative friend is another Leo, the energy comes back full strength, and the pair of them can literally bask in each other's warmth.

The combination looks very positive until you remember that only one of you can be the dominant partner, but that both of you have a real need to dominate. Once one of you is established as the dominant partner, the other one must do one of only three things: he could displace you and be dominant himself, he could go somewhere else and become the center of a new group, or he could stay in your shadow, which would lead to much frustration and eventually illness. As you can see, all three lead to the dissolution of the partnership. The obvious conclusion to be drawn is that if the relationship is to survive, then neither of you must be the dominant partner. The only way to implement this is for you to take turns. Since you are Fixed signs, you have a natural reluctance to change roles more frequently than you have to, and you're much better off in one position over a long period of time. The best compromise seems to be to divide your areas of responsibility, and for each of you to take absolute responsibility for your own areas. Stay inside your own territory for things that matter, but share the limelight for the lighter and more social side of life, where you're not so likely to be fighting for position. In some ways, it's an artificial answer, but it's the only workable one. A business relationship may be somewhat unbalanced, unless you have someone else around who can do the paperwork and cope with the routine chores.

As a friendship, the Leo - Leo pairing is a lot of fun. When the friendship becomes an affair, then the gestures become even grander until one of you feels that the other is taking too much of a controlling interest. Then you'll disengage with polite dignity, maintaining as much of your self-respect as possible, and quietly look for someone more suitable. As a marriage, you should work very well, if you can avoid trying to control each other. You both have expansive ideas and the enthusiasm to match. Given time, you'll be able to achieve almost everything you decide to do.

Leo - Virgo

This is the second of the adjacent-sign relationships open to you, and it's no easier than the Leo - Cancer relationship. Oddly enough, this one works very well as a business partnership, because you have all the expansive ideas and the Virgo looks for ways to put them into practice in the most effective and economical way. You provide the fuel for him to work with, and give him the enthusiasm and breadth of outlook he needs in order to succeed.

On a personal level though, the partnership is not so cozy. A Virgo needs to examine things at a very close and fine level, and unless he's familiar with the detail of things, he's not happy. Broad concepts have no meaning for him; he can only take things in by building a large picture from many small ones. He tends to look down rather than up or outwards, and his attention is focused on the actual workings of things rather than how they look or what they mean. You'll see at once that his insistence on understanding the detail of things will lead to difficulty when he examines much of your behavior, where the detail is missing altogether. You start at the top and often neglect the smaller details, because they are not important to your scheme of things. Worse still, you're concerned with ideas and activity rather than actual things. How can there be any real communication between you if you deal in different universes and on a different scale?

Obviously, what communication actually takes place is going to be misinterpreted, and that's what happens. To you, the Virgo is always picking holes in your arguments, pointing out inconsistencies or impracticalities, and generally acting like a wet blanket. This is not actually true, but it's how it seems to you. What is happening is that the poor Virgoan is genuinely trying to understand what you're saying, but he can only do it by building up a picture a piece at a time, like a jigsaw. If there aren't enough pieces or if a piece of the jigsaw is missing or if the pattern changes, he complains, and there you are, trying to get him to do his own painting with a broad brush.

He appreciates your energy, but he can't get over your apparent sloppiness. I know that you're generous and expansive rather than sloppy, but to the Virgo, it seems that way. He does things repeatedly, building up familiarity through practice, but you prefer to let someone else do that sort of thing, and he can't understand how you could possibly think that way. It's not just that you're different, it's that neither of you can see what the other is trying to do, and are thus unable to communicate.

As friends, you stand no real chance unless you can find some common interest that will allow you each to see what the other is doing; as business partners, on the other hand, you would do very well. If you want a Virgo as a lover, you'll have to be very patient and try to do things on a small scale. They don't appreciate your theatrical gestures, firstly because they are rather shy and restrained emotionally, and secondly, because unless the intention is matched by something material, they won't be able to understand it. They will appreciate your warmth though, and will repay you by doing all they can to please you, which will do much to win your heart.

For a marriage, there are vast differences in outlook to be overcome. You may not be able to stand the Virgo's narrow point of view, and even if your optimism cures their constant worries, they may not be able to join you in your grand schemes as you would wish.

Leo - Libra

Librans are supposed to be the nicest people in the zodiac and to an extent, it's true, but it depends an awful lot on your definition of nice. You'll find them delightful company, but they are a little on the lightweight side when it comes to making firm moves. As long as you're prepared to provide the motive power for both of you, this partnership can be very rewarding.

A Libran sees you as the personification of his ambitions. Put simply, he would like to be like you. He's outgoing and sociable in the same way that you are, putting his energy out into friendly chat. He makes friends with everybody he meets. Everybody likes a Libran. A lot of this is to do with the way his planet, Venus, works. Venus looks for something similar, and needs something to which it can relate. A Libran finds something likable about everybody he meets and something in the other person that's similar to something in him. Then he talks about how similar he is to the other person, and how he has always liked being like this or like that. It's a sure-fire way of making people like you, but it's not a deliberate device, any more than your generosity is, it's just the planet behind the person making all the moves in accordance with its nature. A Libran is the original source of communication between people. He's also the source of all that is harmonious, balanced or beautiful, because his insistence on drawing together those things that are similar eliminates contrast, disagreement and imbalance. It's not difficult to see why Librans have a reputation for being nice.

The trouble with being nice is that nobody thinks you're important or effective. We only sit up and take notice of things that stand out from, or disrupt, our previous steady state. Leos, now, they're different. When a Leo walks into a room the room sits up expectantly, and when he speaks, everybody listens. A Libran would love to have that kind of effect on people, but while he doesn't lack confidence, he does lack effectiveness.

That's one of the things that attracts him to you, and the other is that you generally get what you want, and live in a fairly wealthy way compared to the rest of your friends. Librans would like to own all sorts of beautiful things and live very elegant lifestyles to go with them, but they just don't have the money. Librans have impeccable taste, but they can't seem to translate it into reality in the way that a Leo can.

What do you see them as? Charming companions who agree with your ideas, who appreciate your tastes, and who can live life on your level with no difficulty. When it comes to being decisive, they are a waste of time, because they always see the other side to the argument as well, but you don't mind that. If they were at all decisive on their own, they might decide differently from you, and that would never do, would it? You see them as lazy, whereas they are simply ineffective, which is not the same thing. Overall, you like having them around. You value their opinions, but that doesn't mean you have to take their advice. They are decorative and companionable, and they don't get in the way when you're putting your foot down about something, Ideal, really.

If this relationship is limited to a light friendship, then the way to get the most value from it is to spend time doing the things where you can both contribute to the end result. This might be some expensive, expansive and artistic pursuit, where the Leo's generosity and the Libran's superlative taste can combine to produce something that could not have been achieved by either of you singly. Supper after the theatre sounds about right.

As lovers, you'll both enjoy traditional romantic gestures, and the more stylish they are, the better. You'll have difficulty convincing the Libran that you're seriously in love, because they take things very lightly, and avoid anything resembling commitment, even though the idea of marriage appeals to them a great deal. If you want to make it permanent, you'll have to be very patient, and not advertise your intention. Once married, you'll have no problems other than making enough money to keep up with the style of life you both enjoy so much.

As business partners, you'll have to be the boss, but that will suit you both.

Leo - Scorpio

This is the partnership to go for if you like playing rough. Scorpios are hard fighters, and have the sort of determination that means that even when they lose, they get even in the end. There's no way that you can conduct this relationship on a light and carefree level, even if you try to. It's strong and deep from the beginning. The rewards are high, and there's plenty of blazing passion on both sides, but the downs are at least as deep as the ups are high, and the road is never smooth. If you fancy something you can get your teeth into, a relationship worth your time and strength, then try this one.

Scorpios do almost everything that you do, but in reverse. They don't put out energy as if it was free; they collect it and store it within themselves. They like to be in control at all times, and this means that they need to know exactly what's going on, and what everybody is likely to do, then they stay one jump ahead. Of course, it means that they have to do things their way, and that's where the opposition to you comes in. You know that you're only going to allow things to happen the way you say, because you like organizing things and being at the center, if not the front, but Scorpios won't wear this at all. In their view, your grand schemes are improperly thought out, and there are possibilities which don't matter to you but that are important to them, and which must be catered for. In a way, you're happiest when they take over but then, on the other hand, you don't like handing over power. The arguments between you start at this point, and get worse.

You see them as unnecessarily interfering. Why can't they trust you to get things right? Everything works fine when you're left on your own, so why do they have to try to control it? They see you as incredibly wasteful and dangerously open in all you do, because how could you let everybody see what you're doing when they might want to use it against you? How could you be so generous with your time and money when it has to be so carefully guarded? They never see that you're open because you've nothing to hide, and generous because your energy comes for free. It never occurs to you that they might have something to hide, and that they might not have your facility for making things happen.

Yet, you're linked to each other in a way. The Scorpio's real goal is to be openly in power and publicly recognized for it, just as you are. It's that which he admires in you above all else, and for which he forgives your excesses. You realize, of course, that your real power comes from within yourself, and you recognize the great store of that power inside the Scorpio, held down by his self-restrictive control. You'd like to be able to share and unite with that power, and it's that which draws you to him, and for which you suffer his attempts to stifle your self-expression.

Any contact you make with a Scorpio turns into a power struggle after a very short time, so you can't hope to have a mere amicable acquaintance. Either you'll dislike each other quite fiercely, as the other elements in your horoscope add to the strain felt by your two Sun positions, or you'll find yourselves exploring each other at deeper and deeper levels as the great energies you represent mingle and fuse with each other. A sexual relationship is the only one capable of handling the sort of current you two generate, and this will become very powerful very quickly. This is real life-and-death stuff, because you're both playing with the energies of life itself. Arguments will be catastrophic, reconciliations sublimely uplifting, and everything about it is more intense and on a bigger scale than a relationship with any of the other signs. As a marriage, the same applies. You'll fight for each other in public and with each other in private. It won't be easy, but it won't be dull either.

Leo - Sagittarius

There's nobody on earth with whom you'd rather waste your time than a Sagittarian. This is the only person in the zodiac who makes you feel dull by comparison, and for whose talents you would gladly trade your own. Everything they do is a delight to you. They are lively, witty and even more optimistic than you are; therefore, when you're together, you feel you could take on the world. Fortunately for the rest of the world, you'll never get round to it, because you're having too good a time imagining it all. Even if you went into business together, you'd need somebody to handle the actual mechanics of things, not to mention the finances. Between you, you're an ideas factory gone mad, with enough sheer ebullience to convince anybody of anything, but neither of you are too good on the practical side of things.

Sagittarius is confident and outgoing, as you are; but his confidence is the confidence of belief and of knowledge, whereas yours is the confidence of feeling. Both of you are very forward-looking, far more interested in the immediate future than the past, and both absolutely sure that everything is going to turn out for the best. The difference in your attitudes is that you feel that things are going to be all right, and the Sagittarian knows that they are.

The Sagittarian seems to know everything there is to know about everything, and to share his knowledge freely. You recognize this generosity of spirit as being similar to your own, but you find the depth of his knowledge new and exciting, so you sit there and soak it up eagerly. There isn't much in the world that you feel you'd like more of or that you wish someone would give you, but you can always take in more of what Sagittarians put out.

You're also fascinated by their mobility. You know that you tend to stay in the same situation if it suits you, and you know inside yourself, that this is because you don't think that you could be so successful if you had to adapt to changing surroundings all the time. Sagittarians seem to be able to deal with things as they come up, and they can move from one situation to another and still come out ahead. Is it all that knowledge that makes them so adaptable? No, it's Jupiter. Sagittarians are governed by a big planet, so they have big ideas, as you do. The Sun is also large, but Jupiter moves and the Sun doesn't. A static Sagittarian is a sad person indeed.

They see you as a reminder that, at the end of the day, it isn't the material things that make life work, but the personal energies that you can put in. They know that you always believe in yourself, and they find that an inspiring thought. Sometimes they wonder, with their changeable minds, whether being a giver rather than a taker is the right way to be, but five minutes in your company reminds them that to be self-confident, generous, and optimistic is the right way for them. You refuel Sagittarians, and that's what they like about you.

As friends, you'll get on brilliantly, but don't expect to put any of your schemes into action! You're wonderfully restorative for each other's spirits. As lovers, your relationship should be energetic and warm; after all, you're both Fire signs. He will like to keep things moving and changeable, where you'll be happy to stay with a good thing once you get one. Sagittarians have little time for ceremony, and when impulse overrides decorum, they don't mind one bit - but you do, so your dignity will be rumpled from time to time. You could find yourself feeling a little old-fashioned as your lover teases your sentimental and romantic streak, but overall it's a stimulating affair, and one that you'll enjoy.

As a marriage, you should have few problems. Even if you rule your household in typical leonine manner, the Sagittarian won't complain, provided that you don't restrict his freedom. He needs to be able to move around and feel free, so give him this and all will be well. In business, you'll need some office backup to deal with the boring chores.

Leo - Capricorn

This one isn't easy. The partnership hinges on the essential difference between one person who is a success simply by existing, and another who makes the attainment of success his life's work. On the surface and in public you can talk to each other as equals, but the approaches that led you both to the positions you occupy are very different.

Capricorn sees you as both the beginning and end of his own existence. You're successful, well liked and have a good reputation. People gather around you, listen to you and take notice of you. You're considered important. Quite often, you're comfortably solvent, and when that isn't the case, it doesn't seem to matter. Basically, you're a star, and the Capricorn wants all that. He wants to be seen as important, to be at the top of the pyramid. He sees you as being able to do what you do through applied self-confidence, which is quite perceptive of him, because that's more or less right. If he has confidence in himself and applies himself, he thinks that he will achieve the same result as you. As you were, he was; and as you are, he will be, as the saying goes. What he doesn't see is that you have the Sun in you, radiating out through a person born when it was in its own sign. He doesn't have that. He has Saturn instead, which is cold and restrictive. When you apply yourself, you're applying warmth and sunlight to everything, and who doesn't feel better when the Sun shines on them? When the Capricorn applies himself, he applies Saturn, which extinguishes warmth, adds weight and gives a serious tone to things generally.

Although the success will come in time, it won't come as easily as yours will, and neither can the Capricorn ever be you. The Sun does not shine out from him in the same way. You see him differently. He gives shape to your achievements by doing what he does without effort; you're seen as a success. It's a strange way of looking at things, I know, but public recognition and the acquisition of status symbols are a Capricorn's definition of success, and you choose them as the means of communicating your importance to the rest of society. He works his way up the hierarchy of an organization, while you place yourself at the top, in the ruling position.

It's very difficult for you to have any sort of a friendship. He's restrained and aloof, where you're open and generous. There's no raging passion inside the Capricorn. He's a genuinely quiet person with a strong sense of duty, a strong work ethic, and a low level of fun. There isn't a great deal to talk about between you.

If you're lovers, it's because the Capricorn sees you as a necessary step in his career. He will be cautious and rather reserved in his response to you, and you'll be disappointed, because you'd have liked some warmth and enthusiasm in return for your own, and you won't get any. A Capricorn won't move unless it's within a carefully defined framework. Phrases like "spontaneous initiative" are not part of his vocabulary. You might get to like his sense of humor as the affair develops though, provided that you like your humor on the dry side.

As business partners, you could do very well. The first thing to do is to forget your personal differences, and let him provide you with a framework for your creativity. Just watch your effectiveness increase. Provide him with the rewards he needs to see for his efforts in return, and you'll never look back.

As a marriage, you'd have to run things similarly to the business arrangement, as you'd also have to provide the warmth and emotional input that a home and family require to be a success, because the cold Capricorn can't do it.

Leo - Aquarius

This partnership is a union of opposites in a zodiacal sense, since the two signs are exactly opposite to each other in the circle of the signs, but it's by no means a tense or argumentative relationship. Provided you stay in the public eye and both spend time in the company of lots of other people, you'll have no problems.

To put it succinctly, Leo is concerned with himself, while Aquarius is concerned with the group, where individuality is lost in the crowd. You're both outgoing people who project your energies outwards from yourselves, rather than collecting the energy that others put out, and this gets the relationship off to a good start. Outgoing people find the active response of those similar to them encouraging, because it reminds them of themselves, which is good.

Aquarius is concerned with ideas and conversation, but he suffers from being rather less able to make things happen than you are, although he's the best of the Air signs in this respect. More than anything else, he's an observer. He loves to be present at everything that's going on, loves the buzz of conversation and the excitement of social life, but he would rather not be deeply involved. This is one of the major differences between you. You need to be at the center of things, to be fully involved and the central source of energy for the whole situation, where he likes to be on the edge looking on and enjoying the show. Don't think he's timid - he isn't; he does just not have his heart in it the way you have. He's another saturnine type, as the Capricorn is. His interest is there, but it's cool, and he doesn't radiate warmth the way you do. He sees you as somebody who is as at home at a party or in company as he is, and as interested in life as he is, but whose personal involvement with everything is strange and mystifying.

If I were as committed to my interests as that, Aquarius thinks, I could never turn my attention to anything new, and I would be unable to see what everybody else is doing. The whole point is to see what everybody else has to offer, and see how different people interact. Leo needs to forget himself for a while. It's a pity that so friendly a person can't really put himself into something one hundred per cent, he thinks. If Aquarius was as warm underneath as he is friendly on the top, and if he stopped drifting from one interest to another, he could be really likable. The Aquarian needs to create something from his own efforts, by himself then he'd see how good he could be.

You can't really understand each other, though you're made of much the same stuff. What you both enjoy immensely though, is any kind of social function. You can become the heart of it and the Aquarian can be the circulation, moving round from one person to another, keeping the flow of ideas and contact going, which as an Air sign, he needs to do. If the two of you have nothing but each other's company for any length of time, you'll find him cold and withdrawn, and he will find you domineering, but in a group, both of you can shine, and enjoy each other to the full. This is the way to conduct the friendship if it's intended to stay as just that: in public, and in company.

Oddly enough, you both want to be different, but in different ways. You want to be the sort of person everybody wants to be, a sort of maximum intensity version of conventional virtues, but the Aquarian wants to be genuinely different, something else. In fact, he represents all the things that the members of a group don't have in common, where you're all the things they do. Funny, isn't it?

The juxtaposition of cool difference and warm conventionality becomes more marked if you're lovers or married. Aquarians work at a much lower emotional level than you do, which makes them intriguing and aloof when they are lovers, but seemingly less caring as spouses. You'll also find that their ideas on the content and management of a household are just as cool. Your ideal of the welcoming hearth with a good table will take a bit of a bashing.

This does work as a business though, as the Aquarian is better at details and he's a back-room person, while you're the front-person and the sales force.

Leo - Pisces

This is a very special relationship. On the surface, it will look very bright and glossy, but you know that it isn't like that underneath. On some levels, this relationship will exhaust you, and on others, it will give you the answers for which you've been searching. If you're happy with your active life, full of friends and things to do, then don't even bother with a Piscean acquaintance, but if you can't help feeling that it's all a bit empty, and that your soul needs nourishing as well as your body, then try this one. A Piscean is the water into which the Leo Sun sinks at the end of its day, and from which it rises again. It's not the sort of relationship you can talk about over a quick half at lunchtime, though it is the sort you talk about by the end of the second bottle late in the evening. Nor are the alcoholic references mere decorations. Pisces has much to do with that substance and its effects.

Pisceans are either transparent or chameleons; I'm not sure which. They can take on the attributes and the life-style of others. When they are with you, they are leonine, as leonine as you are; and for that precise reason, you project yourself onto them, and they let you see exactly that. You're both creative, and you like that in each other. The difference is that you create your own world from the real world and live in it, while they create their own world from their imagination, and live in that as if it were real. Read the last sentence again, it's not easy. You're successful in the real world because you make it work for you, but they are in a different universe altogether. Life to you is simple and bold, like children's building bricks, but life to them is all colors at once, impossibly complex and yet undefined, like the colors you see when you close your eyes.

You see Pisceans as frail and sensitive creatures, whose talent for playing roles to suit their surroundings amuses you. You see this as a parallel skill to your own ability to impose your personality on your surroundings. They seem to be from a different reality, and that interests you, because you'd like to see what this other world is like.

They see you as hefty but essentially jolly individuals, whose genuine goodness of heart and optimism shows them how they could use the strength of their own personalities to make sense of the mass of impressions and emotions that seem to flood their minds. When life seems uncertain, you remind them of the goodness, the simplicity and the fun of just being yourself.

Pisceans respond to everything. They find it difficult to focus on any one thing to the exclusion of everything else, and you can help them to do so. At the same time, you'll gain from having their heightened sensitivity at your disposal, especially if the two of you have some common interest that you can spend time on. This is how your friendship actually works, and the more of this you do, the better you'll appreciate each other.

As lovers, you'll have an interesting time. Pisces won't have met your sheer creative power before, whereas it's the range and intensity of his emotional response that will surprise you. It's a union of the soul as well as the body - difficult to explain unless you've tried it and made it work.

Once you've formed a relationship that works on all levels, and there are many levels to explore with a Pisces, you should have the basis of a lasting marriage. They offer you the long-term satisfaction that you could never quite define, but knew you needed, and you offer them a reliable reference point from which to build a life in the real world.

As business colleagues, you both have creativity and salesmanship, but the Piscean is even less able to cope with details than you are.

The Approach to Relationships: Virgo

SYMBOL: THE VIRGIN	♍	ELEMENT: EARTH
PLANET: MERCURY	☿	QUALITY: MUTABLE

Mercury's energy works best on a small scale. Virgoans are often portrayed as fussy and critical, but this is a misunderstanding of the way they function, even though it may be true to some extent. Mercury notices that which is different or out of place; it also notices things on a small scale. An article of clothing left lying about by its owner will be noticed at once by a Virgo, because it's out of place, and it's a small-scale event. What happens next is that Virgo analyses and digests the situation, comes to the conclusion that the best and most effective action would be to put it where it belongs, and he proceeds to do so for the benefit of the owner. Then, because Mercury is a communicative planet, Virgo tells the owner what has happened, so that he will know where his clothes are when next he wants them. Now, *from the other person's point of view*, it looks as though Virgo is being critical of the incident.

It's impossible for the Virgoan to see the whole picture until he has mastered the detail. This is similar to doing a crossword puzzle; until every piece has been inserted, the picture is incomplete. It's always the physical and practical aspects of things that capture his attention.

Virgo - Aries

This relationship, like many of the five-signs-apart relationships, works very well on a professional or business level, but less well on a personal or emotional level.

You see the Arian as a source of boundless energy. He always seems to be full of life, and to be eager to get things done. He seems to be much more forceful than you are, and much stronger. He has an immediacy that astonishes you: as soon as the idea is in his head, he will want to put it into action, and won't waste any time in doing so.

What you find so appealing about him is his directness and his practicality. You're usually sure about what has to be done, and see no point in wasting any time about it. It's true that the Arian wants to get things done, because the actual doing of them is what interests him, whereas you're driven by rather different motives, but your approaches are parallel for the most part. You worry about things. Arians never seem to worry about anything. The fact that they are, or appear to be, untroubled by second thoughts, seems wonderful to you. They are never tired out by the struggle as you often are. People never take offence at their actions, as they frequently do at yours. Overall, they are a reliable source of strength and effectiveness, which you feel you can draw on when your own are waning.

There are one or two things that concern you about Arians, though. They are not perfect by any means. The most important thing is that they appear to act before they think, and they will frequently do things the wrong way (it seems to you) because that's the way that first occurred to them. It annoys you that somebody with such an endless capacity for direct and effective action can waste so much effort by misapplying it. What you'll never understand is the immediacy of the Arian mind. It's not his own effectiveness that interests him; it's the fact that he lives for the moment. From his point of view, you always seem to know a better way of doing things, and that's interesting to him. You also seem to lose the spirit of the moment by considering whether now is the right time to do it, and that infuriates him.

One of the areas of your concern he simply can't grasp is the way you need to do things for everybody's benefit. The Arian is concerned primarily with himself, and he never gives a thought to other people. It's not that he doesn't care, it's just that his energies are all used in his own interests - which is why he's as effective as you see him to be. He also finds you pessimistic. It simply never occurs to him that things won't turnout the way he wants them to, so by comparison, your consideration of the possibilities of failure is deeply pessimistic.

As friends, you'll get on very well if you have some project on hand. His energy and your methodical approach should ensure a satisfactory result for both of you. If you have nothing to do, you'll turn your analytical mind to him personally, and then tempers will flare.

As lovers, you're not really very well matched. What he wants is to be energetic, forceful and passionate. You'd feel uneasy if you had to respond in similar fashion, and you'd prefer a cooler appreciation. As a marriage, Aries is a good partner if you want the marriage to function as a team effort with set objectives, such as improving your careers or building a house together. If you just want a quiet and intimate environment, he isn't the ideal match for you.

As business partners, you'll get on very well indeed. Do things at his speed, but your way. Make sure you get somebody else to take care of forward planning and overall management though, because these areas are weak in both of you!

Virgo - Taurus

This is one of the more comfortable relationships that are open to you. There's a feeling of understanding and mutual sympathy between any two signs of the same element. It's as though you both know that the other one has the same priorities and prefers to work in a similar way to yourself. You know that what upsets or disturbs you is likely to do the same to them, and what pleases you is likely to please them too.

You both have the element of Earth in common, so life between you is very much concerned with the real and material world. There are no wild ideas or fancy phrases that sound like one thing and mean another. There are no over-sensitive or over-secretive emotional states, and no tactless or tasteless wasteful projects, just common sense and practicality – along with good food, as likely as not. Taureans feel better when there's food around, and you enjoy the processes of cooking and eating too, so the two of you are likely to amuse and please each other by eating together. Over dinner, you'll have time to analyze the Taurean, and work out why it is that you like him so much.

The first thing you like about him is how much he cares for the things around him. Material objects need the proper kind of upkeep if they are to stay serviceable and presentable, and the Taurean has an intuitive grasp of this. You find it relaxing not to have to explain this to him all the time, so this is one of the essential features of your view of life and he shares it with you. The other thing you like about him is his great steadiness, and his preference to think before he acts. In time, you'll realize that he may not act, and this will annoy you, but at least he isn't hasty. One thing you really don't like is people who are faster to act than you are.

The Taurean is slow to see ways in which he could do things better, but once he's convinced, he will gladly accept your recommendations. This is very satisfying for you. You can be of service and you can make constructive observations both at the same time, and you're likely to be thanked for it into the bargain. Perfect, from your point of view. Only the Taurean's refusal to make major moves, even when it's really necessary, and his unwillingness to surrender anything that was once his, ever irritate you. You're probably more than willing to trade his obstinacy for the sense of security he offers you, and the reassurance that you're doing things for the right reasons after all.

The Taurean loves you because you seem to know what to do. He has a deep appreciation of the things he knows and loves, but he doesn't know what to do with them. You seem to know exactly what to do with them, and in your hands, they seem to improve and grow more useful still. This is true, of course. Virgoans direct their energies towards the perfection of whatever they have around them, but the Taurean sees this and is appreciative of it. He would dearly love to be able to do it for himself, but at the same time is more than willing to let you do it for him. He does see you as a bit of a meddler at times, because there are things that he's content to leave as they are, which you feel compelled to do something about, but he simply shakes his head and sighs. On balance, though, the fact that you can't sit still is a small price to pay for all the wonderful things you do for him, and he knows it.

A friendship formed between you will be fond and long lasting. Friendships are about people with similar views. Should the friendship deepen so that you become lovers, you'll find that the Taurean is a much more powerful person than you would perhaps like. But he's gentle and fairly slow in his advances, so you'll neither be overwhelmed or taken by surprise, and you'll be able to adapt your responses quickly enough for you both to find the affair rewarding. As a marriage, this pairing looks very good indeed. If you want the marriage to be active and expansive, you'll have to goad the Taurean into moving a little faster, otherwise you'll have a dull but secure and comfortable, existence. It really depends upon what you want.

At work, you cooperate well with each other, but you'll need a more outgoing colleague to be the front person or sales person.

Virgo - Gemini

This can be a rather argumentative pairing, but in many ways, you're better suited to each other than most other three-signs-apart combinations. The ruling planet for both Gemini and Virgo is Mercury, so you're motivated by the same kind of energy, so neither you nor your friend have anything in your characters that the other can't understand or deal with. Whether you want to put up with the way the other person insists on doing things is another matter, but essentially, there are no real problems here.

Probably the most relaxing thing about this relationship, and yet one that will seldom be recognized let alone mentioned, is that you're both rather cool emotionally. Your energies are mental rather than emotional, and both of you find it difficult to deal with things that have any kind of sentimental content. You're not at all sentimental in your approach to things, and it never occurs to you to pay much attention to your feelings when they might interfere with your analysis of the situation. Having a partner who works the same way and who prefers life without embarrassing sentimental outbursts, as you both see them, is a great help in maintaining the relationship as far as you're concerned. Even better is that you don't have to say how pleased you are that things work this way.

You both have enquiring minds, so you each take a great interest in the way the other operates. You never have much time for words and ideas, so this is fascinating to you. You've always preferred the unmistakable feel of real physical objects because they tend not to change from one moment to the next. Gemini seems to have developed a whole range of techniques to allow him to use and manipulate such intangible and formless things as phrases and concepts, and you really admire this. Note what it is that you're actually doing. Do you understand the things he holds so dear? You can watch him at work with interest and admiration, but you wouldn't want to do it that way yourself.

Gemini sees things in a similar way. He has never been much good with the real and actual detail of things as they exist. He has always been more interested in the idea of their existence. There's nothing he likes better than to have something new and intricate shown or explained to him. He may not choose to remember it or use it, but he likes it anyway. He has great admiration for the skill and patience you display in your dealings with the real world. Patience and skill have never been high on his list of talents, but he admires them in others, especially when they are displayed and used in a rapid and analytical manner, as they are in you.

Gemini is immune to your critical observations; he sees them as interesting points in the form of verbal communication but nothing more. You both like to work quickly, as is always the case when the energy of Mercury is in charge, and you're both far too busy to sit and brood over the possible meanings of what one or the other of you has just said.

You live in very different worlds, but you employ the same energy to make your separate ways in them, and this gives much opportunity for discussion. Too much in fact, since Mercury looks after communication. Gemini loves arguing for its own sake, and you think you're nearly perfect! In fact, you both think that the other is very good at what he does, and wish you could do as well, so this is a very verbal friendship, but a very loyal one.

As lovers, you're well suited, as neither of you wants to be very deeply involved. You're likely to be upset if the Gemini takes other lovers besides you at the same time. He's only indulging his love of variety, after all. Friends will try to comfort you, but they won't understand. What upsets you is the implication (in your eyes) that there must be something wrong with you.

As a marriage, this can be very good. Remember that you'll strive to provide all the stability and security yourself, though. It certainly won't be dull - or quiet. A working relationship would be easy and successful.

Virgo - Cancer

This is a very easy relationship for you, as you're both careful not to upset the other, respectful of each other's needs and preferences and above all, not aggressive or assertive in your demands. This one is easy, because you have a lot in common, although this is not due to any shared astrological features, but via the concept of caring. Both of you care for others as a way of displaying your energies, because what you really need is for those who you care for to respond favorably to the care more than you need to run around others.

Ideally, you see the Cancerian as a confidante and advisor. You're ruled by Mercury, so your emotional nature is rather shallow and brittle, and you don't have the capacity to deal with the emotional content of a situation. You're unsure what to do with the powerful but irrational force of sentiment, and it worries you. The power you can understand, but the irrationality you can't. What do you do? The Cancerian will comfort you. Somehow, all this irrational feeling can be absorbed, re-directed and taken care of by the Cancerian without any fuss at all. It's the sort of thing that they are good at, and you're very grateful.

When things get out of hand, you'd appreciate some help in getting things back in order, but not everybody can do it in the way you would like. You want your helper to accept things your way. You want them to support and reassure you, to tell you that you're on the right track and you want them to be discreet. Making public the fact that you're letting things get out of order is something you'd rather not do. Where do these strong but pliable, supportive but silent people come from?

The difference between the signs is that Cancer works on a one-to-one basis, and you work on a one-to-many basis. You feel that you'd like to be of service to a great many people, but Cancer would like to care for you alone. They don't have your facility with things, and they often get things wrong on a practical level. They don't always think things through, because they tend to act on their hunches rather than their deductions. They are often too shy to be really effective. None of these things matter to you, and you can remedy most of their shortcomings by taking those roles from them. In doing so, you can be of service, which is what you want.

They see you as confident versions of themselves, able to put into words and actions all the things that they feel to be right but can't define. It's very satisfying to have a friend who does this sort of thing for you. It makes your own life more exciting, in a similar way to the plain girl who goes with the pretty girl to the party. One is the extension of the other and the other is the support for the first. Cancerians like to change things for the better (better from their point of view, of course), but they want to do it with consideration and care. Only Virgoans seem to understand this need to preserve and change at the same time, and the Cancerian appreciates this. You're the vehicle for his plans.

As a friendship, this pairing works very well. You'll be intuitively considerate towards each other. It may not be as verbal a relationship as you would like, because you enjoy speech in a way the Cancerian doesn't, and you may find them moody. This will certainly be the case if you become lovers. The Cancerian works at a much deeper and closer emotional level than you, and you may well find that you're out of your depth. If you keep things light so that you're working at a level you feel comfortable with, the Cancerian will feel under-compensated.

As a marriage, you'll have to take steps to ensure that you don't take things too seriously. You both have a strong sense of duty, and you'll both be concerned to do things right for the benefit of the family's future. If both of you spend too much time worrying, you'll forget how to enjoy the present. You can work well together in business, and the Cancerian will be better at the bookkeeping than you are.

Virgo - Leo

This is a remarkable relationship. It's almost as difficult a match as is possible to imagine, but then again it may be just what you want. There are many things about a Leo that you hate, because you can see them in yourself. There are many things that are secretly how you'd like to be. The Leo can't see much in you to envy, but there are things that you do which he can't, and he thinks that it wouldn't be too bad a thing if he were more like you in certain respects, albeit on his own terms. It may well be that you don't like each other much, but that you can't live without each other.

A Leo is not subtle. You can't overlook him in a crowd. He's big and boisterous, he makes himself the center of attention, and he loves it. He acts as though he owns the place, and it never crosses his mind that he doesn't. It never occurs to him that his actions might inconvenience others. In a way, he's right, because most people are more than happy to do whatever the Leo's doing, anyway.

It's precisely this behavior that you find so appealing and appalling at the same time. You're proud of the fact that you consider what is best for everybody before you do what pleases you, and you tell yourself off for occasionally being selfish like the Leo. Selfishness is your pet vice. You enjoy catching yourself out being selfish, and treat it as a much more serious failing than it really is. On the other hand, you'd love to be as imperial as the Leo is. Surely, you reason, everybody would like to do things your way, since it's obviously the best and most efficient way of doing them. Many people like doing things the way Leo does them, simply because it's more fun. Leos are warm and kind, and they don't really care when things go wrong. For this reason, you can use them as a safety net, and probably do. When you're tired of trying to set the world to rights, the Leo will cheer you up like nobody else can.

They see you like bees, buzzing here and there, eternally busy doing good things, like making honey and looking after everything for the benefit of the hive. To continue the parallel, they enjoy the honey like everybody else, but they are sometimes irritated by your presence. There's nothing that you can offer in a personal sense to a Leo. There's no companionship or support that they need you to provide. What you offer is a means of expression. Leos are full of warmth and generosity, and they like to see it put to some use. They are much too lazy to do much with it for themselves (and why should they? They don't need its benefits), but they enjoy seeing how you can put it to good use. You're the technique that refines the fire of their energy, gives it direction and purpose. Between you, you can get a lot done, but you'll have to remember that you're going to do most of the actual doing, because the Leo will take a much less active role. Without him, you wouldn't be able to do any of it, though, and you'd probably prefer to be left to do things in your own way, so you won't be too upset.

In any relationship between you, you'll have to function like the Sun and Mercury, with the little planet speeding round the mighty star, while it sits radiantly and majestically in the center of things. He doesn't necessarily need you to orbit him, but you get a great deal more in the form of heat and light when you do.

A friendship between you will only work if you place him at the center and let him radiate. There's no other way to work it. Don't criticize or change him, because he will move away from you and then you'll lose his warmth forever. Should you become lovers, it will be because he wants it so, not the other way round. He will be able to offer you more energy and heat than you've ever imagined. The best you can do is to lie there and enjoy it.

As a marriage, this can be good provided you stay within your roles. You must let him be master of the household, and don't attempt to change the way he likes things done. Where Leo invites you to suggest ways of doing things that's fine, but if he doesn't ask for your opinion, there will be an argument. If you don't think you can stand the life of an orbiting satellite, then don't try this one.

Virgo - Virgo

Like all relationships of the same sign, this one magnifies the faults and shortcomings of the sign as well as the virtues. The big advantage is that you know what you're letting yourself in for, which is another version of yourself. This particular pairing is the easiest of the same sign matches, because Mercury is so adaptable. There are no heavy planet energies to cause imbalance, and no overabundance of emotion or sentiment to throw things out of control. Moreover, both of you pride yourselves on being reasonable and rational, so a flexible understanding or compromise of your requirements is going to be that much easier to achieve.

You have a great deal to teach each other. You're both proud of how much you know about the correct way to do things, and you both stress the importance of proper learning. It's unlikely that you'll have had exactly identical experiences in life, so you can teach each other what you've learnt. You'll appreciate learning from another Virgo, because he sees things in the right way according to you, making sure that no detail is missed out, and covering all the possibilities. You may not appreciate their criticism of your own ways of doing things, but you'll have great fun arguing over them. Virgoans are a strange mix. Unless something is theoretically impeccable, you don't want to know about it, but it has to be workable and practical as well.

There's a danger that a long-term relationship between you could become smug, self-satisfied and rather prim. You'll soon iron out all your minor differences, and then spend your days in a spotlessly clean, absolutely neat environment congratulating yourselves on how perfect you are. The way out of this is to open yourselves out so that others can enjoy your skills and expertise; on a simple level, throwing a lot of dinner parties, or at a higher level running some kind of charity or public service.

The early stages of a relationship between you will be the most enjoyable and the easiest. Mercury is always at its best with something new and the problems come when familiarity sets in. You're both eager to please in a practical and everyday way, and you're quick to respond to new things. If you have different interests and pastimes when you meet, each will soon convert the other. There's a joy both in learning a new skill, and in teaching somebody else to enjoy it and both of these give a Virgoan satisfaction. On a light and practical level, then, this friendship is easy to manage and enjoyable.

If you become lovers, you should still be happy, as it's difficult for a non-Virgo to understand this aspect of a Virgo's life, since the Virgo most emphatically is not in it to express his emotions. More important is the need to use one's body well. You'll understand each other's needs and help meet them.

A business partnership between you would be good if both acted in an advisory capacity. Neither of you have enough of a sense of organization to take full responsibility for things, nor sufficient personal drive to make things happen for yourselves without outside help. As a marriage, this partnership is fine provided that it looks outwards and shares its achievements with friends and relatives. Left to its own devices, a Virgo plus Virgo marriage becomes cold and rather unyielding, with needless worry being more likely than laughter. Linking it into a wider community is essential for its health.

Virgo - Libra

The trouble with having a partner who is one sign onwards from yours is that your partner often seems not to recognize your efforts as being at all important, as the things that are important to you aren't interesting to them. In terms of astrology, having moved on by one sign, they are past that stage. Nevertheless, it makes for a powerful irritant, especially when, as in your case, you want people to recognize all the things you're doing on their behalf. Librans are almost as different from you as you could imagine, and their minds work in a very different way. Where you analyze things to see how they work, trying to master the intricacies of everything so that you can make better use of it, they simply pick the bits that they like. It's not at all important to a Libran to know how his car works. If it goes, it's comfortable and he likes the color, that's fine. It never occurs to a Libran to dig beneath the surface of anything or to try to understand anything fully. The only things he's interested in are the ones that appeal to him personally, and if there's no appeal, then he has no time for it. There's a certain surface judgment in a Libran, from your point of view.

Librans are lazy. Bone idle, in fact. They inhabit a world of people and friendships rather than your round of work and duties, and this makes them do nothing all day, in your eyes. Why should they, if duty isn't rewarding to them? Anyway, they are busy doing other things. Every time you find something out of order or in need of correction, they find two things with an affinity that can work better together. Every time you upset somebody, the Libran reassures and sooth the other person. What Librans actually do is bring people together and promote friendships. It's not something you can do. Your job lies with organizations and objects rather than people. They look outwards where you look inwards. You're aiming for individual perfection and they want individuals to become friends. It's another step on in the process. You want to be of service to the community, but there wouldn't be any community to serve if Libran energy didn't create it. That's what they do for you.

What do you do for them? They see you as the dull boy who is all work and no play, and your constant frown of concern and mild irritation at the world that besets you doesn't help them at all. They like to be relaxed, surrounded by pleasant things and pleasant people. They take things at a leisurely pace and enjoy themselves while they do it. There are times, however, when they can't cope. Sometimes there are too many problems that require serious effort, and they can't be nice to everybody at once. The smiles fade. At these times, you're a support to them, and you can help them tackle their problems in the same way that you do, which is one bit at a time. Your system of repeated small-scale victories leading to overall triumph is just what they need, and that's what you do for them.

As a friendship, this pairing isn't likely to last unless it has strong bonds at a deeper level. Your surface attitudes are entirely different, and you're unlikely to find each other good company unless other factors in your charts lend their energies that way. As lovers, you'll need a sense of humor. Librans are great romantics and you see such stuff as sloppy nonsense. You feel that you can't cope with something as undefined as sentiment, because Mercury gives you no facility for it. Nonetheless, it's the way the Libran works, so you'll have to try to accommodate each other somehow.

This pairing makes a good team if either of you is ambitious, because you can support each other very well. It isn't really a love-match, though. If you want a hard working, achieving marriage, then fine; if not, look elsewhere. In business, you can do the backroom work, while Libra swans around attracting customers and soothing ruffled feathers.

Virgo - Scorpio

This is probably the easiest relationship of the twelve for you to form and maintain, but it isn't really much to do with hearts and flowers. The planetary energies flow easily and strongly together. If the two of you ever decide to go into business, run a detective agency! Let me explain. Scorpios are strong and powerful people whose strength is not so much in their muscles, but their motivation. They need to find out exactly what's going on, to think through all the possibilities, and stay in control of all of them. They are absolutely determined that everything will take place the way they say it will and under their control, and that way there will be no mistakes. It all sounds good to you, I know. This is exactly the sort of person you've always appreciated and admired, and their way of working sounds like what you've been saying all along. What's more, they are brilliantly effective. Where's the catch?

The catch is a small and subtle one, as befits Scorpios, and it may not bother you a great deal, either. It's this: the more you do for them, the more they'll let you. Make no mistake, the Virgo works for others beside himself, but the Scorpio just works for himself. They work with a different material from you, and one with which you're unfamiliar. You work with physical, measurable things, such as making something out of a chunk of raw material, doing a job and getting paid for it, being helpful in a practical way and being thanked for it, and looking after the objects. Scorpios don't work with any of these things. They work with the unseen powers that lie over and above all our everyday business, which involve motives like loyalty and ambition, love and enmity, pride and fear. These motives are all products of emotional energy, and it's this that the Scorpio collects and maintains as surely as you manipulate and work the material things.

Since you're so unfamiliar with the world of emotions, you admire his facility with them, and are quite content to leave him to it, though you may be a little apprehensive about his motives towards you. Relax. As long as you're useful to him, the Scorpio won't abuse you, and you're very useful indeed.

Scorpios need somebody who can actually do things for them, whose skills are firmly based in the real and tangible world. They also need this person to have the same high standards as themselves, and this is precisely where you come in. You're just the sort of friend a Scorpio is looking for, being careful, controlled, dutiful, eager to please and with high standards of performance and finish. What's more, you're no threat to him where his real concerns lie, which are in the emotional control of his own life.

This has all the makings of a great friendship. You love finding out about things, and going into the causes and origins of things in great depth. You seem to complement each other perfectly, as the Scorpio does the digging and you do the sifting, so that between you, you find things. From the outside, you're an unapproachable couple, seemingly completely occupied in yourselves and laughing at private jokes. From the inside, you're having a great time.

When the friendship grows into an affair, you must be prepared to be overwhelmed. This is the Scorpio's home territory, and you won't have previously met anything so intense. The physical strength is similar to the Arian's, but the emotional strength is truly massive, so you'll be blown flat like a reed in a hurricane. As a marriage, it will be fun at first, but their unrelenting emotional grip, occasionally becoming obsessive jealousy, may be too much for you to deal with. In business, you'll have to fill in the details while they find the business.

Virgo - Sagittarius

You're curious and want to find things out, and Sagittarius knows it all already. You want to be appreciated for what you do, while Sagittarius is a born winner. You want to be able to use what you know to get results, and he already does that. You don't want anything emotionally demanding, and Sagittarius makes no emotional demands. It sounds too good to be true, but can you stand the pace?

Sagittarians have a better view of you than you do of them, but there again, they have a fairly good view of everybody and they are so irrepressibly confident that it unnerves you. Like you, they are driven by the desire to change things from their existing state by their own efforts, and make something better and different. The difference between you is that they are the originators of ideas, and you're the means of putting them into effect. They talk about changing things, and you worry about how you're going to manage it. They see everything on a large scale, and everything seems possible to them, so problems never cloud their vision. You have your nose much closer to the ground, making sure that the problems that arise are solved in an effective and proper fashion; you've lost sight of the original vision, so you see things on a smaller scale.

As a consequence of all this, their impractical idealism makes you angry from time to time. They never see that they will need so much time, so much money, and this and that before their wild schemes can come to fruition. What you don't see unless someone tells you is that the point is the idea itself, and not the fruition. The idea is exciting, because it has possibilities for the imagination to play with. Once you make it normal, all the fun has gone out of it. Sagittarians play in the realm of the creative imagination, and you always forget that. On the other hand, they can't understand why you can't see the whole project in a flash in your mind's eye, as they can, or why you only seem to get interested when the project's nearly finished. Virgoans play in the real world at an individual component level, and Sagittarians always forget that.

Although it sounds as though you have an insuperable communications gap, it's not in fact, so you recognize that you're aiming for the same thing in different ways, and this gives you a sort of companionship. As a result, you indulge each other's excesses good-humouredly, with you muttering, "he's dreaming again" under your breath as you listen patiently to the latest wild idea, while they dismiss your practical objections with "details, mere details". One area where you'll clash is in that of standards of work. Sagittarius would rather you did things quickly, while the passion of the moment is still there, and he's prepared to overlook small inconsistencies, but you must attend to every little thing, and this takes time.

As lovers, you're in for an interesting time. Sagittarius has a childlike eagerness that you'll find very attractive, but he's not the slightest bit constant or even consistent, so you'll have to be prepared for some difficulties. He's spontaneous and sincere in his affections, and you'll appreciate that. As a marriage, this is by no means bad. He has expansiveness, optimism and energy, and you can help his ideas become realities to the benefit of both of you. You'll have to be careful that his bouncy and playful manner doesn't exasperate you: try not to take things too seriously! In business, he will have the ideas, and you'll bring them to life.

Virgo - Capricorn

All your fondest ideas seem to be embodied in the person of the Capricorn. They seem, somehow, to be a fully developed version of yourself, with all your own promise brought forth into glorious fruit. That's how you see it, anyway. Capricorns are not usually on the receiving end of such an enthusiastic press from the rest of the zodiac, but you see them this way because the Capricorn is an Earth sign person, like you. That means that they work in essentially the same areas as you. Like you, they appreciate things that are good and firm. They take reassurance from the actual presence of things. They can value themselves by reference to a physical measure, which is money. Emotions and words are not theirs, nor half-thought-out projects and whimsical fantasies. Capricorn likes things firm. If he can feel it, weigh it or buy it, it's real to him. You can understand this. It's familiar to you, and you don't have to make any allowances for the way he thinks, because you also think that way. When you're so in tune with somebody, attraction is instant and friendship is easily brought into being.

The major difference between you is that he's at a different phase of the Earth element from you. Where you spend your time working on things to improve them, using your mind to analyze and probe, trying to find the best way of doing anything, he has it made. The achievement of the finished item is his. You seek the technique for improvement, but he wants the recognition for his achievement. You'll no doubt protest that you'd like some recognition for your efforts as well, but it's not his prime aim. If you receive recognition without earning, you feel guilty, but the Capricorn wouldn't. You need to feel that you can do something properly before you get the applause, while he simply needs to be at the top.

If you think for a minute, you can see the nature of the interaction between you. You'll spend a lifetime trying to reach your own standards of perfection and never reaching a stage where you think that you deserve the number one position. You'd like a foretaste of what that position's all about, though, and in a Capricorn, you can have it. From his point of view, you're something he can believe in. He believes that everything in the world is ordered and structured, that there's a hierarchy of things and that his position in the structure is at the top. When he sees you busily examining and repairing the structure of things, he's reassured. In his imagination, the world is like an anthill or a beehive, in which Virgos are workers and Capricorns the queen bee.

As a friendship, this one will run and run. You see eye to eye on almost everything. You both have a strong sense of duty, and of what has to be done, and you both like working hard. You have similar tastes, albeit for different reasons. You both like expensive and well-made things, in Capricorn's case because they are status symbols, and you because of the care and skill that has gone into their manufacture.

As lovers, you could do worse. It all depends on whether you come up to each other's expectations, since you're a perfectionist and Capricorn only wants the best. Emotionally, the Capricorn is rather cold, but that won't worry you, since Mercury is uncomfortable in scenes of either great passion or sentiment. This is a respectful affair then, but satisfying to the people concerned.

As a marriage or for business, you could hardly do better. Both of you are determined to improve yourselves, and through his determination and your application, you'll work wonders.

Virgo - Aquarius

On paper, this one shouldn't work, but it does. One of the signs is oddly attractive, the other is attractively odd. The attraction is probably that you're both unattractive to others, not in a visual sense, but because you prefer situations with a certain emotional distance. This distance helps you form an opinion of others without feeling tied to them. Aquarians are as fond of the "cool appraisal" method as you are, and you recognize that in them. You probably bring it out in each other, since one of the features of any partnership is that common personality traits are emphasized.

Aquarians, like Librans and Geminis, work in a world of speech and relationships, where people are far more important than things. That said, Aquarians are the least changeable of the three, which makes them function at about the same level of intensity as you. You're the most changeable of the Earth signs, which are usually very solid and heavy, so this brings a kind of meeting of your emotional levels.

Aquarians like to be a face in a crowd. They are not necessarily shy, but they don't really have the force of personality required to hold the stage on their own, and they are much better in a group. Indeed, they really shine in company, becoming in some strange way the representative of the group without being part of it. They have tremendous organizational talents, in a way that you don't, and not only can they see the larger picture that you have difficulty with, they see it in terms of people, which you almost never do.

If you're going to try to analyze and define an Aquarian so that you can get to know him better, you're in for a hard time. They like to keep themselves at a little distance from everybody and to stand apart from the crowd. They don't try to be superior or inferior - just different, and a little distant. You'll find that there isn't really a lot for you to take hold of, for you to say that's what makes them different. Your inability to pinpoint exactly how this strange person works will either enrage or captivate you. If he enrages you, you'll obviously break off the relationship, but it's far more likely that you'll rise to the challenge offered.

They will have been forming their own opinions about you while you've been busy. They see you as a friendly person with an inquisitive mind. Later on, they will realize what a talent you have for seeing how things work, and how to get the best out of every thing, and they will see that as an admirable thing. Like you, they are concerned to get the best out of things, but what they want to get the best out of is people, not objects. They keep thinking what a pity it is that you don't have their sense of organization and that they don't have your eye for detail or your analytical powers. They are pleased to find that you like to work with a group of people and not just for yourself.

Neither of you are initiators. You both prefer to do something with what you already have. Neither of you are comfortable with the idea of being directly and personally involved with another person, but you both like company. Outside of that, you're wildly different, but there's a fair body of similarity of approach, if not of motivation, and it may be enough to make you seek out each other's company.

As friends, you'll talk non-stop, but in a rather clinical and scientific way, about everybody who you know. You seem to be on each other's wavelength, at least on the surface. You'll need a bit of pushing to become lovers, because you're both rather cool emotionally, and the enjoyment you get from talking to each other doesn't get any better when you become sexually involved. If you want to explore this side of yourself with somebody of similar persuasion, who is unlikely to offer you more than you could comfortably deal with emotionally, and who would maintain the pretence that the relationship is strictly experimental, then the Aquarian would make a good partner. You'd both find it greatly amusing, and that's half the pleasure.

For marriage or business, the only obstacle would be your lack of involvement. Although you both like things cool, the bonds could do with being a little stronger if the union is to last a long time. Otherwise, you drift apart and become two individuals again.

Virgo - Pisces

Relationships between opposite signs are never going to be easy, but your planet, Mercury, is particularly unhappy in the waters of Pisces, so this is the most difficult of all the opposite-sign pairings. What's more, it's unbalanced, because it's slightly easier for the Piscean to get on with you than for you to get on with him.

What you have in common is the idea of giving to others. Both of you are very good at that, and many Pisceans make their careers in the caring professions, such as medicine. What astounds you, at least until you're used to it, is that the Piscean gives to others by taking from them. He soaks up their worries, fears and anger. He lets them unburden their guilt, share their secrets, voice their frustrations. All of these go into the Piscean, and he dissipates them. It's difficult for you to cope with this as an idea. If everybody approached you on an intimate level, you'd find it very difficult to make anything useful out of it all. Perhaps the Piscean is the same with fixed procedures, rules and regulations. Had you thought of that?

Pisceans can thrive on a diet of other people's emotions. Indeed, they can't live without it. A Piscean lives in a world formed from his imagination's response to what he hears or sees, and if he doesn't like it, he moves it around a bit until it suits. Imagine living on a giant rubbish heap, made from everybody else's belongings all piled up. Apart from everything else, you'd find it unbearably scruffy. Now imagine taking out a few choice items to use, and if they weren't what you wanted, or you got tired of them, you could throw them back in the pile and choose something else. Now forget the idea of doing it with real pieces of hardware, and imagine doing it with emotions and feelings. That's Pisces.

Impossible though it must be to believe, you're both involved in the same process, which is changing things through your own efforts to make something better. You simply use different materials. Go back a few pages and read the Virgo-Sagittarius section again, and you'll see how they come with an original idea and leave it to you to make it into something, well, Pisces is where it gets recycled after people have used and loved it, and worn it out.

Pisceans like you more than you'd think. They are as definite as you are and as precise, but it's all in the mind rather than in reality. In addition, from time to time, they change their mind. You're quite certain all along about which way you're going to do things, and about what has to be done, and it's all in the real world of rules and regulations, which don't change. Pisceans admire that.

As friends, you look miles apart, but you should appreciate what the other is doing, and that will lead to understanding and cooperation. Besides, the Piscean will adopt Virgoan traits when in your company, so you won't have to compromise your principles!

As lovers, you'll have to be patient. You're much stronger minded than they are, and you could become demanding. You'll have to allow their sensitivity to function, and not crush it with your insistence on common sense. You could both learn a great deal.

In a marriage, you have to give them a flexible but practical framework and try not to restrict their imagination. Don't tidy up after them to an obsessive extent either, and this way, you could have an unusual and rewarding marriage. In business, they will come up with the ideas and you'll put them into practice.

The Approach to Relationships: Libra

Symbol: The Scales	Ω	Element: Air
Planet: Venus	♀	Quality: Cardinal

The whole area of forming relationships is what Libra is all about. Much of your time will be spent talking to other people, forming and sustaining friendships, and generally being sociable. It doesn't sound much, but it's what you do best, and what you like doing best; in fact, you can do it better than all of the other signs, and you also need to do it more than they do. Some of the other signs don't need friends in the same way that you do, and don't really care if they are left on their own: Aries and Capricorn are often like this. Aquarius likes the social scene as much as you do, but he prefers larger groups; he doesn't have the personal touch that you do, and he is uncomfortable in a one-to-one situation. So, you see, personal relationships are the specific concern of the Libran: it's your *job* to be nice to people.

For you, it's enough just to be with someone you love; you don't need to control their whole life, dictate and arrange what they do or what happens to them, or anything like that. You might want to, but that's really the concern of the next sign on, Scorpio. His job is to control and maintain things for whole groups of people: yours is just to make contact and to get people talking.

Libra - Aries

This partnership is formed from two people representing different sides of the zodiac, but there's a lot more going for it than you might think. People from different sides of the zodiac are not entirely opposite in their motivations, as a quick glance at the zodiac circle will prove. You're both Cardinal signs, so you both have outgoing natures rather than "collecting" ones. This means that you're both eager to make something of the relationship. Both of you approach things by giving your energy to them rather than seeing what is given to you, and both of you are of the firm opinion that your own efforts are sufficient to make the situation develop in a way that is satisfactory to you. Given that kind of willingness and capacity for input on both sides, the relationship can hardly fail, and whatever else happens to you, it can't be said that the partnership suffers from lack of effort from either partner.

What will strike you most about the Arian is his determination and energy. He seems almost to be on fire; so keen is he to get things moving. He's involved with life in a way that you're not; everything that he takes on is a thing of great importance to him and it matters to him that he gets something out of it. It may seem to you that he's too intense, that his whole approach is much too urgent, and that he will surely wear himself out if he continues to live at such a pace. You're wrong on two counts. Firstly, Mars is the planet that drives him at that rate and gives him the strength to live at that speed, so there's no danger of him wearing himself out. Secondly, he's selective in what he does. He ignores the things that are of no interest to him, and attacks the things that do interest him with force and enthusiasm.

He is his own man. He does things purely to satisfy himself, without thought for others. This does not make him selfish, because he simply exists through his own actions and for himself. You're at your best when in a relationship, because the relationship is what your planet moves you towards, while his planet moves him towards individual and personal action. He's not really interested in what anybody else does, because what matters to him is what he does. He will see you as somebody interesting and variable, and who seems to be in changing circumstances all the time. That will appeal to him. He needs new challenges to keep his interest and test his abilities. He's not really capable of sitting still. He also has no time for pessimists, because he would rather be up and doing than sitting and worrying. He sees you as light, changeable and optimistic, and he will be happy to stay in your company.

You find him irresistible. His confidence, outgoing nature and capacity for achievement attract you at once. The Arian planet, Mars, is associated with the metal, iron, while your ruling planet, Venus, has an energy that's like a magnet. The resounding clonk that you hear occurs when the two of you meet. Once you've got the Aries stuck to your magnetic personality, you'll both be completely uninterested in anyone else. It could take as much as five minutes before the two of you will consider a sexual relationship. Arians aren't exactly romantic, but they are definitely passionate, and you'll gladly settle for that.

As a marriage, this one could last. The inner secret of it is that the Arian would rather be busy and active than sit around baring his soul, and you get more out of being in a relationship than from the person with whom you're relating... especially if that person expects very close personal involvement. It's the very slight emotional aloofness that you both have which keeps the balance perfect. Odd, isn't it?

As a business relationship, there are no problems if you both decide to go in the Aries' direction, but you must deal with the clients yourself, and do the talking along the way.

Libra - Taurus

This is a better relationship than it looks. Astrologically, you have nothing in common, as you're Cardinal Air and Taurus is Fixed Earth. You're outgoing, and he's collecting, but you have the same guiding planet, which is Venus. What it boils down to is that you're both using the same energy, but using it in different directions and for a different purpose, What you can both say is, "I can see what you're doing, but I wouldn't do it that way if I were you". It would be nice if you could both say in addition, "I must try it your way, because it looks quite interesting", but with people being what they are, you're more likely to find yourself saying, "Why don't you do it my way? It's much better like that."

What is it that the Taurean is trying to do? Like you, he's using Venus and its power to attract, but what he's attracting are objects that he can value and cherish as his own. Sometimes he will attract people, but his central desire is still to keep, value and cherish property. All of the magnetism is used to pull inwards, you see. As more things become part of the collection, the Taurean becomes more and more unwilling to make any changes, and less and less interested in anything new; what he's determined to do most of all is to hang on to everything he has, and to let none of it go. You see him as a stick-in-the-mud. You appreciate his desire to attract beautiful and satisfying things because you do the same, but you're actually more concerned to create beautiful things rather than to collect them. You'd like to share everything you have with everybody, so that everybody gets a chance to enjoy all that you've done, but the Taurean wants it all to himself and may not want to share any of it with anybody. This is a very biased view of course, and there are many good things about Taureans. Their genuine kindness to those close to them and their steady, reliable presence in an emergency, to name but two. However, despite all that, it's the differences that become more apparent to you than the similarities.

Among these, you notice how personally they seem to take everything. A whimsical jibe becomes a deep wound and they become defensive. You can restore their trust, of course, and you're good at that, but why should they be so touchy? They see you as ineffective and indecisive. They watch you juggling your opinions, and mutter to themselves that, while others may not agree with the way they do things, at least they know where I stand, and I am consistent. They see your obvious talent for color and style on display in your home and in the way you dress, and they shake their heads in despair. They hate to see all that talent running to waste instead of being used to make something lasting, solid, and durable, despite the fact that they wouldn't actually get round to making the objects themselves, either.

Taureans keep their thoughts to themselves, and they keep much of what they feel inside themselves. They have a capacity for endurance and putting up with discomfort that you could never understand. This is a friendship that will center on the things of beauty and value you both love, and as long as this interest is maintained, the friendship will continue and could make a good business partnership as well. However, your personal requirements are too far apart to make much more of it on an intimate level.

As lovers, one of you will have the double bass part and the other the flute's line, so you're unlikely to be playing the same tune at the same time, and you're not even on the same page of the score! Marriage? Yes if the Libran has stability and material comforts high on his list of requirements, otherwise, no. A business relationship can work though, as your partner will deal with the practicalities while you charm the customers.

Libra - Gemini

This is one of your easier relationships. Two people from the same element, in this case Air, share a similar approach to life. Somehow, the Gemini understands your motives without you having to explain yourself, and without you having to adjust your behavior to compensate for his preferences and fixed ways of doing things. A sign that's ahead of you in the circle is more exciting to be with than one behind you. In this case, Gemini is the earlier sign, so he finds you more appealing than you find him, but the difference isn't great. You're likely to be attracted to each other on sight anyway, and you'll have plenty of conversation. This is an instantaneous, perhaps even spontaneous, friendship.

Perhaps that's the level on which to keep it, because what makes this relationship is the mingling of the energies of Venus and Mercury, and they are essentially light and personable planets. The weighty and serious matters that are usually assigned to Jupiter and Saturn are not here, nor the force of Mars, nor the vital and life giving energies of the Sun and Moon. What you have here is bright mentality, wit, conversation, good times, small pleasures and things like that. Overall, this is a brilliant recipe for a lively and hugely enjoyable friendship.

What isn't in the recipe is anything deep or powerfully emotional. This relationship is in the mind rather than the soul. It's a relationship for sunny days and lively parties, not for long nights and heavy responsibilities. If you want the sort of partnership where you examine your motives deeply, where your innermost needs and fears are constantly in play, where obsession, worry and tortured passion are the usual emotions, then this isn't it. Even if those things are in you, and need expression, then this relationship won't express them for you, because it will skate over them. Mercury and Venus really can't handle things that are big and ponderous; they concentrate instead on the lighter side of things, bringing a lively sparkle to all social activity, and making sure that everybody enjoys himself or herself in an entertaining way.

Entertaining is exactly the word for it. Even if you deepen the friendship into a sexual one, it will still be entertaining. You'll find yourselves laughing and talking as you make love, and you'll have a very mobile and playful physical relationship which is never heavy and ponderous, and which doesn't include the kind of collisions that other combinations of signs like. This friendship brings two light planets together. Because of this, you'll find that the relationship itself brings more social contacts than you'd otherwise have had, and your circle of friends will grow and grow. At the same time, you'll force yourselves to deal with everything in a lighthearted and rather shallow way, because this is the nature of this relationship.

What do you see in each other? You see him as a dazzling wit with a quick tongue, and he sees you as charm itself. It's as easy as that. As business partners you'll do well, provided your business can be handled in a light and fast-moving way, involving many social contacts. If it can't, then you'll lack the necessary power and determination to make a success of it. Marriage will be similar. You'll have plenty to talk about, and a very enjoyable time, but deep down, the heavy differences between you may not find adequate expression, so the partnership may not grow very long roots, despite its busy growth on the surface.

Libra - Cancer

It isn't impossible to make this one work, but it isn't as easy as it looks. Once trust has been established, you'll have a very strong relationship indeed, as is the case with all the relationships where your signs share quality but not an element. Here you're both Cardinal, but one is outgoing Air while the other is collecting Water.

You'd love to make friends with the soft and fragile Cancerian. Your Venus energies would go so well with his delicate lunar ones. The trouble is that the Cancerian is afraid that you're some kind of a threat, or that you're not serious, so he needs time to get used to you before he makes a full response. If you push too hard, he will clam up. If you lose interest and go away, he will know that you weren't serious and won't take you seriously in future. Be patient, gentle and reassuring if you want to make a lasting relationship here.

Cancerians are concerned with the emotional content of everything; they like to be in a situation where the feeling is the most important thing and they are concerned with the way the atmosphere of a place makes them feel. Do you see the difference? A place can have a bright atmosphere, or a gloomy one, but you stay if you like it and leave if you don't. You're self-sustaining, and you can cheer yourself up if necessary. This is part of being an Air sign. Cancer is different because it absorbs the atmosphere of the place it's in, and develops an emotional response to it. These emotions are the normal way for Water signs to express themselves, just as speech and social contact is the normal way for you. You'll see at once that a Cancer is going to be much more vulnerable to external influences than you are, and is not going to be as optimistic as you are for much of the time.

They know this too. They have developed a tough exterior to prevent themselves being damaged by contact with people whose intentions are less than kind, and it's in their own interest to maintain this, at least until they have got to know you a little. When they have accepted you, you'll be thrilled to discover how sensitive and subtle a Cancerian can be. They are intensely personal, too, but not in the brash way of the Arian. They take great care of themselves, in a gentle and sustaining way that your Venusian sensibilities will admire very much. They take care of those they love, too, so you'll be able to enjoy the wonderful feeling of having somebody be as nice to you as you'd like to appear to them. Above all, Cancerians are so soft and so genuine, that you'll feel quite ashamed of the little bit of airy aloofness that stops you giving yourself completely to another.

They see you as a more open version of themselves. Because you're graceful, refined in manner and perhaps a little ineffective in action, Cancerians see you as having no harshness or cruelty in you, and therefore warm towards you at once. They sense a similarity between your need to be with other people, and your willingness to do what others want, and their need to care for other people. They see your emphasis on relating as an initial stage in the process that leads to their maternal and nurturing instincts. They are reassured by the fact that your prime interest seems to lie in the other person rather than yourself. As you will realize, they are viewing the reality of the situation sideways on, but they like what they see nonetheless. The only thing that makes them shiver is the openness of your way of life. It's all seems too risky for them, but they are more than ready to let you get on with it, and they will also be ready to pick up the pieces when mishaps occur.

As a friendship, this one is happy but quiet and reflective, as it smiles rather than laughs. Should the friendship develop into a love relationship, it will be very soft, very loving, and as romantic as you want to make it. It will lack any hard qualities, so if you fancy something of a challenge this isn't it. It will also become set in its ways after a while. Cancerians gain strength and reassurance from familiarity and regularity.

As a marriage, like most of the three-signs-apart matches, it will be strong but a little stormy. You both recognize that the other has qualities you would like, but seems to concentrate them in a way that's at odds with the way you would like them. The same goes for a business partnership.

Libra - Leo

This is almost the easiest relationship you'll ever fall into, provided that you can make one simple allowance. Just one. It's ever so simple: Leo is the boss. Leos conduct life on that principle, so you'll have to learn it sooner or later, and to have it in mind right from the word go saves a lot of heartache later on.

The reason is simple and it makes an easy mental picture to remember. Leo is governed by the Sun, and you're governed by Venus. The Sun stays where it is and Venus orbits round it, shining brightly as it goes, because it reflects the sunlight. Note that last phrase – which is that the Leo is the light source. Not too rosy a picture perhaps, but the reality is in fact hugely enjoyable. Leos are enormous optimists, and the thing they like doing best is showing off and having a good time. You mustn't tell them this, of course, because they prefer to see themselves as magnanimous and big-hearted philanthropists. Whatever the reality, a relationship between you will be a very warm and enjoyable thing, and well worth embarking upon when a Leo comes your way. Like Aries, the Leo pushes out energy in a steady stream. He wants to make things happen the way he likes them to, and he's more than ready to put in the necessary effort to achieve this. If a relationship with you is what takes his interest, then his full radiance will be turned upon you, and you'll certainly feel the warmth. Lavish entertaining, beautiful gifts and all sorts of good times together will start to fill your life and you won't have to do a thing in return except appreciate his generosity. As long as the Leo is appreciated for what he does, he will continue to do it.

There will be some special quality in you that he particularly admires, and it will be this to which he's paying court. He would not have chosen you if you were not, in his opinion, the most wonderfully talented person that he has ever met. Isn't it a fantastic process? Mutual ego-massage, convincing the other that both of you are absolutely wonderful. It's all to do with the infectious warmth and true generosity of spirit that the Leo displays. He radiates it outwards, and it reflects off everybody near him, as we noted in the astronomical parallel earlier.

You see him as a wonderful friend and a creator of friends. You'd love to be the way he is. Everybody likes him, and that's the center of it. Your planet, Venus, has much to do with the business of liking and you feel attracted to somebody who is universally liked. Somehow, nothing gets him down for long. He can always find something exciting to do or rustle up a few friends to come round and start a party going. This would be a world of warmth, optimism, friendship and companionability. It sounds like everything you've ever wanted.

He sees you as Jack to his King. Light, likable, and companionable, but not having anything of his regal might and power. Are there any pitfalls? There aren't many, although the main one is lack of movement. As an Air sign, you need variety and movement, so staying in the same place for too long does you no good. Leo is a Fixed sign, and that means that he likes to stay with an existing situation once he has it working the way he wants it to be. You could end up finding the endless hilarity with the same old friends just a touch boring, while you all grow older and fatter together. Leo won't be moved unless he says so. He's the center and people go round him. He won't have it any other way.

As a friendship, this one is of the best. As lovers, you may find him a bit heavy and a slow mover, but he's warm and generous, and that's worth something. As a permanent relationship of any kind, this one has a lot going for it. The only thing for you to consider is whether you'll trade lack of movement in return for generosity, warmth and guaranteed success. This is a good business relationship as long as you both employ someone to do the boring chores that neither of you like.

Libra - Virgo

You would be forgiven for thinking that your Venusian energies allowed you to form a reasonably enjoyable relationship with absolutely anyone, but sadly, an encounter with a typical Virgo will make you wonder. Of all the possible combinations of Sun signs, this one gets maximum marks for difficulty. Why? Virgo embodies all the qualities you'd like to forget, but know that you shouldn't really. Worse, Virgo is the sort of person who will literally tap you on the shoulder and remind you of these qualities when they feel you need it.

You work in new ideas and hopes for the future, but the Virgo works with the minor details of the here and now. You read holiday romances and fantasize about meeting wonderful strangers on sun-kissed shores, but they tell you that you can't afford it. If you continue to holiday with the Virgo, you'd have to be very careful what you say and do if you didn't want to ruin your entire holiday. They are not killjoys; at least not on purpose. They are unimaginative, or at least they are not imaginative in the way that you are. Grand feelings, such as optimism and romance with a capital "R" or art with a capital "A", which mean so much to you, are simply beyond their grasp. How are you going to communicate, great communicator though you are, the importance to you of something whose existence they can't even imagine?

A seemingly impossible situation. Yet, for all that, there are definite points of contact between you. You know, as well as anybody ever can, that little things can cause imbalance in the whole. You see it when something is inelegantly arranged, when someone's clothes don't really go together or when you spot clumsiness of speech or movement. The Virgo spots the detail that's out of place while you notice the overall effect. Do you see the difference? You're dealing with the ideas being put forward, and the Virgo is dealing with the actual things used to do it. The difference between you is that you're capable of thinking backwards in the zodiacal sequence to Virgo, so that you can appreciate the small details of things, whereas he's all but incapable of thinking forwards and grasping the overall intention and effect.

Virgo, like all of the "collecting" signs, takes things seriously, so he analyses what he sees, and most importantly, what he touches and handles. He needs to build up a physical familiarity with things, and to understand them. You don't have time for this. Things aren't people, and familiarity of the kind achieved by the sense of touch takes far too long and is too silent anyway. Speech, dialogue, interactive thought; these are what you want. You can't readily understand a person who would rather understand one thing fully than know about twenty to a more superficial extent.

They see you as much too hasty. Why will you not take the time to become fully familiar with things? Above all, why do you waste your obvious talents on such changeable and insubstantial things as relationships? If you could learn to appreciate the values of physical things, you could be the sort of artisan they long to be. You wouldn't, of course, because you'd be an artist, which many Librans are anyway. There's the difference between art and craft; it's the difference between Libra and Virgo.

It's not easy to make this relationship work at the level of an amicable friendship. There are too many little irritations, such as their habit of hanging your clothes up for you when you leave them on the floor. Given that friendship is unlikely, becoming lovers or getting married is even more unusual. Should it happen, the relationship would work in a frenetic sort of way, because you both want to make things better for the other, but get in each other's way. Oddly enough, as workmates within a larger organization, you could get on quite well, although problems would arise at the higher levels of management.

Libra - Libra

At least you know what you're getting when you start a relationship with another Libran, or at least you should do; after all, you're one yourself! This would actually be better if you weren't too alike, in either looks or the proximity of your birthdays, as that would provide differences in you, from which you can build a stronger relationship.

When you meet each other, you'll be attracted to those similarities in yourselves that you find admirable. If you take pride in your appearance, you'll be pleased to see that they do the same, and if you're very interested in some artistic activity or music perhaps, you'll be delighted to note that their taste coincides with yours. It's enough to start a friendship, and you'll tend to concentrate on the things you have in common, because it's the Libran way.

Doing things the Libran way is all very well when relating to other signs, but it works against itself when used with another Libran. The trouble begins when you start presenting the other person with the parts of yourself that he would like to have, and if you both do that for long enough, you find yourselves playing roles the whole time, so that reality never enters into it. You may well be having a grand time of it, chattering away nineteen to the dozen, but it isn't productive, because neither of you is actually communicating. The important thing is being able to hear yourself think, and you do this best by having proper conversations with somebody else. If you're both saying things that you don't mean, you're defeating the purpose of the relationship, and you'll feel the strain as a result. Your answer will then be to start a more honest and productive relationship with somebody else and to let this one decline, but what a waste of energy it will have been. Just think how useful it could have been to have a friend who really understood what you were trying to do!

It will be quite easy in this relationship to produce an atmosphere of "Grand Romance", complete with pink ribbons, handmade chocolates, weekends in Paris and all that sort of thing. Both will enjoy indulging yourselves, and will be even more pleased to find that the other person enjoys it just as much as you do. You'll tell yourself that this is perfection. However - and this is important - you won't get anything from it that you couldn't have provided for yourself. Monstrously unfair of me to spoil your fun, I hear you shout, and I don't understand how lovely real romance is. Ah, but two Taureans could sit and eat cream cakes all day (and would, given half a chance); two Arians could leave their families behind, and rush off to explore the Himalayas. You'd be quick to spot the disadvantages of these actions, even though they're all only doing what they like best, and the same applies to you and another Libran.

The satisfaction in being Libran is in balancing your abilities against the different values of other people. If their values are the same, there's no balancing to do, is there? The whole point of a pair of scales is that they tell you when two amounts of different substances are or are not equal in weight. If the two items are the same and of the same weight, there's no work for the balance to do.

This is an easy and enjoyable friendship, and it will develop into an easily manageable and reasonably enjoyable sexual relationship if you so wish. It will form a fairly relaxed marriage, short of enterprise and rather untidy domestically, but good-natured and friendly. It's an easy-going business partnership that's ideally suited to an office environment. What it won't do is stretch you at all. If you want an easy life, with no ups or downs to speak of, then this one will suit you, but if you really want to exercise your Libra nature, and feel that you're getting somewhere, choose someone different rather than the same.

Libra - Scorpio

You'll love this one. It will leave you black and blue and you'll love every minute of it! You don't stand any chance at all of making it work, but you'll try hard. This relationship gets a maximum difficulty rating, but you actually enjoy your time within it. As you will see by the time you've known him a while, a Scorpio is the sort of person your mother warned you about, but who listens to their mothers?

Scorpios are an alarming mixture of the solidity of a Taurean, with his ability to attract things to himself, and the pure energy and force of the Arian. Librans make themselves attractive to others, and use their charm to enhance their appeal. Scorpios don't need to do that, and they are not really interested in such vague methods, either. A Scorpio is magnetically attractive to everybody anyway; it's just how he is. Note that attractive doesn't mean attracted. Scorpios don't do the moving. Nor do they need to be particularly charming, though that doesn't mean that they are rude. Far from it - they are accomplished manipulators of the emotions of those around them, and they usually offer a very polished performance. When somebody is attracted to them, they know that they won't have to work at keeping them there, it's just a question of reeling them in, in the Scorpio's own good time. You'll be hooked, of course. If you're the sort of person who goes out looking for relationships, and you are, then you're actually going to accelerate towards him, the closer you get. Scorpio is governed by Mars, and Venus and Mars just seem unable to keep their hands off each other.

You see them as deep, mysterious, alluring and impossibly sexy. You also see them as the sort of thing you'd like to be. After all, you manage to form relationships by working at them and putting your energy into them, but he seems to do it all without even trying. This has a lot to do with him being the next sign on; everybody finds the next sign on from them rather enviable, because they can't get to it. The grass is greener on the other side and all that. As usual, you pick on the aspects of their character that you have in common, forming links, via Venus, between elements in both of you that are similar. What happens in this instance is that you bring out all the parts of you that are dark and exciting, and you rather enjoy playing the role. "He's made me a more exciting person", you say to your friends. No, you've made yourself more exciting. What you don't notice about the whole affair is that you're turning back flips to appeal to him, and trying to get closer to the heart of all that delicious magnetism, but he isn't changing one bit. You aren't even close to changing him. He's in control; he was at the beginning, and he is now.

He sees you as somebody light and friendly, but in no way a threat. He knows that you're about to give yourself to him body and soul, and he's looking forward to the experience - not from any sense of malice, but because he's a sensualist who is in for a treat. Your ideas of romance, your way with words, your perfect taste and grace of movement are exciting to him, and he can hardly wait. He is, however, determined to stay in control of everything, because you're just the sort of person he could lose his heart to, and losing control of himself is something he fears, in the same way that you fear loneliness.

You're so open, so optimistic and trusting in your approach to people, you see. On the one hand, he thinks you're naive and foolish, whereas he has learnt to stay in control, but on the other hand, he knows that he will never have your generosity of spirit. He also knows that the secret of relationships is to be open and optimistic, and he feels ashamed. You'll never know this. Only he knows this, and he won't even let himself realize it fully; but he will be doubly determined to stay in control.

As friends or working partners, the relationship will last for as long as it takes for you to become lovers. You don't chat - you flirt. As lovers, you'll be knocked flat by his power and intensity, and it's likely to be more than you want over a long period of time. As a lasting partnership or a marriage, the outlook is not so good. You really represent too much of what the other would rather forget about, for a deep relationship to thrive.

Libra - Sagittarius

Now we're at last reaching the easiest, friendliest, and most optimistic relationship of them all as far as you're concerned, and yet one which has more to offer than just light conversation and a pleasant time. The reasons aren't difficult to understand. The sign that's two signs on from your own is always the one that's easiest to talk with, and somehow you always have things that you want to say to them. The things that interest you interest them too, but with enough of a difference in viewpoint to make an engaging conversation.

Sagittarians, on the other hand, are like Leos, but slimmer and more mobile. They are not much slimmer, but they are a lot more mobile! What they want most of all is to see and do new things, to find out about them, and then somehow to make something useful out of them. Most of the time, this takes the form of telling other people about the things that they have discovered. It never occurs to them that the rest of the world doesn't really want to know, and on those occasions when they misjudge things, they bounce back with irrepressible optimism.

Having a relationship with a Sagittarian is an ever-changing experience. They are constantly changing their opinions as new information comes along, and they don't like to do the same thing for too long. A steady job with the same firm for twenty or thirty years is heaven to a Capricorn, but it sounds like a jail sentence to a Sagittarian. This means that there will always be something new for you to relate to in him, some new feature that you'll have to match or counterbalance with something from yourself. This will do you no end of good.

They will also join in most enthusiastically with your wide social life, because they are outgoing, effervescent people who, if truth be told, love showing off to an audience. It suits you perfectly: you need to keep circulating, because you're an Air sign. Put you near a moving Fire sign like Sagittarius, and there's a circulation of warm air to keep you comfortable. Great, isn't it? They see you as the perfect friend: lively, chatty, optimistic and interested in everything that they are themselves, while your habit of picking up on common interests is at work. They are more than happy to stay with you as long as you're prepared to keep moving, as they do. Since you're an Air sign, there's no problem, and all goes well.

Sagittarians are capable of enormously wide-ranging and profound thought. They are the philosophers of the zodiac, and they are capable of seeing the grand view of things better than any other sign. You're also interested in the idea behind things, though you don't often stretch this part of you. Sagittarius will help you do this, and he will be thrilled to have a partner to whom he can communicate his lofty ideas. Such a relationship does both of you a power of good at levels that other relationships don't touch. Communication on the surface is your stock-in-trade, but communication in depth is hard for you. Sagittarius makes it easy.

This partnership is good at every level. You're lively friends, and laughing lovers; as husband and wife you'd fulfill each other's every ambition, and as business partners you'd be full of enterprise and confidence. It really is a wonderful match; its only flaw is that your feet aren't always on the ground. Too many ideas, too much optimism, not enough practicality, your Virgoan friends will say. However, is this really such a bad idea?

Libra - Capricorn

This is a three-sign relationship. You're both Cardinal signs; so both like to start things off, make new things happen through your own efforts, but in very different spheres of influence. Like Virgo and Scorpio, your most difficult partners, Capricorn is a "collecting" sign, and he will want to gather things in to himself rather than offer his energies to the world at large.

Capricorn is quite difficult to get to know, even for a Libran. You're not likely to run into him killing time in a bookshop, because he's far too busy. Capricorns are workaholics. Assuming you do actually find him somewhere, you'll get the impression at once that he isn't a great talker, and doesn't have much to say when he does speak. While this isn't entirely correct, it's not far off. Capricorns are tremendously reserved. Reserved but not repressed, because they have plenty of energy and they use it to the hilt, but it doesn't come out in the form of words or ideas.

What they are interested in is their standing in society. They genuinely believe that the world is a well-ordered place, or at least tries to be, and that everything in it has a position within the structure of things. They also believe that if a person puts in enough effort, then he will be able to advance and be recognized for his efforts. Everybody starts out equal, and everybody has the same opportunity to advance themselves. It's the familiar work ethic of the past, and the only thing wrong with it is its assumption that the system is indeed fair, and that work and reward are directly related.

You're wondering where your relationship with him comes into all this. You both recognize that you work in different worlds, one with material rewards and one with relationships and ideas, and different directions, one ready to give and the other to receive. Yet as you pass by on different roads and in opposite directions, you notice that you have something in common: the absence of self-centeredness. You have a sense of fairness that lets the other person have his say or his turn, a sense that accepts that things don't always stay the way you like them to be, or even end up in your favor. You can live with the difficulties, and you even welcome them, because they keep you on the move. You can usually keep your balance. It's what Librans do, after all.

Capricorn recognizes this. His whole view of life depends on the balance of effort and reward, and the universal order that gives everyone a fair chance. You represent that, and he knows it. He's interested in you for that. You know that you have to think about what your partner wants if a relationship is to work, and you're quite used to going along with majority decisions for the sake of the unity of a group. You can leave your own preferences out of the reckoning when you have to. Capricorn understands that too. He knows that there's work to be done, that certain things are expected of him and that he has to come up to the mark. When his reputation is at stake, he can leave aside his own preferences.

There, then, is the relationship between you. You're both prepared to put something other than yourself first. What can you build from this? You can build a wonderful business relationship, for a start. You can make a good marriage, one that works for the good of the team rather than the gratification of its members. You could create a cool but affectionate friendship, spiced with his dry humor expressed in your words. You may have to work at the sexual side of things, but given time, the results may surprise you both. This may be an offbeat relationship, yes, but it's by no means impossible.

Libra - Aquarius

This is an easy relationship, and it's the one you see most often quoted for Librans in books on astrology. This is a visual relationship as much as anything, something to be seen having: sharp, cool, stylish, wryly humorous and quite possibly platonic. He's from your element, Air, and like you, he's concerned with words and ideas. Like you, he tries not to be on his own, and loves being in a group of people. He's a stage further on in the scheme of things from you, though; so, where you're keen to make friendships and to continue doing so, he's concerned to keep groups going and he's far less keen to take the initiative. He works on a larger scale than you do. He likes the group or large numbers of people, whereas you prefer the intimate world of the one-to-one relationship. He finds that a bit too intense for comfort, and dislikes being pinned down by one person. He will find a way of bringing more people into the situation, until he has the comfort of a group once more. If you want to find an Aquarian, they are either in the pub or with their friends on holiday, in fact anywhere where large numbers of people do anything collectively.

There are other ways in which he is a larger version of you, too. Just as you can make yourself attractive to your partner by highlighting the qualities you have in common, so Aquarius can make himself represent the best of everybody in his circle of friends. In company, he's the brightest of them all, and yet without showing off. Take him away so that he's on his own and he seems much more ordinary, rather gray, even. He seems aloof, and while he's much in his group, he's not of it. You can see him keeping ever so slightly apart from them, watching what is going with a faintly detached air. You see him as a larger-scale version of yourself, but one who doesn't have the same talent for initiating things as you. He sees you as an earlier and slightly unreal version of himself. If ever he doubts what he is, you'll be able to remind him.

As friends, you'll get on like a house on fire. There's something about being in a large group and yet somehow separated from it. It's like being in a film that you're watching. It's not an easy thing to understand, but both of you can do it, and together you'll develop it into a continuing source of amusement to you both. Aquarians like to be just a little different, if they can. You simply like to look beautiful. Between you, you develop one of the most original visual styles in the zodiac. What you manage to express is social confidence blended with a sense of humor, and the result is terrific.

Your friendship is very much a meeting of two similar minds; you pride yourselves on how much you're not involved with each other, and you both feel that it would be rather ponderous to have a physical relationship. Consequently, this pairing is likely to remain platonic. If you do decide to become lovers, your activities will be conducted with style and wit but without passion, because the combination of Saturn and Venus lacks that essential warmth.

As a permanent relationship or as a business partnership, you'd have to overcome the fact that you might not achieve very much in the conventional terms of success. Fire signs are the enterprising people, and Earth signs end up with the rewards, but Air signs have trouble converting theory into reality. You'd also be rather self-satisfied and uninvolved with those around you.

Libra - Pisces

This is a peculiar relationship, and yet one that occurs more often than some books would have you think. It's probably the most difficult partnership in the whole zodiac to define, and that's exactly the problem. The success of this one depends on whether you can put some kind of framework into it and make it work. The most engaging feature of this union of signs is that it's so fluid. It can be anything its participants want it to be. The problem lies entirely in finding a suitable vessel to hold the fluid, so to speak.

How are you going to begin a relationship with someone who absorbs everything you offer them, and takes the shape of everything they contact? You can't try to find a common point with somebody unless he or she offers you something you have in common. Perhaps you like dancing. If the Piscean is with you at the time, he will like dancing too, but not when he's with somebody who doesn't dance, though. The thing about Pisceans, as you will quickly learn, is that they are not active, but re-active. They absorb the emotional energy of other people, and make something out of it to offer in return as a reaction. What you have to be is firm for once, and offer some firm opinions and definite preferences. It's going to be hard, isn't it? The Piscean embodies the very technique you've always used yourself, which is that of taking the other person's point of view as your own. What he forces you to do in this relationship is to take some of your own medicine, and analyze your own motives, which is quite hard.

He sees you as a source of ideas. He needs new ideas to react to, and he needs people too, because they generate the emotions that are where he feels most at home. What he can't do is achieve your balance or your sense of detachment. Emotions aren't detached things and neither are they balanced. In many ways, you're too cool for him and you don't give him anything to grasp. What he needs is some good old-fashioned bigotry, a point of view or a way of doing things to which he can react. What you're offering is pure theory. You want him to respond as well, so you want a dialogue. Pisceans aren't very quick with words, because they are never sure what they want to say.

It will he difficult for you to establish exactly what it is that you want to do with each other. Left to your own devices, you're apt to drift apart, simply because your energies can't focus enough. If you have some definite objective or shared project, then everything becomes a lot easier, because within that framework, you can start exploring each other's imagination. There's almost no limit to either of your imaginations, and the Piscean is very receptive. You'll both enjoy ideas and moods, and have a splendidly theatrical relationship that will fulfill every fantasy you've ever managed to think up.

Note that the real development of the relationship lies in the wealth of imaginative details and style that the pair of you can produce. If you want the sort of relationship that produces durable results in the form of big houses and a Rolls Royce in the garage, then this isn't it. This one is conducted on an emotional level or even on an artistic level, and the only way you will make things work is if you're both in the film business.

Actually, as a business partnership this isn't too bad; provided you managed to be in the right business, and your roles were clear within it, you could both provide a wealth of new and interesting ideas. A marriage would work in much the same fashion. You'd need to be firmly committed to the partnership to supply the guiding structure, but within that, you'd have a very satisfying time. As lovers, you'd be imaginative and expressive, but private. Perhaps the deeper levels of your friendship would be conducted the same way; you'd have to get used to that, and the Piscean would have to get used to the amount of time you need to spend in social circulation. You could both adjust, if you wanted to.

The Approach to Relationships: Scorpio

SYMBOL: SCORPION	♏	ELEMENT: WATER
PLANET: MARS	♂	QUALITY: FIXED

Scorpio is another Fixed sign. You like your environment, and you find that you can manipulate it or work with it so that you can gain profit from it. You feel safe and familiar among the hopes and fears of others; you know that with a little bit of effort here, you can make them grow the way you want. Like the gardener who makes his vegetables grow bigger with care and attention, so you work with the motivation of your companions. What you want out of it is the security of being in control: the idea of not being in control terrifies you.

What you are trying to do is to maintain your emotional responses to things at the level they are at right now. You think, somehow, that if you get over-emotional about things, you will lose precious emotional energy, which must be kept intact. You are right, to some extent; you have a very great deal of emotional energy, but you don't *generate* it, as the Cancerian does. Nor does it benefit you to let it loose and be swept away on it, in the Piscean manner. To do so would be contrary to the nature of your ruling planet, Mars; Mars gives things direction, and letting things loose is just not Martian.

Scorpio - Aries

This is a relationship that should give you plenty to think a bout. You live in different universes, you have different targets and the things you each consider vitally important don't even exist in the other one's way of thinking. You've absolutely nothing in common at all - except for the fact that you're both driven by the same planet, namely Mars. You'll be fascinated to compare yourself with the Arian, and amazed to see how the same familiar energy works in such an unfamiliar fashion through him.

Aries lives for the moment. He never plans forwards and he very seldom looks back to see what he has done in the past. Each moment is full of opportunity in his view, and there are many new possibilities open to him. What matters to him is not what could happen if he did not do something, but what he could achieve if he did do something. His view of things is intensely personal. It never occurs to him that other people's reactions or intentions are in any way relevant to his own existence. He exists for himself first, and makes the assumption (wrongly) that everybody else must be doing the same.

You'll recognize his energy and his drive, but it will seem strange to you that he appears to use it in an unconsidered fashion. It's not really so. He lives in a world where emotions are not as important as they are to you. He only really exists when he's in action, and the action itself gives him purpose and direction. He tries to be active all the time, because that way he stays in contact with himself and knows who he is. It's your emotions and your mind that are the most important thing to you, but it's his body that's the most important thing to him. Where you'd like to think around a problem, using your mind, and testing your emotional responses to it in various ways, he would like to use his body to attack the problem directly, by physically doing something about it.

Physical energy is powerful and immediate, but it isn't subtle. You'll probably find the Arian too trusting, and even rather naive. Be careful in your analysis. Arians are not great thinkers, but they are not unintelligent, even though their mind may not be their greatest asset. Carefully laid arrangements of intrigue and secrecy can be shredded by one bold stroke from the simple and honest Arian. His greatest weapon against you, but one of which he is entirely unaware, is his spontaneity. He can do anything he wants at a moment's notice, and probably will. You can't possibly allow for that in your careful assessments, and it would be useless to try.

In many ways, you admire him. He has a capacity for getting things done and converting thought into action that you don't have. It's simply a matter of your elements and qualities. Aries is Fire, so he can make the material world that we live in move the way he wants. He's also Cardinal, so he can impose his will upon things to provide new beginnings at any time. You have the ability to start again, too, which you get from Mars as Aries does, but you can't make a new situation from nothing: you're not an originator, which he is. You see him as willpower in action, the personification of your own concentrated energy. He sees you as the master of all the things he intends to look into some day when he gets a minute, because he knows that they are somehow important.

It' you want him as a friend, you'll have to be more outgoing, because he isn't prepared to play intricate and intimate games. If it's not easy to see at once, he isn't interested, so you'll have to arrange things so that he sees enough to catch his eye. You'll be infuriated at his transparent simplicity of outlook, and he will be puzzled by how closely you examine everything. The only thing you'll actually feel at home with in each other is the intensity of energy, supplied by Mars. Mars will also help you form a strong and energetic sexual relationship, one that you'll enjoy very much. Aries uses his body rather than his mind in sex, and he won't notice you keeping your true, emotional, self out of the relationship. That's fine as far as you're concerned, and you need have no fear about overwhelming him with your forceful Martian energy - he's every bit as strong.

Marriage? Not really any good at the end of the day, because he doesn't really understand you, and if he did, he wouldn't like it. Similarly, you can't live with his childish trust and simplicity on a long-term basis, either. As a business partnership, though, it's brilliant.

Scorpio - Taurus

Pairings of opposite signs run into difficulties because of the similarities of the signs rather than because of the differences. At the same time, those similarities give the relationship a much greater chance of success than you might think, and this one is no exception. You're both cautious souls, moving in a deliberate manner after due consideration, and you both feel a lot safer when you're surrounded by things that you can call your own. Novelty and instability bother you. Taurus is much more concerned with material things than you are, but that doesn't mean that he's insensitive to the world of the emotions. Far from it. Taurus is very sensitive indeed to what people think of him or say to him, but it's not his way to show it. You'll understand this very well because you also keep your emotions well hidden. He will be wounded quite deeply when criticized, but because he endures the pain in silence, he gets a reputation for being thick-skinned. You'll know, as a representative of an animal whose insides are so sensitive that you need a shell to keep them safe, how he must feel. The great difference between you comes in what you do in response to that injury. You bury yourself in a secret world of plot and counter-plot, thinking about how to ensure firstly that you're never hurt again, and secondly that you're always in a position of control over your enemies. Taurus simply retreats and comforts himself with physical pleasures. Many Taureans use food as a comforter, or the pleasure of having a beautiful house where they feel secure, or the enjoyment of beautiful possessions that are unchanged by unkind words. Taurus puts his trust in material things in a way that you don't.

You'll find him thoughtful and reliable, but you'll also find him slow. Taureans are much more willing to accept things as they are than you are, and they will simply sit out difficult circumstances, waiting for better times to come along, where you'd be working hard to advance yourself from that position to a better one. They find you careful and thoughtful, which they like, but deep and unfathomable, which they don't. Rather than try to fathom the depths of your Fixed Water sign, or drown in the attempt, they decide that as long as you're no threat to their well being, they will be happy to stay with you and enjoy the bits of you they can.

Friendship between you will probably form as a sort of mutual defense arrangement. Something that you both like most about each other is that you don't have to be on the defensive. After that, you'll develop the friendship through the growing sense of reliability and support that you each find in the other. There is a very strong sexual attraction between you, but it's a little on the slow side, because it comes from so deep down inside. There will be no brilliant flashes of sexual electricity, either. The union is likely to be fruitful, and that's what you get when you mix Water and Earth.

As a marriage, this one would work well, because your energies will continue to grow towards each other over time. Some relationships are definitely short term, but this one isn't. Once Scorpio has learned that he can trust Taurus, he need not be suspicious and can turn his mind towards making a successful life for the two of you. Taurus will provide stability, support, and warm affection for the two of you. As a business partnership, this one is less good. It lacks the inventiveness and confidence necessary to make profitable progress.

Scorpio - Gemini

On the surface, there isn't a lot of contact between these two signs. Gemini is an Air sign, which you will see as being insubstantial. He fails to take things seriously enough. He seems to have no emotions that you can gather in and work with. He's also Mutable, which means that he readily accepts change for its own sake. In fact, you can't get hold of him at all, and that exasperates you. You don't have to get hold of him, though. He will come to you of his own accord, because he's interested in the way you work.

Like the birds that follow the ploughman, he wants to see what turns up. Scorpio and Gemini share a common characteristic, which is curiosity. The idea of the ploughman is worth continuing with for a few moments longer. The ploughman isn't searching for worms for the birds, because he has another purpose in mind, and his work is a necessary preamble to that. In a similar manner, the Scorpio does his investigation and his analysis as necessary groundwork for his larger ambitions, but the Gemini is interested in what he turns up anyway. The larger ambitions are not of the slightest concern to him.

Gemini is the great assimilator of trivia. His energy is mental, and it's so concentrated in the rational side of his mind that he leaves almost no emotional shadows at all, which makes him almost invisible to you. Remember that you only see people through their emotional responses, but Gemini responds intellectually and verbally to his circumstances, not emotionally. How you'd like to have his mind! What a waste, it seems, to have so fine an instrument at your command and use it to collect trivia and to make witty remarks!

You're clever and devious, but Gemini makes you feel ponderous and dull. He's so much faster than you are, and quick to see the different sides of things, so you wish you could match him. He even has the capability to throw away his best ideas as though they didn't matter. You keep all of yours, because they were so costly to produce. It's because he never takes anything seriously, and the novelty of an idea is worth more to him than its content, and novelty cannot be kept.

He sees you as somebody with the strength to finish the job. One of his own great failings, and he knows it, is his inability to stay doing one thing for a long time. Somehow, he can't raise the enthusiasm. You, however, are thorough, purposeful and successful. He can see that, and he likes it. He will never understand your need for emotional restraint, but then he doesn't deal in emotions, except as an abstract concept, and he will never understand why you take things so seriously. What he does know is that his own energies are mental and that he lacks the forceful application that brings ultimate results. Your energies are primarily mental, too, and you have exactly the forceful application he needs.

A business partnership between you would be very productive, because you can each contribute what the other partner lacks. With your force added to his incisiveness, you can really get somewhere. Marriage would be similar, though it would have to allow for his need for movement, and for you to realize that any attempt to dominate and dictate his behavior would end up by both of you adopting a policy of deception and intrigue.

As lovers, you're ill matched, because his needs are for gentle teasing and mental rapport, whereas yours are deeper, more physical and more emotional. It's like matching a rapier against a cannon. Both are weapons, but so different that no engagement is possible. It's far better to stay as friends, and let your shared passion for finding things out amuse you both.

Scorpio - Cancer

This is the first of the partnerships within your own element of Water. There are a great many similarities between you, just as there are between the two animals that represent your signs. You both have hard shells that symbolize how your true selves are not on show to the world at large. Both of you have pincers with which to defend yourselves against those who get too close without being invited. What must strike you very forcibly about a Cancerian is how very private they are. They are polite enough, but it really isn't possible to see what they are thinking from the outside. You'll understand this without any trouble, but you might like to remember that this is how others see you, to a great extent. An interesting thought, isn't it?

You both live in a personal and internal universe where emotions and feelings are the things that matter most. In the early stages of the relationship, you'll edge round each other cautiously, trying to get some idea of how the other one works without exposing yourself to possible attack. Both of you like to be quite sure of how the other person behaves before making any kind of firm commitment.

You see the Cancerian as someone with a special talent that you would dearly like to have. They can generate emotion. They are capable of giving themselves to and caring for another person without first asking themselves what they are going to get out of it, and what it will cost them in time and effort. You can't do that. On the one hand, you can dismiss it as sentimental weakness, but you know that you're lying to yourself, because this is real care of which we're talking. The stuff that's like gold dust to you, and the Cancerian ability to create it from inside is something you find inexpressibly moving. There are dark mysteries within you somewhere, so deep that you can only just glimpse them yourself, and they have to do with the meaning of your existence. Somehow, Cancer seems to have mastered them in a way that you have not. They are clearer, softer people who can manage to exist without the strong harness of self-control that you've had to wear for as long as you can remember. You feel clever and powerful most of the time, but in their presence, you feel almost ashamed of yourself.

They see you as unbelievably powerful and successful individuals whose willpower borders on the manic in comparison to their own. They know that they are not always as effective as they would like to be, and their well-known sentimental streak often prevents them from being as ruthless as is sometimes necessary. It's one thing to make a lot of emotional energy, they say, but another thing altogether to direct it and make it work for you. You can do this and they can see that. They are in awe of your ability to direct your energies towards a specific goal with enough force to make it bend to your will. In terms of the Water element that you both represent, you're a high-pressure hose, while they merely rain softly over things. They would gladly trade some of their sensitivity for some of your intensity.

This is an easy friendship to form, as you both find things in the other to admire, along with similar likes and dislikes. You respect each other's privacy instinctively and avoid the vicious circle of suspicion and withdrawal that would otherwise come into being. If the friendship develops into a liaison, then you should find it deeply satisfying, with your partner meeting your needs and understanding you deeply, due to being of the same element as yourself. It will be passionate, but it needn't necessarily be energetic.

As a business partnership, this one lacks the pioneering spirit, so it might not be as successful as you would think. As a marriage, it would be a much better proposition, although you'll have to make sure that you develop an adequate means expression for your differences, because jealousy, suspicion and resentment are all too easy to generate from an overabundance of the Water element.

Scorpio - Leo

This one will either work or it won't, and you'll soon know which it is. This elemental mixture is Fire and Water, and both of you are Fixed signs, so it may be impossible to overcome the problems between you. Fire and Water make steam, and it remains to be seen if the steam that you generate between you can be put to any useful purpose. The essence of this is that one of you wants to be in command and the other wants to be in control. You get a commander's hat if you're in command, but unless the Leo gets to wear it, he won't play.

In many ways, a Leo leaves you breathless with disbelief, but you can't help but admire him, because he seems to be able to achieve without apparent effort all the things for which you work so hard. He's a natural winner, everybody looks to him as the leader of any group and it's generally regarded as enjoyable to be in his company. He radiates warmth and energy without wanting anything in return. He's genuinely generous, and it's probably this, more than anything else, that unnerves you. Water signs never understand that warmth radiates outwards naturally, and that Fire signs have it to spare. Indeed, if they didn't do something with it, they would probably be ill. Aries and Sagittarius put that energy into movement, but Leo prefers to sit still and radiate.

He represents what you're aiming for. What you really want is to be as popular, as well liked and to have the same regal status as the Leo. What you find so amazing is that he can be so open, so self-centered and so lazy and still make a success of his life. Have you not spent valuable years of your time making sure that you do everything in the most effective way? How can he be so careless, so ignorant of anything except himself and still be where he is? Because he gives energy out and you take it in, that's why. The world loves a giver, especially when it's all for free. At the end of the day, you can find plenty about him to despise, but you love him just the same and you'd love to be in his shoes.

He sees you as somebody with the same sort of inexhaustible power as himself. He also sees that yours is restricted and controlled by your own effort of will. He's attracted to somebody who is as powerful as he is, and recognizes you as a sort of earlier version of himself, someone who lacks the confidence to let loose the power inside himself. He's intrigued, interested and a little irritated by the way that you try to organize him, restrict him and control him. What he doesn't want is for you to be able to contain his light, to soak him up as it were, and he will turn his light up even brighter if he thinks this is happening, while you run for cover. He needs to be the one in command, the one that people look to and he will fight you for that role if he thinks that you're going to take it from him. What he won't do is fight you for it if he can see that it was yours in the first place. In this case, he will simply go elsewhere. If you want him, you'll have to give him first place.

Really, you need him more than he needs you and he probably knows it. Any friendship between you will develop into a power struggle in a very short time indeed, and this will still be the case if you have a sexual relationship. In fact, it will be even more so, because the two of you represent the fundamental forces of life and death in the zodiac, so your power games are played on a cosmic level as well as an individual one.

If there's some interest outside the pair of you that you're keen on, then the combination of your energies will be very strong indeed. For this reason, you'd do well in business together. Privately, however, you'd be fighting for power in the home, which would make for a marriage lived at a fairly high volume, with flying crockery from time to time. It really depends upon how much you like a good fight. You hurt yourself each time you hurt him, you know, and you must ask yourself if this is what the sting in your tail is for.

Scorpio - Virgo

Most of the relationships between signs two signs are quite amicable, but this one is really special. There aren't many people in the zodiac whose company you really enjoy, but Virgo is one. The funny thing about it is that it's the very unemotional qualities of the sign that you like best. The thing that you really appreciate about the Virgoans is their no-nonsense attitude to life.

Virgos like getting things right. They approach things in a practical way. They analyze their own approach, and decide on the best way to tackle the problem. When they get down to work, they work in a structured, methodical way and they get things right. They waste nothing, and when it's all over, the result is nice and clean. You like this sort of thing. It's almost good enough to sit and watch, but even better is the knowledge that you can rely on them to do things properly in your absence. Anybody who does things to your standards is the sort of person you'd like as your friend, and it's this shared attitude of perfectionism that attracts you to each other. It's true that you're like this for slightly different reasons, but the effect is the same, and that's what you recognize in each other.

It will surprise you, when you get to know a Virgo, that they are very willing to do things for you. It will also surprise you to find that they do things for the sheer pleasure of doing them and getting them right, much like a child at school who likes getting ten out of ten, even when they don't care much for the subject itself. This makes Virgos undemanding friends and good ones from your point of view, because they don't examine the emotional motives that underlie all your actions. Indeed, it seldom occurs to them that such motives even exist, which suits you admirably.

They see you as exciting, larger versions of themselves, dealing with big projects with the same correct and effective procedures that they use on a smaller scale. They like your attitude: or to be more accurate, they like your apparent attitude. Your true motives are beyond them, because they live in a world of material and practical details, where the emotional content of things is almost non-existent and where human hopes and fears are dismissed as unreliable and. uninteresting.

A friendship between you is most likely to start as a working partnership, and it works brilliantly on that level. They are likely to be the most enthusiastic and reliable helpmates you will ever find, knowing instinctively how you'd like to go about things, and gaining as much satisfaction as you do when things go according to plan. It's probably a mistake to attempt a sexual relationship with a Virgo. They are completely unfamiliar with your Martian energy, in both its quality and its intensity, and you'll overwhelm them. At the same time, you'll be irritated by their inability to respond to or even understand the strength of your emotional needs.

As a business partnership, things will go well. It's absolutely imperative that you're in the leading position, so that they are working for you rather than with you, but you're likely to arrange it that way anyway, so there should be no problems. A Virgoan isn't really happy leading the way, so he will voice no protest if you take the driving seat.

Marriage is probably not a good idea, despite the fact that you work so well together. The Virgo will never come to terms with the intensity of your emotion, and you'll wear them down after a while. They do worry so when they are unsure of themselves, and you will in fact make them ill after a little while. Keep them as friends and helpmates and leave it at that.

Scorpio - Libra

This pairing gets the maximum difficulty rating, if such a thing exists for a relationship. You're different in element, quality, and just about anything else that there is. In addition, they are the sign behind you in the zodiac, and so embody all the qualities that you'd rather not think about, or feel that you've already dealt with and let go. Despite all that, though, the relationship seems determined to form itself, whether you want it or not. It just happens that way, because there's an attraction between you.

The attraction is the easiest thing to explain. Libra's ruling planet is Venus, and your traditional ruling planet is Mars. These two seem to have a magnetic effect on each other. Librans are always on the lookout for a partnership to form, and they have a very romantic view of life. They can be attracted to anybody, and if that person gives them the right sort of response, they will form a partnership. You, of course, respond to them as you respond to everybody, which is with a concentrated blast of emotional power. They read that as everybody else does, as sexual energy, and take it as a favorable response. In this way, the Libran falls victim to his own capacity for attraction. He finds himself hopelessly attracted you. You may find this amusing, but if you're busy, you might not.

You see Librans as rather pathetic figures, but at the same time rather discomfiting. They are much less sure of their purpose than you are, and you see this indecisiveness as an annoying weakness. Not only do they have no idea what they are aiming for from one week to the next, but they are also likely to have a completely different opinion about things from one week to the next. If you like things to stay as they are, that's annoying. They have a knack for saying the right thing, for putting people at their ease. They are friendly to everybody, and everybody has them as a friend. You see this as a useful talent, but when you look a little closer, you're surprised at how shallow the content of their conversation really is. Why waste a talent for dealing with people so well, you think to yourself, by keeping it to so trivial a level? You can't understand that the Libran is being nice for its own sake and that there's no ulterior motive.

You're actually made uneasy by their apparent happiness, the more so because you can't understand where it comes from. Can they really have no purpose other than to make friends with everyone? Where does their energy come from? How can they afford to be so open and welcoming to everybody the whole time? The answer is actually very obvious, but you're unlikely to see it, and when you know what it is, you'll be even more upset. It's simply this: they are happy to share things.

Sharing is the last thing you'd think of. It's completely alien to the way that you work. What's worse, you know that it makes a sort of sense, but you'd rather not be reminded of that. Now you see why the relationship won't work unless you're prepared to make a special effort. How can you be happy with a person whose definition of happiness is the very thing you'd most like to avoid? Libra does not have this trouble. He's simply besotted with you, and you can do with him as you wish. He's helpless in your hands.

A friendship between you will last only for a few minutes before Venus and Mars, acting through you, make you decide to become lovers. In this area, the energies are most unevenly matched. Libra will be expecting something loving and romantic, but your powerful passions and concentrated power will completely stagger him. From your point of view, his inability to match you with similar strength to your own will leave you unsatisfied.

As a marriage or as business partners, this pairing would probably take more than it was worth to make it work properly. If you were prepared to change yourself and to become more flexible and less obsessive, and if the Libran were particularly strong willed and creative, then you might make a marriage with something to it.

Scorpio - Scorpio

At least you know what you're getting here. Have a look in a mirror. Make a fist. Do you notice how the mirror image makes a fist in his other hand to oppose you exactly? That's what this relationship is going to be like. Some signs go rather better with themselves than others, due to the accommodating nature of the signs themselves, but Scorpios don't qualify on that count.

The trouble, of course, is that you both want to be in control and neither of you is prepared to give way. You're frightened until you find out more about him; he's busy finding out all kinds of things about you. You'll attempt to find his weaknesses, and when you've done that, you'll feel a lot surer of yourself. He may also have found yours, and you'll be aware of it. He may have deceived you as to his weaknesses. There are all sorts of possibilities. The pair of you may actually enjoy this game of secrets a lot more than you're prepared to, and if so, all well and good, especially if it takes place within a sexual framework. If it becomes at all serious, really serious, as opposed to ordinarily serious (Scorpios have a wide range of seriousness) then you'll be in danger of destroying each other forever. The venom in the scorpion's sting is not for pretend battles.

You're both very possessive. This possessiveness extends beyond the individual to cover a vast territory of people and experience, all of whom you regard as your exclusive property. You think that you own them in a material sense, but you're sure that you control them, and that your partner's actions and thoughts are always referred back to you. This wide sphere of influence is your own special world, and if it overlaps with that of another Scorpio, then one of you must be mistaken. If you control him, then he might be able to control you. The idea of being mistaken is one that you do walking backwards, in order to avoid turning your back on your adversary, and scorpions, like crabs, prefer to walk sideways or forwards.

The way out of this constant feuding is quite simple. Go back and look in the mirror again. Now turn to face right. Take a step. You're both walking in the same direction. You'll need a common goal large enough and far enough into the future to occupy the pair of you. If possible, it will need to have different facets, so that one of you would like to control one side of it and the other another side. You can both use your considerable organizational talents to attack this target, and you can help each other up through the structure of the thing so that eventually you both stand at the top. It's the only way. You both need a purpose and you both like being busy, and the feeling that you're getting somewhere. You must simply ensure that you help each other, and that you don't trespass on each other's chosen territory as you do it.

As your working partnership flourishes, your day-to-day friendship will look after itself, though it may come to be inward looking, and discourage outsiders from joining in. As lovers, you'll have to be very sure of your own territory. With confidence and a feeling of mutual trust will come the ability to let go some of that awesome Martian force at full strength at each other, and you'll enjoy that very much. However, if anything undermines that confidence and trust, then the imbalance in the relationship will have disastrous consequences. You must be particularly wary of giving any cause for jealousy. It's quite simple, really. If you're going to work with high voltage, observe the safety regulations. As a marriage? Yes: very powerful, very private, very successful, if you can maintain each other's total trust and confidence.

Scorpio - Sagittarius

Sagittarians are wonderful people. They will remind you of this fact, using those very words, whenever they feel that you need a reminder. Their arrogance makes you cringe at times, but they seem to get away with it, and you find them very attractive. They don't find you anything like so enticing though, and a lasting relationship between you is a hard thing to achieve.

You spend a lot of your time finding out about things. Background information, mainly, such as how things are, how they got that way, who does what, that sort of thing. You do this so that you'll have an effective plan of action and a sure chance of winning. Sagittarians are better than that. They know everything already; it comes built-in, somehow. They also know how people are going to move, because they are perceptive that way. In addition, they are very successful because they have energy, talent and luck. It makes you sick.

You see them as having all the knowledge that you'd love to have, but they appear to give it out to everybody free of charge. If it were yours, you'd put it to good purpose, capitalizing on the advantage it gave you. This is Fixed sign thinking. Sagittarius is Mutable. He spends his time doing things for other people and giving his talent away. He's Fire, whereas you're Water, so if he doesn't parade his talent and show off a little, he will become ill. Energy is indeed free, to him anyway, and he does not have to collect it the way you do. He would be more than happy to offload some of it in your direction, and this suits you fine for a short while, but he will begin to wonder what you do with it all.

Energy and friendliness, according to him, are for spreading around and giving out, and it isn't fair for somebody to attempt to control it all. He has an almost childish sense of honesty and fair play, and he will tell you off if you attempt to take more than he thinks is your fair share. He will also resent your attempts to contain his movements. He needs to be on the move all the time and to experience new things.

He sees you as an inverted version of himself. He appreciates your inquiring mind and admires your effective way of working. He recognizes something similar to his own enthusiasm in your intense dedication to your own interests. What he doesn't like though, is the way that your world is inward facing. He's sure that you're missing the point somehow, and that knowledge and talents are to be shared. He doesn't care for money in the same way that you do, either. As far as he's concerned, it's only useful when spent, whereas you can appreciate the power it has for its own sake. Power of any kind doesn't interest him, it's knowledge that does. You can understand that, you think, but you can't really. You understand the power of knowledge, but he has the joy of knowledge, and it's not the same.

Since he can offer you more than you can offer him, the friendship will be one-sided. He's quite willing to be friends with you, but only for as long as it interests him. If you're interesting, different and communicative, then you'll gain his attention, but not otherwise. You'll have to work very hard indeed. How you do captivate somebody who you're desperate to know but who doesn't want what you have? Once you get talking, you'll be surprised how easy it can be. Sagittarians talk about almost anything. They will talk about grand concepts and universal deals rather than personal and individual matters, and you'll find that you know more about this sort of thing than you thought you did. You'll certainly make bright company for each other, or at least until the Sagittarian fancies a change!

As a lover, you'll find him strong and imaginative, but playful in a way that upsets you. He will refuse to take the affair as seriously as you do, and you may get the feeling that he's thinking about something else some of the time. This leads to jealousy, and of course, this is detrimental to the situation.

As marriage partners, you'd have to make some major adjustments. You'd have to live with his changeability, and he would have to realize how little you like moving unless you really have to. He would accuse you of not being honest with him, and you would accuse him of not taking the situation seriously enough. It could all work out well, but the odds are very much against it, as they would also be against a successful business partnership.

Scorpio - Capricorn

This is the one you've been waiting for. Capricorns and Scorpios get on well. This is quite possibly the easiest and best suited combination of signs in the whole zodiac, and the two of you just can't help but get on with each other. What's more, you can actually do something positive for each other, which pleases you both a great deal.

Capricorn is the Cardinal Earth sign. What a Capricorn likes to see is a structured approach to life. To him, everything has a framework into which it can fit, and everything has a set of rules. He likes to play by the rules and he likes to succeed. What he likes best of all is the recognition he gets for his position, and the status it brings him, and this is similar to your own outlook.

The difference between you is that Capricorn is very unemotional. Quite cold, in fact. He's not interested in the emotional side of things, and he doesn't trust people who are. To him, such people are unreliable, weak and ineffective. He likes you, though. He sees your intense Martian energy and the way you pursue your objectives and he's mesmerized. Your emotional objectives are very successfully hidden from him.

Because he's an Earth sign, Capricorn values material possessions. He uses these possessions and his status in his career as the yardsticks for his existence. The harder he works, the more money he has, and the higher he rises. As he goes up the ladder of success, he acquires larger cars and larger houses. Each of these things represents the amount of work necessary to obtain them, in his eyes. What he's doing, in fact, is converting energy into material form, and everybody accords him respect according to the size and quantity of his status symbols. This is a very interesting process to you. You want to be a success too, and you want people to recognize you as somebody with obvious power. They way to do this is with material tokens, similar to the ones a Capricorn uses, but you're unable to do this on your own, because you're a Water sign. Capricorn, however, can help. He sees you as a tremendous force of concentrated energy.

He's a hard worker himself, but he has to do it with patient toil over many years, because his ruling planet, Saturn, has none of the immediate energy and force that your planet, Mars, has. When he gets very tired, he knows that he has to press on, and he also knows where he wants to be at the end of it all, but it takes a lot out of him and it takes a long time. When he sees your talent for concentrated activity and organized control, he sighs with envy. It's exactly the sort of thing he would wish for if he had three wishes (except that he's too down-to-earth to believe in fairies).

What makes you such firm friends so quickly is mutual approval. You're both likely to find the other visually attractive, since you both dress in a way that suggests a businesslike approach. As you get to know each other, you encourage each other to talk about plans and projects, and voice your approval of the other's approach. With the Capricorn's perception of structures and capacity for long-term effort linked to your sense of purpose and ability to discern motives, you'll make a formidable business partnership which will bring you greater rewards than either of you could achieve on your own.

As an intimate relationship, this combination suffers a little from being too regimented and goal-oriented. As a marriage, it would be very successful in terms of your careers and material success, but it lacks warmth and the ability to comfort itself in times of trouble. Sexually, you find the Capricorn a bit of a puzzle. Capricorns are strong and potent like the goats of their sign, but they don't have passion, and depth of feeling just isn't in them.

Scorpio - Aquarius

There's a lot that you two have in common, or to be more accurate, you indulge in similar behavior for different reasons, and you can recognize it in each other. The essential idea is one of remoteness, of keeping your own business to yourself. Aquarians are funny creatures. You'll not be able to notice anything unusual about them at first, because they don't do anything that sticks in your memory. Your particular memory, remember, works with the emotional responses and motivations of those around you, and an Aquarian is an Air sign, so he's emotionally rather cool. He's also ruled by Saturn, the coldest planet astrologically, so you can't expect him to generate a lot of emotional heat for you to pick up.

Aquarians are sociable. So sociable, in fact, that you'll seldom find one on his own. In a group of people, he really comes to life, somehow taking on all the characteristics of the group as a whole. He loves meeting many new people and being in their company. He's not too keen on personal and intimate relationships, because in them, the emotional temperature tends to be high. He'd rather be cool, so larger groups are where he's at.

The interesting thing about all this socializing is that although he's part of the group, he keeps himself aloof within it, as though he was watching a play unfold around him. He's interested and amused, but not really committed to the hopes and fears of any of the individuals in his group. He's kind and friendly, and he likes his surroundings to be full of friendly people, but his best friend is still himself. The things he feels most strongly for are ideas that affect a whole group of people, such as a political opinion or a protest movement. He's dedicated to being friends with everyone, and that means that everyone has to be on the same level as he is. He's opposed to all kinds of hierarchy and any system in which one person more power than another. Nobody has power over him, because to his mind, he's unique, special, independent and his own man.

You can recognize in him the idea of keeping your own thoughts to yourself while appearing to be an active member of a group, because it's the sort of thing that you do all the time. You're not so sure about his egalitarian ideals, though. To you, power is one of your main aims. He is, of course, the outgoing part of the cycle of which you're the incoming; what he is doing is putting his energies out into a large group of people, and you collect it back in. Both of you need large numbers of people to function productively, and you both keep yourselves effectively one step ahead.

In you, he sees the principle of emotional control taken to its ultimate form. He doesn't like your love of power, but he likes your ability to analyze and gauge any situation, because it's a similar process to the one he uses. What he would like to have is your passionate belief in yourself and your own purpose. Saturn doesn't give him as much heat as other people do, and he finds that attractive.

As friends, you may be too remote to risk real communication. The friendship will be firm but cool. You realize how necessary the other is to your own activities and you appreciate your similarities, but you don't feel the necessity to talk about it all the time. It's an instinctive thing.

As business partners, you're too far apart in your basic principles to make much progress, but as marriage partners you could suit him better than he would have you believe, because you wouldn't get in each other's way. However, the Aquarian would appreciate some of your Martian heat. Sexually you'll find him cool, but strong and inventive. From time to time, he will really surprise you.

Scorpio - Pisces

Some relationships are good for your career and others good for your health, but this one is good for your soul. Pisces is the last of the Water signs, and it's the most fluid of them all. Completely unstructured and infinitely flexible, he represents the ultimate challenge to your ideas about yourself.

Pisces lives entirely in his imagination. Like the two fishes of his symbol, he lives in the emotional world of the Water element, and often seems to swim in two directions at once. Self-control isn't important to him, as it is to you. Instead, he lets his emotions flow wherever he wants and forms his reality out of them. He's completely caught up in whatever he's feeling at the time, and his version of the truth is formed from the feelings he's experiencing at any given moment. The randomness of this horrifies you. You want to tell him to get hold of some sort of plan, some set of rules, so that he can at least be consistent in himself, and then to impose some sort of order on his surroundings. His whole existence seems so disturbingly loose.

For a Piscean, the essence of life is to feel the force of emotion and to be carried along by the experience. Even if the emotion is a bad one, there's no need to worry, another one will be along in a minute. There is, of course, the awful thought that the world might run out of emotional energy, but luckily, there are people like you around to store it up and keep the flow going with your intensity.

If you allowed your emotions to go free, you'd soon find that the tremendous pressure subsides and you start to feel better, as they would now be nothing more than a gentle flow for you to swim around in. The Piscean is the next stage in your emotional development, which occurs after you've sacrificed control and have gained the confidence never to doubt your own identity; then, you can allow yourself to let go a little and see where it gets you. Your problem is that you don't actually have that confidence.

As you can see, on a day-to-day level, the Piscean is so different from you that you can have hardly anything in common. It's only on a life-long level that you can see how they are always one step ahead of you. Still, life is lived on a day-to-day level, and that's where relationships are formed.

As a friendship, these two signs get on very well and possibly rather better than you would like. Let me explain. Pisces will take the form of anything that his companion wants him to be, so if you're going to be forceful and dominant, they will respond in a similar manner, which you'll find most encouraging. What you won't find encouraging is that they will instinctively know what you really mean, because they are almost psychically sensitive. It's no use at all being devious with them, because they can perceive your real meaning at once. It's no use trying to control them, either. Water runs through your fingers, you know.

If you want to extend this shadow boxing into your love life, you'll find that they are a lot more subtle and sensitive than you had at first supposed. They are capable of matching your emotional strength when it suits them, but you can't match their changes of temperament. You'd find them difficult business partners, unless you defined the rules very closely indeed. Their mutability means that they will frequently modify their way of working as it suits them from time to time, and that would infuriate you. Marriage would be rather better, because the private side of your life needs to be developed as well as the public side, and they can show you how to do that in a way that's beneficial in the end.

The Approach to Relationships: Sagittarius

SYMBOL:	CENTAUR	✗	ELEMENT:	FIRE
PLANET:	JUPITER	♃	QUALITY:	MUTABLE

Sagittarius is the last of the Fire signs, the final version of that creative force which is so athletically displayed in the Arian, and so warm and cheerful in the Leo. A Sagittarian is a little of both of these, and more besides. Aries uses his energy for direct physical action; he decides on a course of action and goes to it at once. Unless he is actually doing something, he is unhappy. Sagittarius works in a similar way, but his preferred work area is that of ideas in social context. He likes to know what everyone else knows. He likes to hear everybody else's opinion. He can see at once what they really mean, even if that's not what they actually say, and he will tell them so - at once, face to face.

Direct, open, perceptive, inquisitive; this is Fire energy at work in the world of ideas and beliefs. What it is looking for is truth; it will burn away anything that has been built up to obscure or disguise the truth, until the essence of the argument stands there, naked, for all to see. Notice how similar Aries and Sagittarius are; one is a physical energy, the other is an intellectual energy, but they share the qualities of Fire - they are effective, direct and pure.

Sagittarius - Aries

This is a very good relationship. They think you're bright and interesting, and you think they are dashing and sexy. Both true, of course: you're both Fire signs, so you see each other in your true colors.

Arians are very active people and they don't function properly unless they are actually doing something. An idea isn't enough for them; it's only the beginning. They are impatient to see what happens to the idea when it's put into action, so they do exactly that. Only in the performance of the action can they understand the idea. You see them as fantastically energetic, and you're envious of their ability to turn ideas into actions. Because you're a Mutable sign, you're very good at breaking things down to see what can be extracted from them, but you're much less effective in getting things going, especially when you have to start from scratch. You need something to work with. Aries doesn't, because all he needs is a direction to go in, and he's away. Where you will turn an idea around in your head for some time, comparing it to other, similar thoughts you might have had, Aries takes the first idea that he comes across and races off to put it into action. What's more, he gets it right first time. Whatever an Aries does is active and effective: in other words, it works. A lot of this is to do with his being a Cardinal sign, but whatever it is, you wish that you could do it.

He has his faults, of course. For instance, he won't think before he acts. It may well be that this is because he can't think unless he acts, but it does have a few drawbacks. He also has no sense of time. Everything for him has to happen right now, this minute, just as it does for a young child.

He's very self-sustaining, and he's self-centered, too. This means that he's very happy on his own; he doesn't need a partner for support or protection, and he doesn't really think of sharing his time with somebody else. If somebody else wants to be there while he's being active, then that's fine - as long as they don't get in the way, and don't expect him to stop what he's doing to attend to them. This sounds rather selfish, but it's actually self-centered. No matter what the motivation, it appeals very strongly to you, because you know how he feels. It has all the action, freedom and movement you could wish for, and none of the commitment you're so keen to avoid. Is it the perfect partnership? No, not quite: it has all the rugby team playfulness that you could wish for, and you could hardly ask for a better companion for an adventure, but the Arian can't offer the intellectual stimulation that you need. He knows it, too: that's what he comes to you for.

He sees you as a great source of inspiration. You can see and understand all the things that he can't quite grasp, and you can tell what they are like. As a young child will bring a book to his grandfather and ask him what's in it, so the Arian wants the Sagittarian to show him the inner meanings of things, to tell him how things work and to fire his imagination. He wants to act on every idea you show him, and everything you say gives him something new do. Between you, you can create real achievements out of the slightest whim, and the idea of that attracts you enormously. However, you'd also like him to be able to converse and argue with you at your own level, and he just can't do that, no matter how much he would like to.

As friends, you're ideally suited. You'll keep each other amused and cheerful, and you'll be able to laugh together at a world that seems altogether too set in its ways to go off and try new things, as you both like to do. As lovers, you're equally well suited. Aries is more physical than you are, and stronger too. Neither of you use sex as a symbol of personal commitment, so you're unlikely to misconstrue each other's intentions. They are simple souls though, and they won't understand your liking for changing partners every so often.

As business partners you'll be unbeatable, provided that you have somebody else on hand to take care of the routine work, and to tie up all the details while the pair of you launch yourselves off into yet another new venture. As a marriage, this pairing will work very well, provided that you realize that you'll eventually have to do things their way. You'd rather do things in an Arian way than in the way of some of the other signs.

Sagittarius - Taurus

This relationship is very difficult, and yet in real life it seems to struggle along somehow. It may be that the best thing about this relationship is that your ruling planets - Jupiter and Venus respectively - are essentially kind hearted and well meaning in their nature. If they were not, you'd end up throwing plates at each other.

Taureans are essentially static people. The very idea of movement bothers them. They are equally disconcerted by the idea of novelty, since that threatens them with the dissolution of their existing way of life. Difficult for you to imagine, isn't it? You couldn't exists without movement and novelty, and the idea of forming a relationship with somebody so opposed to your own way of life seems difficult to comprehend. What they are trying to achieve is a stable way of life, where everything is secure and where every physical need is met. Taureans are very much lovers of home comforts, so they measure themselves by the size and comfort of their homes and by the amount they have in their larders, just as you measure yourself by how clever you are, and how much you know. They are physical where you're intellectual, and they want comfort where you want excitement.

They are very slow to anger, and will endure a great deal of strain and stress before they eventually take steps to rectify the situation. Their stability and reliability can have a sort of appeal to you; you wouldn't like to be that way yourself, but somebody who represents constant values in a changing world isn't hard to appreciate. At the end of it all, you realize that what they have is what you're trying to achieve. You want things to take shape as a result of your ideas, for your Fire sign energy to become established in the world as Earth sign energy, such as Taurus has. You know that when you shoot one of your Sagittarian arrows into the air, it will eventually fall to earth, but Taurus is the end product. If you were to get there in the end, you would no longer be Sagittarian, and that's why you fight shy of it. You appreciate their stability, and you admire the care that they lavish on their home and possessions, because you know that you just couldn't give that much time to that kind of activity.

The Taurean sees you as somebody who changes their opinions from one moment to the next, and who seems determined to undermine all that they hold dear. Their eventual reaction to you is to ignore you. They see you as unconcerned with the world that they inhabit and uninterested in possessions, so you don't threaten theirs. Taureans can safely ignore ideas, because what matters to them is material wealth. This infuriates you. You don't mind them not accepting your ideas, but to be ignored for having ideas of importance in the first place really drives you wild.

Friendship depends to some extent on having similar viewpoints. Since you have to struggle even to recognize the existence of each other's way of thinking, you're unlikely to be close friends. Should you become lovers, you'll find that the Taurean is capable of a tremendous passion. You'll find them hard to deal with, because the emotional content is at least as much as the physical one. You'd prefer things to be a little lighter in tone.

If you marry, it's obviously because you want a secure home base, which the Taurean will gladly provide for you. Don't complain if they are unwilling to change as quickly as you'd like them to, or if they place constraints on your personal freedom.

As business partners, you do much better than you might think, as you would do the selling and let them do the buying.

Sagittarius - Gemini

Gemini is the sign opposite to you in the zodiac, and that means that they have all of your talents, but displayed in the opposite way, which you find irritating. They are so like you, but so different. They seem to be interested in the same things and for the same reasons, but they use them in very different ways, and you find yourself wondering why they won't do things the right (i.e. your) way, when it would be so easy for them to do so. They wonder about you in the same way, of course. Had you thought of that?

A Gemini is the only person in the zodiac who could find you dull. While you're reeling from the shock and the insult to your intelligence, think about how much smaller and faster Mercury is than Jupiter. They are quicker on the uptake than you are, and cleverer in their manipulation of words and ideas. They also move more quickly physically, and their hands can do quick little tricks that yours couldn't begin to. The idea of little tricks is one of the things that bother you about Geminis. There's always the suspicion that they are somehow less than honest. You, of course, are absolutely straight, so the slightest deviation from that will show in comparison. You're right to think that Geminis aren't always honest. They're not consciously dishonest, either, but the idea of honesty just doesn't apply to them, because their energies are directed towards their own amusement and not towards public duty. If it amuses them to twist an argument a little for a better effect, then they will do it. Similarly, if there's some fun to be had from a little sleight-of-hand, then they will do that, too.

Geminis seem to spend their time accumulating surface knowledge; it annoys you to see them wasting their talent this way, when they could be investigating the higher intellectual pursuits. It does not occur to you that they like doing things their way, that they don't really have your capacity for pure knowledge, and that they can't see why you spend your time with worthy causes when you could make an absolute fortune using your perception commercially. Essentially, they use their powerful mentality to amuse themselves while you feel obliged to use yours for the benefit of everyone. Your attitude seems pompous to them and theirs seems selfish to you.

It must have struck you by now that there's more to forming a relationship than matching mentalities. There is, but in this case, it's the area that you keep returning to again and again, because it's the single thing that, more than anything else, you pick up on in each other. Everything else gets pushed aside.

As friends, you'll get along wonderfully. You'll be eager to tell each other new things that you've noticed, and your love of news and gossip generally will keep you chatting away forever. Gemini will have a little fun at your expense from time to time when he thinks that you're being dull, but you'll forgive him. In your opinion, being dull is a punishable offence anyway, so you're grateful for his reminders.

As your lover, Gemini will surprise you. He's even lighter in his affections than you are. Not only does he not want to be involved, he doesn't really want things to be excessively physical anyway. He doesn't have half an animal for his sign in the way that you do. Sometimes you'll be left thinking that you could really do with somebody a little more basic in his tastes.

As business partners you'll do very well, but neither of you can spare the time for boring routine work, so this could be a problem. Neither of you have much tolerance when things go wrong, and when they do, you'd rather be off starting something new than helping an ailing project through a sticky patch.

These two signs work very well when married to each other, and while this is not a relationship that values stability and wealth, it will give you what you want in the form of bright conversation, plenty of variety and a not-too-serious outlook.

Sagittarius - Cancer

This is a difficult pairing, and the main problem is how to match your openness and love of company to somebody who is very shy and reserved. Cancerians don't live their life on the outside in the way that you do. They are extremely sensitive, and they respond very quickly to the emotional needs of others. Understandably, they have to have a mechanism for shutting off this response, or they would become exhausted just by walking down a crowded street. Remember, Sagittarius, that these people absorb energy from others, so they don't pump it out as you do. As absorbing types, they often don't have much of a choice in what they take in, so they have to take what comes. This makes life a much riskier business than it is for a Fire sign like you, and they will make very sure that they trust a person first, before they allow themselves to absorb his influence.

When they find that somebody is in need of their care and protection, they respond at once with love and care. You probably wouldn't notice that anybody needed help, because it's not easy to feel a lack of energy in somebody when you're an energy source in yourself. This is why Sagittarians get their reputation for being unsubtle and insensitive - it's not that you don't care, it's that you can't see when care is needed, or how much.

A Cancerian shields and protects himself, his family and his friends. Fire signs like you act of your own accord, but Water signs react to the actions of others. Cancer is governed by the Moon, so it reacts by reflecting the kind of light that you shine at it. Treat a Cancerian harshly, and see how the crab's pincers nip, but treat them with kindness, and they will respond with kindness.

A Cancerian will treat you very warily at first. Your ever-changing point of view means that he has continually to re-evaluate you, and see whether he needs to change his responses or perhaps retreat into his shell. His own security comes first. This process takes time. When you have a new enthusiasm that completely captures your imagination and makes you want to devote the rest of your life to it, as is usual for Sagittarians at weekly intervals, the Cancerian is rather slower to react than you would like. He's also decidedly short on enthusiasm by your standards. He just doesn't have the energy to waste in the way that you do. He also worries about what to do if things don't quite work out. He doesn't have your ability to recover from setbacks in a matter of minutes, you see.

He gasps at your openness and closes his eyes in fright at the risks that you take, but on the other hand, he loves your warmth and genuineness, and he finds your eternal optimism very cheering. You tease Cancerians for being so cautious, but you appreciate their selfless devotion to the care of their families and friends. You're always aware of higher motives, and anyone who displays them gets your approval. On a selfish level, there's something that they do for you, which no other sign can. When one of your imaginative schemes has collapsed, leaving you temporarily floored, they will care for you, and you appreciate that. A friend whose life you brighten when you're up, and who comforts you when you're down, is no bad thing at all, and you know that.

As friends, you're an odd couple, but you like each other's company. It's not easy for an outsider to see why this is, but perhaps it's because they reflect a little of yourself back at you, and that's the kind of audience you like. As lovers, you're a long way apart. They are very emotionally involved, whereas you're not. Their enthusiasm comes and goes in phases, like lunar phases, which will surprise you at first.

Marriage will take some working at, for this pair of signs. Cancer loves his home and seeks always to make a safe retreat for himself and his family, while Sagittarius wonders why they are making such a fuss. You'll have to adjust to each other. The same goes for a business partnership. If you handle the marketing, and they handle the financial side, you won't have any problems, but don't try to tell each other how to do the job!

Sagittarius - Leo

This is the other partnership possible within your own element, and you enjoy each other's company, but Leo is a bit static to your way of thinking. He's bright and warm, generous and friendly, but he isn't keen on seeing new things in the same way that you are, and when he travels, he does it surrounded by familiar things, so that he isn't really changing his surroundings at all. He doesn't have anything like your intellect; what he's got is warmth and generosity, but you have enough of that yourself, so you don't find him very remarkable.

The truth is that he likes you, but you aren't sure you like him. Not that you dislike him particularly; he's optimistic, open and lively just like you are, and that's more than can be said for most of the other signs, but he doesn't have anything that would make you want to trade places with him. He adores you, though.

What you have that he wants is wisdom. Leo has enough capability to be going on with, but more importantly, he has social confidence, which is the stuff that makes everybody cluster round him and want to be his friend. Sagittarius has spiritual confidence. It's his soul that's bright and strong, and the Leo finds that desperately desirable. A Leo wants to be recognized for what he's doing. In the Sagittarian's high principles he sees the perfection of his endeavors, and action accumulated into experience, wisdom distilled from that experience, then handed on to influence others, and gratefully acknowledged.

Leo is fine as long as he stays where he is. If anything displaces him from the center of the action, or something new comes along and changes the order of things, he's troubled. How envious he is of your confidence and mobility! He's confident enough on his own, of course, but only as long as he has people around him. He can't take his achievements along with him the way you can. Leo is expansive and generous, but Sagittarius is expansive, generous and mobile, and Leo would love to be like that.

He gains approval and friendship from everybody. Everybody loves a Leo and he loves being generous to his friends in response. This process is self-sustaining, and everyone benefits. Not everybody loves a Sagittarian, as you'll have learned by now. They work in the same way, but Leos hand out material comforts, whereas Sagittarians hand out spirituality and knowledge, and this doesn't always go down so well.

As friends, you get along very well, provided that you can slip into the subordinate role necessary for the friendship to succeed. Leos like their friends to consider them to be important, but your dislike of pomp and ceremony could be a hindrance to this. As lovers, you'll have a lot of fun. Leos are pretty traditional in their tastes, but they are strong and they like a good time. There will probably be quite a bit of rolling around on the floor, because both of your signs are animals, remember.

The drawback about going into business together is that you won't be able to work for somebody who knows less than you do, and the Leo won't play if he can't be boss. The same applies to marriage. Leo has to be the master of the house, and if you won't want that, then don't marry a Leo. He won't want you to go wandering off on your own either, as you'll inevitably feel drawn to do.

Sagittarius - Virgo

Relationships with those who are three signs apart aren't usually a good idea – not unless you like having rows, anyway. This one is less of a strain than most though, because both of you are pretty flexible in your approach to things, and because both of you enjoy doing things for other people's benefit. All this helps the pair of you to make the compromises necessary to form a relationship.

The essential problem is one of scale. You have a boundless imagination that needs to roam free, to form great universal concepts and apply them to the whole of humankind. They have very little imagination, and even less time for hypothetical concepts, preferring to concentrate their energies on the actual job in hand and to make sure that every detail of it is attended to. You see things through a telescope, and they see things through a microscope. Quite some problem, as you will appreciate.

What you have in common, and it's worth building on, is an interest in how things work, and how to do things for the best. In their case, the emphasis is on the actual mechanics of the process and they need to take a screwdriver to it to see how it works. You want to know what people do with it, how it helps them and why they want it.

It's important that you should not cross over into each other's territory. As partners, you can accomplish a great deal together, with one of you looking after theory and application, and the other one giving time to technique and efficiency. If you start to apply your generalized grasp of things to specific tasks, you'll make errors of detail. Similarly, he lacks both the facility to deal with the theoretical instead of the reality, and the scope to handle things on your scale. Don't criticize him for being fussy over details. Somebody has to be, and he has a talent for it. It's not your field, so leave him to it. In the same way, you can cheerfully ignore him when he criticizes you for having your head in the clouds. After a while, you'll recognize each other as experts in parallel fields that don't touch or overlap in any way.

Mentally, you're quite different. Both of you like to see the inner states of things, but the Virgo analyses carefully, bit by bit, whereas you grasp the whole thing at once, and perceive its meaning in one go. You're similar but different emotionally, too. Neither wants to feel tied down, but in your case, that's because of a love of freedom, whereas for the Virgo it's simply that he feels lost with irrational things like emotions, so he tries not to have much to do with them.

As friends, you should be able to understand each other. You have similar views but for different reasons, as we've just seen. If you come to an understanding about the difference of scale in your views of life, then you'll probably enjoy comparing your experiences. As lovers, you're not really suited. Virgos are too careful, while you prefer things to be a bit more boisterous. In any case, the Virgo doesn't have the energy of the Fire sign, nor any of your sense of exuberant fun.

As business partners, you need a third person. You work on a large and impractical scale, while Virgo's scale is too small. Most things happen in the middle, and who will look after that? You can work together as a marriage, though you'll find their small-scale view very frustrating. You attack common problems from different ends in your own ways.

Sagittarius - Libra

This is the best of the lot as far as these relationships go. There's more to matching people astrologically than just comparing Sun signs, but having said that, you won't get far if the Sun signs don't match, and as far as you're concerned, this is the one to go for.

You like Librans. It's as simple as that. When you have one of your great ideas in your head, they are interested; when you tell them about it, they like listening. They talk back too; in just the way that you like them to, brightly, with interest and humor. Their attitude is one of optimism like your own, and they are sure that the next thing is going to be even better than the current one, just as you are. They are friendly too, as they positively relish company, and don't like being on their own any more than you do. When you decide that it's time to get up and do something, they ask to come along for the ride, but they don't get in the way, and that's just how you like it. They will fall in love with you, which you find flattering, but they don't get emotionally dependent on you, and they don't cling. Nor do they get moody or temperamental. In fact, they will do almost anything to avoid an argument, and would much rather think about something else instead, preferably something new and entertaining, just as you do. If you were to sit down with pencil and paper, and make a list of all that you wanted in a partner, you wouldn't come up with anything better than a Libran.

You can't find anything wrong with them at all. In fact, they are suspiciously well suited to you, and you may wonder why. To be fair, they are just as pleasant to everybody, because that's how they are, and you may have suspected this. On the other hand, not everybody finds their light and friendly outlook on life to their taste, but it happens to suit you very well, so you might as well make the most of it.

Librans are Air sign people. They live in a world of thought, speech and ideas, where what you say is more interesting than what you do, and where nothing lasts for very long. They are also the Cardinal Air sign, so they are the most active and assertive of their element. You, on the other hand, are a Fire sign, which is to do with creative physical activity, but because you're the Mutable Fire sign, your activity tends to have a mental rather than a physical emphasis. Therefore, you're the sign of mental activity and they are the sign of active mentality, which is pretty much the same thing. Now you see why you like each other.

They see you as being much more assertive and effective versions of themselves. They also see you as the ideal conversational partner. They love talking and you never seem to run out of things to say. They like being entertained, and you seem to know so much (their own minds don't hold deep knowledge like yours does). As friends, you're perfect. You lead your own lives but in parallel, and you love to tell each other everything that has happened to you. Your conversations can never become heavy, so there's always laughter and entertainment in them somewhere. Even after many years, you should be able to note how genuinely pleased you are to see each other, and how much you have to say to each other. Arguments just never seem to surface and you're completely sympathetic to each other's point of view.

As lovers, you should be almost ideal. Librans are a bit on the cool side sexually, but they are very friendly, and being a Cardinal sign will give them enough strength to match your fiery power. Neither of you take it too seriously, and both of you like the affair to be flexible and full of variety. These two things alone make it more enjoyable for both of you than your other relationships, even if they have more passion.

As business partners, you will dominate. They are your partner, not you theirs. There are some areas where you're lazy, but it's no good expecting them to fill in the gaps for you, so business is not necessarily a good thing for you to share.

If you marry, you should be very content. The Libran will make your day-to-day existence very pleasant indeed, through his talent for making things relaxed and graceful. Neither of you are much good at fighting your way out of tight corners, though, and you might need to at times.

Sagittarius - Scorpio

There are quite a few Sagittarians who have relationships with Scorpios. Like everybody else in the zodiac, they are attracted to the intense energy that the Scorpio puts out. With this particular pairing, however, the Sagittarian finds that the Scorpio is nothing like as much fun as he had hoped, and the Scorpio finds that holding the Sagittarius in check is more trouble than it's worth. Eventually, the Centaur, tired of being made to rear up by having the Scorpion under his hooves, takes his quiver and brains the little beast; then he gallops off into the sunset wishing he hadn't been so hasty as to get into the relationship in the first place.

Scorpios are all the things that you hate most, and what makes it worse is that you can see why they are doing it. They are secretive where you are frank, underhand where you are honest, and manipulative where you are generous. What they are trying to do is to stay in control of everything. To them, it's important that the result of every action is known; if it is not, a situation leading to a possible loss of control could result, leaving the Scorpio vulnerable to attack. They take great pains to assess the condition of everybody they come into contact with, and are the masters of interpersonal politics. If there's any plotting going, the Scorpio knows about it, is doing it or they suggested it in the first place. The amazing thing to you is that nobody can see this process going on; Scorpios take great care to keep their actions and feelings well hidden, and for the most part, it works. It doesn't work with you, though; you can see into the situation without trying, and the devices of the Scorpio are quite visible to you. How angry this makes the Scorpio!

The fact that you don't seem to care about your own safety, and that you're absurdly honest in your speech, makes him cringe in embarrassment, but the fact that you seem not only to get away with it, but to benefit from it, makes him grind his teeth with rage. He sees you as a holy fool, protected by angels from the consequences of your naivete. You see him as raging at his own insecurity, somebody who would be a lot better off if he could have the confidence to trust other people with himself. It's not really a good basis for a relationship.

For you to be good friends is unlikely. When you talk, you'll be aware of how much the Scorpio is trying to take from you and how little he's willing to give in return. You'd welcome his views on things even if they were different to yours, but you know that he isn't going to let you know what he really thinks, and that annoys you. When you lose your temper, he just smiles. Other people's emotional outbursts are like food to him, because it puts him firmly in control of the situation.

A much likelier reason for you to be together is sexual attraction. Your ruling planets have much to do with it. Scorpio's Mars is a power for containment from outside, and your Jupiter is an irresistible expansion from within. Both of you enjoy the way the pressure rises when you're together. Scorpio is actually stronger than you are sexually, but it won't be exhaustion that will make you decide you've had enough, it's his obsessive and possessive emotional energies that will get you down.

You don't like each other's methods enough to be reasonable business partners. As marriage partners, you'd have to accept that the Scorpio will want to contain your energy, and that you'd be unable to roam lest his awesome jealousy erupts. You'd attempt to influence him for the better (as you would see it), but he will find it difficult to be as open or as flexible about things as you are. Present him with a variety of things and he simply tries to control all of them at the same time, because he just can't let go. Eventually you'd just get up and leave for good.

Sagittarius - Sagittarius

As with all the pairings between identical signs, this one has plenty to recommend it, and a few drawbacks as well. At least you're both Mutable signs, which means that you're both interested in examining a different point of view. If you were dogmatic and unwilling to change your views, you'd be in trouble from the start. You're both outgoing signs, which again brings benefits because you're both willing to contribute to the situation. If you were both "collecting" signs, you'd sit there each waiting for the other person to put something into the relationship.

The trouble with this relationship is that you're both right. You both know all there is to know about everything and you both know it. You're both right all the time. It's a difficult thing for a Sagittarian to understand that truth is essentially a personal concept, and that what seems true to one person may not be acceptable or even credible to another. If the other person is a Sagittarian like yourself, you're doubly confused. You had thought that somebody like yourself would be able to see things your way, but it turns out not to be like that. You're also bothered because they are just as persuasive as you are, and their arguments are as clear and convincing as your own. It's all most unsettling.

Not that you spend much of your time deep in philosophical discussion, even though it does interest you greatly, because you have other things to share. One of the great things about being a Sagittarius is your capacity to be inspired and excited by everybody else's interest, especially if it's new to you, and if they communicate their own enthusiasm for it. Other signs will retreat into themselves when faced with something unfamiliar, but you welcome it cheerfully. Obviously, another Sagittarian will have much to show you, and indeed much that he wants to show you, and you welcome all of it. When you have a shared interest, you go off and do it together, but you don't get under each other's feet and you're not dependent on each other. These are the qualities you expect to find in others (because you have them in yourself) and you're delighted to find them in another Sagittarian.

A friendship between you may well be episodic in nature, because you both have other things to do, and will go off and do them. When you have time, perhaps you'll see each other again and talk about what you've been doing. Your friendship doesn't need to be regular to be enjoyable. It isn't formed from emotional dependency, but from a shared love of action and excitement. Something to look out for in a Sagittarian friendship is a tendency to talk about what you're hoping to do, rather than what you've already done. Sagittarian thought looks ever forward and upwards, and the future is more exciting to you than the past.

As lovers, you'll be evenly matched in terms of energy and inclinations. You'll be able to indulge in as much horseplay (don't ever forget the animal that forms your bottom half) as you want, and you gain much enjoyment from the knowledge that for both of you it's the spirit of the moment that counts. Love may well be forever, but for you it must be right now as well.

As business partners, you're hopeless. You both want to do the interesting bits and neither of you can be bothered to stay up late doing the accounts. The same goes for a marriage, because someone will have to do the chores. Not that either of you are great homebuilders; as long as you have books to read, maps to plan your next journey together and somewhere to sleep, you're quite happy.

Sagittarius - Capricorn

This is the most difficult of all the Sun sign relationships for you to handle. It isn't that the Capricorn has any real trouble dealing with you - though he could think of other people he would rather have as a friend - but that your planet, Jupiter, has a particular dislike for the sign of Capricorn. Jupiter tries to break out of all restraints, while Saturn forms closed frameworks. You dislike Capricorn quite strongly. He seems on the one hand to have all the qualities you're trying to gain for yourself, and this makes you envious, but he also seems to deserve them, which offends your high principles.

If you remember the sequence of the zodiac signs, you'll get better idea of what I mean. Sagittarius, as you know, is proud of his knowledge and perception. What he wants to do is to distribute this knowledge for the benefit of everybody, and to gain recognition and reputation as his reward. Capricorn, the next sign on, represents that reputation and recognition. Capricorn is what everybody sees as a man of reputation. He's the head of the company, the managing director, the big landowner, and the plutocrat. You'll notice at once that all these definitions are images of money. That's what makes you mad. Why is it, you ask, that the only reputation that seems to have any weight to it is a financial one? Why can't you be recognized for your ideas, in a Sagittarian way? The answer to that is that Capricorn is an Earth sign, and weight is a physical properly, and thus connected to physical matter, and hence the element of Earth. Anything that has weight and importance on this planet, is of the earth. How do you think the planet got its name?

Anyway, at the end of it all, the Capricorn has the money, the power and the reputation, and you don't. You could live with this if it weren't for the fact that he doesn't have a fraction of your knowledge. Nor has he your warmth, your compassion, your imagination, your willingness to help, your spiritual depth, the nobility of your soul or any of your optimism. In fact, he strikes you as a thoroughly uninspiring individual, and yet he has all the success that this life can offer. Few things make you really angry, but this does.

Capricorn is a quiet, methodical and a really hard worker. He likes things ordered and regular. He likes things to be in their places, and for there to be well-defined links between these places. He fits brilliantly into any corporate structure and rises through it by regular hard work and identification with the corporation. In other words, he's a company man.

You couldn't imagine anything worse, could you? He has no imagination, freedom, impulsiveness, and no far horizons, knowledge or vision. He sees you in an equally unflattering light. You have no organization, no structure, you won't wait for anything and you have no sense of time. You have no reserve and no tact, and you pay no respect to your superiors. Worst of all, you give things away, such as your gifts of knowledge, warmth and companionship. Why can't you see that if you have things that other people want, then you should sell them, not give them away? No wonder you have no money. From this you'll understand that a friendship between you will be almost impossible in your terms.

When you tell a Capricorn something, he will use it to advance his reputation rather than yours. In addition, if you refuse to recognize him as the successful person he is, he will end the friendship. To the Capricorn, if there's no reward, then it isn't worthwhile.

Physically, you can cope with each other as lovers, because Capricorns have a goat for their animal, so you know what to expect, but deep down, you make love for fun and they make love as part of a career plan. As business partners, you can do very well, if you're prepared to take things as seriously as they do. Capricorns are wonderful business persons, but they lack your entrepreneurial spirit. If you provide that, and direct your energies firmly to the job in hand, then Capricorn will see to it that you both become very wealthy.

Marriage? Possibly - but it isn't a love match; it's an arrangement, a private deal. You give all your warmth and knowledge to them, and they give all their practical management skills to you. The result is that your ideas and personality are converted into money, and they have the pleasure of your company and talent as an exclusive right, which appeals to the snob in them.

Sagittarius - Aquarius

Aquarius is a bit of a paradox, but since both sides of it appeal to you, there are no problems. On the one hand, an Aquarian loves company, and is always involved with some social group or other, but on the other hand, he feels that he's different from everybody else. He's attracted to anything unusual or which, like him, stands apart from the crowd. All of this is fine by you, because you like a varied social life too, and anything that's a bit different interests you.

Aquarius is an Air sign, so this is one where you seem to have a lot to talk about. Aquarians don't have your depth of insight, but they do have a refreshingly wide range of interests, and they get quite passionate when talking about issues that arouse their concern. This means that you can have a good argument with an Aquarian, with you both pulling at the subject between you like two dogs with a bone, and both enjoying the affair enormously. Only the two of you will realize that you like this process; other signs will be horrified at what they see as bitter feuding. The fact is that most of the time you're in agreement with the Aquarian's principles, and that makes your arguments much more playful affairs.

Principles are funny things, because you have to look outside yourself, and think of the wider implications of things. Both you and Aquarius have high principles and you appreciate this in each other. In the Aquarius, it often shows as a particular political persuasion, or a devotion to humanitarian causes. Another thing you might notice is how determinedly egalitarian they are. In an Aquarian's world, everybody is equal, and all hierarchies or master-and-servant relationships are seen as a bad thing. This isn't so far removed from your own view that respect is given rather than demanded, and that everybody should be free to do what he or she pleases. You see them as talkative and sociable people who believe in good causes and are prepared to argue their case. They see you as refreshingly enthusiastic friends, honest and loyal, not afraid to speak your mind, and with the right sort of ideas about most things.

A friendship between you is a very easy thing to produce. You find a great deal of comfort in knowing somebody who is likely to understand what you're trying to say, but is not necessarily going to agree with your opinion in every case. It's also good, in your eyes at least, to have a friend who doesn't want to be too closely tied to you emotionally. Aquarians are quite cool in that respect; they understand your need for freedom very well, since it's similar to their own need to be independent. As lovers, you're very well suited. They have plenty of physical stamina, and they like playing but they don't need deep emotional commitment.

Business partners? Maybe, if you can find something that maintains your interest and doesn't offend your principles. You're good as a team, but are you really businessmen at heart? Marriage would be a much better bet, as a lively, open partnership, looking forwards to a better future. You might find that it lacked a sense of traditional family values, but you could supply that too, if you wanted to.

Sagittarius - Pisces

Pisces is a sign that contains every possibility, but often doesn't know which one to choose. Nothing about the Piscean is clear-cut, so when you try to pin them down, they run through your fingers. It's what you'd expect from Mutable Water, if you think about it.

The zodiac comes up with some strange combinations, and this is one of the strangest. Although you're of different elements that represent different directions (they are incoming while you're outgoing) and different universes (they are imaginary, you're real), you're ruled by the same planet, which is Jupiter. All that expansion and growth, all that energy for increase, is inverted in Pisces; whereas you radiate energy and enthusiasm outwards, exploring distant lands, and gathering experience and knowledge, Pisces expands inwards, discovering new and more fantastic realms of experience and sensation inside themselves. They paint increasingly complex patterns on the inside of their heads. This is a fascinating idea, isn't it?

They are sensitive and imaginative like nobody else in the world. These people can think in terms of color and music, drama and poetry, and sometimes all of them at once, in a way that you find compelling. They can be anything they want, because they take their cues from the situation in which they find themselves. They somehow manage to be all things to all men. The whole business fascinates you. Your curiosity wants to know what the real nature of the Piscean is, under all the disguises.

There isn't one. They really are who they say they are at the time. There's a fundamental difference between you, which, although it sounds far removed from daily life, actually underlies everything you do together, and it's this. You think that once you know something, it's an unalterable fact and the truth never changes. The Piscean knows that today's answer may not be quite so true tomorrow. To him, truth is defined by the person to whom it seems true, and it can change. The Piscean is as keen to know things as you are, but he sees that the way of what he knows changes as time goes by, You sense this somehow, and you're very curious to experience it for yourself. You see them as fascinating creatures, so sensitive that the slightest stimulus will set their imaginations off into flights of fantasy. You can't quite see all this as being useful, and you have the sneaky feeling that a lot of your own knowledge may be similarly viewed by others.

They see you as great sources of creative energy, enough for you to wear your ideas on the outside, which they find very impressive. They see your clarity of thought as particularly desirable, because in your case, you do appear to have compromised your imagination to obtain your logical approach. Because you're so much more confident and expressive than they are, they see you as an admirable blend of creative imagination and worldly success. This isn't quite right, as you'll no doubt tell them, because you're honest that way, but you must admit that it's very flattering of them to see you in those terms.

Friendship between you is formed out of mutual curiosity and admiration rather than what you have in common. You have conversations like magicians practicing their art on each other. You give them ideas to see what the Piscean does with them, and they give you impressions of things from which you try to guess the original stimulus. Like art, these encounters work on more than one level at once, which you find exacting but satisfying, and although you think you know what you get out of it, you probably couldn't explain it to anybody else.

Should you become lovers, you'll find yourselves communicating on two levels simultaneously - the animal and the spiritual. You'll have to be a little less robust in your approach than is usual for you, but when it all works, you'll discover dimensions of yourself you never knew you had. As business partners, you'd only do really well if you were in a media-related business. You're both too good with ideas but not with routines, finances and organization to feel at home in a traditional business structure.

If you married, you'd be happy enough, but unless one of you has a practical streak somewhere, you'd need all sorts of help to manage your finances and to fix the plumbing. In this marriage, material things are definitely a low priority.

The Approach to Relationships:
Capricorn

Symbol:	The Goat	♑	Element:	Earth
Planet:	Saturn	♄	Quality:	Cardinal

Capricorn's ruling planet is Saturn, the last of the traditional "seven stars"; after all the growth and change that the energies of the other six have made possible, Saturn puts on the lid and gives things their final form. He is the planet of framework and containers; he is the much-quoted "bottom line" of long and involved contracts. When all the fancy words and promises have evaporated, the reality of the affair is Saturn. The hard work necessary to keep things going is Saturn, along with the rules and regulations necessary to stop the whole thing falling apart. Hard work, duty, being serious, getting results, being disciplined, keeping to the rules: all of these are Saturnine energies, and this is what Capricorn is all about.

Not that it's all bad - hard work and patience usually bring promotion, and doing your duty gets you a medal. These are visible rewards, and as such, they are much appreciated by Capricorn. Saturn is the Lord of Structure and Time; he puts things in their place and keeps them there. Saturn isn't as explosively powerful as Mars, nor as creative as Jupiter, but he can maintain his efforts over a long period of time Saturn is a marathon runner rather than a hundred-meter sprinter.

Capricorn - Aries

This relationship needs a fair bit of work if it's to be successful, though initially there are many things you have in common, and you'll find that attractive. Both of you like to be effective in your actions, and you like to see things done rather than sit around thinking about them. However, the motivation behind your preferences is very different.

The major difference between you is your idea of time. Aries lives for the instant. It's pretty difficult for him to imagine tomorrow with any degree of seriousness, let alone next year. In extreme cases, he may have difficulty with this afternoon. You can see next decade as though it were today, and have no problems laying plans for five or even ten years hence. What you're doing is building structure while what he's doing is living for today. If you go into a partnership with an Arian, you can't expect him really to understand how important it is to you that things be done at the right place and time. To the Arian, if he wants to do it, he does it at once. Neither the future nor the past has any bearing on what an Arian does at this moment; only what he feels at this instant is of any importance. As you can see, his capacity for immediate action can be very useful for getting things started, but he needs (in your view, at any rate) careful guidance if his talents are not to be wasted, and if he's to help you realize your plans.

There's something very simple about an Arian, and it's rather noble at the same time. Quite simply, he does things for the joy of doing them, not for the reward at the end. You know very well that what makes you a hard and willing worker is the recognition you hope to enjoy at the end of it all: in your world, the harder you work, the higher you rise.

Aries is simpler than that. He doesn't care what people think about his efforts. It never occurs to him to do something purely to enhance his reputation. He only knows whether the task at hand appeals to him. If it does, he will do it, and if it doesn't, he won't. What he actually works for is the pleasure of being at work. For him, the enjoyment he gets from experiencing action is as important as the pleasure you get when you're promoted to a new position, His whole existence is centered around the physical sensations of being in action. What he does something for doesn't matter, what matters is that he does it, and that he does it now. Aries is a pure physical force.

You appreciate his direct approach to things, his energy and the fact that he completes everything he attempts. You like his confidence and his capacity for effort. If you had that kind of strength, you think, you could do anything. However, there again, you remind yourself, that kind of explosive energy can only last a short time and what you'd really like is sustained energy over a longer period. What you want is steady heat, whereas the Arian provides ignition or explosion.

He sees you as a father figure. You have a longer view of events, and you're more sensible, in his eyes. You're surrounded by all the material tokens of seniority, and he sees you as older than you are because of them and because it's obvious that you think and move much more slowly than he does. One day, perhaps, he would like to be like you, but not yet! As friends, you'll be pleased to find that you're aiming for the same goals. You share a dislike for indecisive people and an appreciation of anything that gives quick results from firm action. You'll probably approve of each other's taste in cars and clothes, but for different reasons.

As lovers, you should be evenly matched. Capricorn has the stamina, while Aries has the strength. Both of you come from the sign of an animal with horns, so you're both strongly sexed. Capricorns aren't usually very keen on experimental sex; strong but conventional is how you like it. As it happens, Arians are similar, because for them the body is more important than the mind and they can't be bothered with thinking up fancy ideas, so neither of you will have much to complain about.

As business partners, you could do very well, provided that you channel his energy productively, and if you do the organizing for the two of you. As a marriage, this would work better than many would think. Be prepared for the Arian's temper, and try at least sometimes to do some things impulsively, for his sake if nothing else. You both appreciate each other's capabilities, and you're willing to share your own in return for some of your partner's.

Capricorn - Taurus

This is an easy relationship. In fact, it's one of your best. If stability and enjoyment of your hard-earned, high standard of living are what you want, then the Taurean is just the person to share it with you. Taurus is an Earth sign, as you are, so he instinctively understands the importance you place on what you have to show for your efforts. They appreciate beautiful things and they have similar tastes to you. Taureans are dedicated to steadiness and the pursuit of a life without disturbance and change. When they are in a situation that seems both comfortable and manageable for them, they do all that they can to keep it as it is. They regard it as their particular territory, and will resist any attempts to dislodge them from it, defending it to the death, if need be.

What you like about Taureans is that they are the originators of the good life. Sumptuously decorated houses, fine foods and wines, cars with leather seats and soft suspension are all Taurean. What a Taurean needs most of all is physical security, and by that he means surrounding himself with objects which he can touch and be comforted by. He needs to know where his next meal is coming from. He needs that meal not only to nourish him, but also to reassure him that he's as fine a person as he thinks he is. If you think about that for a moment, you'll realize that, not only must the Taurean have a very full freezer at all times, but it must be full of luxury food as well. If all he has to eat is basic foodstuffs, then he doesn't feel reassured. The same kind of ideas apply to his clothes and house as well. To you, work is energy being converted into money, while in the Taurean, you have a person whose existence is devoted to the appreciation of what that money will buy. You find that in itself reassuring, and when you wonder what you're working so hard for, five minutes with a Taurean will remind you.

The only problem with Taureans is that they are so static. You appreciate stability as much as anyone else does, but you do like to feel yourself making progress and moving along through life. Taureans aren't interested in moving, only in making their present location more comfortable. There's a puritanical streak in you, inspired by your dour planet, Saturn, which enables you to do without life's little luxuries on the way to better things; Taurus won't do without anything.

They see you as exactly what they would like to be, which is financially successful. They miss the point to some extent, in that you're financially successful as a sort of side effect of being at the top of the pile, and that's because the idea of position doesn't have a lot of meaning for them. What they would like is to be able to afford all the lovely things they are so fond of, and it seems that you have the ability to turn time into money, which is true.

As friends, you'll enjoy each other's company immensely, and will particularly enjoy spending money together; they will find your sense of the status of objects as interesting as you find their sense of texture and color. You could both end up extremely fat, of course, because food is a major pleasure with Taureans. When matters get serious and you need to discuss your next move, you'll seek advice from elsewhere, because their defensive approach to business isn't always what you want to hear. Should you go into business together, they make wonderful partners, because they will always be supportive and reliable; the initiative, however, has to come from you.

Although having a lover of the same element as yourself is usually a good thing, you might find that they are more sensitive emotionally than you had realized, and you could be out of your depth a little. On a sexual level, you may be surprised by their strength and possessiveness. This pairing makes for a good marriage provided that your main aim is to have a secure and enjoyable home life. In business, you may be more interested in getting on than in enjoying life, so you'll find the Taurean more hindrance than help.

Capricorn - Gemini

This is a very dry and crackly sort of pairing. There are plenty of things that will produce sparks between you, but almost no heat. Emotionally, this one is conducted at a very low level, but that may be just the sort of thing you're looking for.

Gemini has the fastest thinking brain in the whole zodiac. He can see the point of a sentence before the speaker has finished. He also likes re-telling stories, with slightly altered endings, just for fun. He can play with words and ideas like nobody else, and he doesn't really believe any one of them. Nature makes ducks waterproof because they spend a lot of time in the water, and it makes Geminis immune to persuasion by the words they use so much.

What a Gemini needs more than anything else is to be amused, and he does this by absorbing huge amounts of new information. He doesn't remember it all, and he doesn't want to. He just wants to read it or hear it, and for it to keep him amused for a few minutes. He's not working to a plan in the same way that you are, and he isn't interested in building a structure, so he doesn't feel that everything is best if it stays in its appointed place. There's a strong streak of the anarchist in a Gemini, which rises to the surface every so often when he feels that things aren't changing fast enough to keep him amused, and that he had better do something about it. Geminis don't share your belief that hard work is the only way to achieve your goals, either. They are, given half a chance, extremely lazy. It's not really their fault. Gemini is an Air sign, which isn't at all practical or down-to-earth, and it's governed by Mercury, which doesn't have the weight or driving force of Saturn or Mars.

So far, it seems you're trying to form a relationship with a fork-tongued anarchist: so, what is it about them that captivates you? To start with, he has a great sense of humor that's verbal and cerebral. Your own sense of humor is wry and dry, so his sharp wit appeals to you a great deal. Because of the Saturnine influence that you bring with you, in your presence his humor becomes even more piercing and sardonic, and in return your own becomes more verbal and better expressed. The pity about this process is that the lighter side of the Gemini's humor gets lost. You've no time for that sort of thing, so your Saturn influence crushes it out of the Gemini before it gets a chance to show itself.

The other thing you like about Geminis is their ability to analyze situations at work. They are fast, accurate and dispassionate, and you admire them for it. If you were like that, you think, you could really make some progress. It never occurs to you that Gemini isn't interested in that sort of progress. They see you as rather slow and too careful by half, but they like your black humor and they would like to enjoy the capacity for self-indulgence that your financial success brings with it. As long as you continue to move up and to be with powerful people, the Gemini will stay around to be entertained.

You like each other as friends because you're both unemotional. Neither will get sentimental about the other and you're both thankful for that. You're much stronger sexually than the Gemini, so if you should become lovers, you'll be the dominant partner. If you keep things varied, the Gemini will perform well enough, but if you become serious or obsessive, he will quickly lose interest.

As business partners you're wonderful together, provided that your ambition is strong enough to override any twinges of conscience arising from the Gemini's very sharp deals.

Marriage? Yes, if you make a few allowances for each other. The flavor of the marriage is hard, though, like bare furniture. Fine if you like that sort of thing, but most people like cushions now and again.

Capricorn - Cancer

This is the union of opposites, and as is always the case in astrology (and real life too), you have more in common than you think. Cancer, like you, is concerned with the structure of things. He's reserved, polite and proper in his dealings, as you are. He's mindful of the rights and requirements of others, as you are also. Cancer is a "collecting" sign, as Capricorn is, and is therefore concerned with taking in energy from others so that he can strengthen his own position. Finally, he's a Cardinal sign, as you are, so he thinks that he won't get anywhere unless he does something about it personally.

Familiar, isn't it? The difference is that his world is internal where yours is external. His purpose and aim is to protect what is his from the attentions of the world, whereas yours is to have the world applaud you for what you've achieved. Imagine that everyone was given a large box to help them live their life. You'd have the outside of the box painted in fashionable colors, and decked out in fabrics that would show off your status to everybody. This done, you'd climb on top of the box so that everybody could see that you were higher up than they were. Now consider Cancer. Cancer would live inside the box. The outside would be completely plain and featureless, unremarkable and uninviting. Their attitude isn't hostile or rude, but private nonetheless. Inside the box would be the most comfortable and cozy home you could imagine, where the whole family would live their lives with much love and affection. The purpose of it all would be emotional nourishment, support and protection. The box represents the structure of your life and your career. To you, it exists for you to be able to get to the top, but for the Cancerian, it exists for his reassurance.

Neither of you can live without that structure. Both of you find it the essential feature of your lives, and if it's ever dissolved, you'll build another one at once, in much the same way as spiders with webs. Cancer has the same sense of time as you do, and is interested in working towards the far future in a patient fashion. You're both builders. He's interested in laying the foundations, and you're interested in the topping-off, but you're both builders at heart, and you can appreciate it in each other.

He sees you as rather too public in your tastes, and uncomfortably Spartan and self-denying in your personal life, but he welcomes your serious approach to getting on in life. You see him as a bit of a worrier, and a little too sentimental about things to be a really effective decision-maker, but you appreciate his determination to succeed. You also welcome his belief that the traditional way of things is probably the best.

As friends, you'll take time to get to know one another; once you have each other's trust, the friendship will last forever. As lovers, you'll find that the Cancerian is as strong as you are, but in different ways. You find his emotional needs difficult to respond to at first.

In business, you should do well, though you're both better suited to rising through a big organization than to starting up on your own.

Marriage between you is a good idea, because it's a long-term thing, and both of you work better over a longer period. You must appreciate how vital the Cancerian's home life is to him, though.

Capricorn - Leo

You don't find Fire signs enjoyable. This partnership is easily the most difficult of the twelve for you. Put quite simply, Leos make you spit. They are lazy, good-natured souls, and they seem to be well liked for it. You can understand being liked for working but not for being idle and the fact that they seem to be able to do exactly that annoys you. It never occurs to you that you can't buy affection, that being pleasant isn't to do with being rich, or that hard work won't necessarily make you popular, but that's just how you are, and that's the disadvantage of being an Earth sign.

You know what confidence is. It's that inner warmth that comes from being in control, being right, and being able to afford to do what you like. You have it in some measure, and the harder you work, the more of it you hope to get. It's expensive stuff, as far you're concerned, because it's only achieved in return for much labor; but there again, if it didn't cost you a lot to get it, it wouldn't feel that it was valuable, would you? You like being in control, being right and being able to afford to do what you like. Leos were born with it. They have warmth, confidence and ability enough to throw away - and they do. The sheer waste of it all offends you. How can they be like that, you cry; though what you really mean is, why can't I be like that?

The truth of the matter is that you're jealous of Leos. Leo represents the Sun, the source of light and heat and the center of the solar system. Against their light, you're thrown into shadow. Saturn's weight, the source of your power, is made to seem what it is in the Leo's realm of sunshine - small, cold, gray and dull. Your achievements are all external. Inside, you're still the same as you were when you started. What you've managed to do is to compel admiration and respect for your position, but that can't compete with somebody who gives out warmth and light for free. Basically, Leos make you look like Scrooge, and you don't like it.

They see you as somebody out to usurp their position as the natural center of the group. They see your structured approach to life as being rather unimaginative and cold, and they would rather not give time to it. Life is one big party to a Leo, but they have to have an audience, and they have to be the star of the show. If you look as though you will threaten that, then they will be most displeased. There's a sense of nobility about Leos, so they show royal displeasure if they feel that they are not given due recognition.

A friendship between you is going to be something of a power struggle. Both of you want the other to admit that you're the prominent partner. The way round it is to give the Leo preference in a social and personal context, and to concentrate your own individual capabilities, yours in the world of power and finance and his in society and family life. The only problem is that you'll both pay too much attention to the other's sphere of influence, since both rate the other's as unimportant and trivial. The power struggle continues on a physical level if you become lovers.

As business partners, you could do a lot for each other. Leo has the confidence and the capacity to inspire confidence that you often lack. Leo doesn't have your capacity for hard work, but he has an organizational ability that would surprise you when you come across it. After a while, you'll recognize that it's as effective and as reliable as yours is, and considerably more flexible. He hasn't your touch with money, so you'll have to look after that for him.

Your marriage would certainly be fun to watch. You should live in the finest style, and have some memorable rows when you felt that your partner was being too selfish. It would need a lot of adjustment from you both to be really successful, though it would be strengthened by children. Leos love children and are natural parents. You both have dynastic ambitions, and see children as extensions of your own excellence, going on to the next generation. Your own children would give you a common goal.

Capricorn - Virgo

This is a thought-provoking relationship, in which you feel comfortable and you're happy with the cool energies of Mercury, which is Virgo's ruling planet. Virgo is a clever and analytical thinker, and his talents are directed towards practical ends, as you'd expect from another Earth sign. The results of his analysis are found in things rather than merely in words and ideas. Virgos are experts on how to do things. They know what to do, how to do it, what skills are needed and how to add the extra little touches to get the result that they want. When they meet something new, Virgo will take it to pieces to see how it works - sometimes literally! They are thoughtful and methodical in their approach. They like to understand a thing fully and thoroughly, right down to the level of its components, before they feel at home with it. You'll appreciate all this and feel reassured by the Virgoan approach. There are times when you're working so hard that you don't have time to think, or when you know what has to be done but you aren't sure why it has to be done that way; Virgo tells you the reasons why, and it all makes sense to you. You have to believe in the order of things. If they are not in their places, if there's no structure and pattern, then you're lost. Virgo reminds you that the order of things carries on down to the smallest level, right down to molecular level if need be, and you find that very comforting.

On a personal level, you're one of the few people who find Virgo's methodical approach praiseworthy, and his obsession with getting things exactly right, admirable. Most people find him meticulous and too critical. He finds your success an inspiring thought. He can see that you work in a similar way, but on a larger scale to himself, and if he had the time and energy, he would be just like you, he feels sure. Whenever he has doubts about the correctness of his approach, he looks at what hard work has brought you, and he feels pleased.

Given that you find each other mutually admirable, a friendship is likely to form very quickly. You fit together very well indeed. He will try constantly to do things for you, and you'll be proud of him for it. This is his way of showing his affection. He can't express himself with soft sentiment; instead, he shows his affection by being useful. Being useful is the finest thing he can imagine, just as being successful is your fondest dream; he feels that if he can be useful to you, and you become more successful because of it, then you have the makings of a fulfilling relationship, though not all of the signs would recognize it as such.

You'd make a good partnership in business. Virgos can't always see the whole situation at once, but you can. There again, you sometimes can't see the details of things, but that's just what they do best. You compensate for each other's deficiencies beautifully, and you both enjoy the actual process of working. This is a really winning combination.

As lovers, you may find each other on a different planet, with Virgo being critical and not really sexual, while your animal-sign symbol makes you strongly sexed. The mutual sense of industry and purpose would go into a marriage between you, and that would make it a success in material terms. The relationship would lack emotional warmth though, and it could be seriously short of laughter, as you both take life too seriously at times.

Capricorn - Libra

This is a very interesting combination. You're two very different people, but each of you has a major talent that the other finds highly desirable, and that's what gives the relationship its initial impetus. Librans are not practical people, because they deal in words and ideas, like all the Air signs do, and they don't care how it happens, as long as they like it when it's finished. In fact, Librans care about how a thing looks, and they care even more that it should look attractive.

The thing that captivates you about a Libran is their taste. They have other qualities too, but you react most strongly to the ones that apply to your world, and you understand material things much more easily than you understand ideas and feelings. Librans have the ability to choose the most graceful, the most elegant, the most pleasing to the eye, repeatedly. You, on the other hand, can't seem to get a lot further than deciding what you want and how much you're going to pay for it. Once your life has been touched by a Libran, compliments start to come rolling in and you're very keen for that to carry on happening, very keen indeed. Librans are professionally nice people. There isn't anyone who doesn't like them. This quality - instant likeability as you see it - is very attractive to you, and it makes you rather ashamed of your own rather low social profile, and your own reputation for being too serious.

There are disadvantages to being everything to everybody though, and one of them is that a Libran has to keep changing his mind. Indecisiveness isn't something that ever troubles you, and it's that very thing which makes the Libran so eager to make your acquaintance. If some of your firmness of purpose, sense of organization or simply hardness of exterior could be transferred to the Libran, he would be delighted. He's never certain which course to take, never able to decide what to do next for the best, and never able to say no to anybody if he thinks that they might be upset. All of these weaknesses are very apparent to him, as is the fact that you have none of them and he would love to change places with you.

There are drawbacks to the partnership. Just because you admire certain qualities in each other doesn't mean that everything else slips into place. Libra is likely to find you rather serious, so he would like you better if you laughed more often, and if you shared his pleasure in going out and being among friends. You'd like him to be firmer in his approach to things that demand it; because at times he can be impossibly lightweight, and it just makes you sigh with frustration.

In many cases, your interests won't coincide enough for you even to think about seeing any more of each other than you have to, but on other occasions you'll feel that you get enough out of each other for you to ignore your differences. In the best instances, you'll admire what the other one is trying to do. Capricorn will understand the importance of the intimate personal relationship to the Libran, and the Libran will understand the Capricorn's need to be seen as the best.

A sexual relationship between you would be a lot more successful than you might think, given that friendship itself is so difficult to achieve. Librans have just a hint of coolness somewhere in that impeccable style, a suggestion of vanity that means that they are always making sure that they are looking good rather than giving themselves totally to the experience. Capricorns understand this. It's part of your nature too. You can build a very exciting sexual partnership out of that.

A business partnership isn't really Libra's sort of thing, or at least not in the same way that it is for the Capricorn. On the other hand, marriage is a very Libran thing. You'll have a stylish home but a lazy partner; because once the relationship is permanent, the Libran's purpose is complete!

Capricorn - Scorpio

This is an easy relationship from your point of view. There are some pairings in the zodiac that fit together so closely that the joins are invisible and the combined strength of the two is more than twice their single strength. It isn't a comfortable partnership to be in, but it certainly achieves its aims. It's ruthless, dominant and wonderfully effective.

Scorpio is interested in the maintenance of power and control. To him, knowing how people are likely to react is essential intelligence, and when he has this intelligence, he can control the entire situation. Everything that a Scorpio attempts is done with tremendous power, directed in precisely the right way to ensure the desired result. Scorpios are secretive people and they go to great lengths to keep their own movements hidden. They also go to great lengths to determine and discover the hidden movements of everybody else. As you can see, they are very powerful yet very private. You're different in that you want to be in power and publicly recognized for it. Certainly there's much that you have in common, and you're close enough in outlook to enjoy each other's company.

Scorpio is trying to be powerful and you're trying to be in a position of power. One is a condition of potential, and the other an established state. You represent what happens when the Scorpio's power is converted into material wealth, and he represents the invisible network of influence that later becomes crystallized within the organizational structure you love so much.

He sees you as being the steady state of permanent control, very much the sort of thing that he admires. He's seeing the weight of Saturn, which restricts and encloses. He works through Mars, that irresistible force applied suddenly and to one point, and so he doesn't have your stamina or your patience. You don't have his immediate power, though, so it balances out.

You're not likely to be friends so much as co-conspirators. You'll have a special vocabulary of code words and symbols that refer to people in positions of power and their position in your schemes. From the outside, it seems impenetrable, untrustworthy and generally hostile; but inside the partnership, you're having a glorious time. This is the only relationship that has what you would no doubt describe as a properly professional and serious outlook on life. It's also the only one where the other partner is at least as ambitious as you are.

You don't generally mix business and your emotions, so be doubly careful with the Scorpio, whose business is emotions. He will be as cool and businesslike as you are, but he will be playing with your emotions the whole time. You'll see just how important they are to him if you develop your friendship into an affair, and you'll also be introduced to the full force of Mars. Scorpio will knock you flat sexually, though it's comforting to know that eventually, after a very long time, you'll prove to be the stronger of the two, simply because of your greater capacity for endurance. It will take too much out of you to find out though; so don't try to match him if you argue on this subject.

As business partners, you were made for each other. There ought to be a law against business partnerships of this sort, to give the others a chance. As marriage partners, you should be reasonably suited. You'll need to be in the seat at the head of the table, but he will actually be in control, because marriages are emotional things, and that's where he's stronger. If he gets obsessive about something, you'll have to let him win, because he will break up all that you've built together rather than lose, and you wouldn't want that.

Capricorn - Sagittarius

Sagittarians seem to embody all the things you'd rather not come into contact with, and being with them just brings out the worst in you. Yet, they are irresistible. There's something engaging about them that you feel drawn to, and wish that you weren't. Sagittarians are open and optimistic people. To them, everything is full of life and interest, and they like nothing better than to have something new and untried to look into. They are insatiably curious and childishly trusting. In their world, there are no hidden pitfalls, and even if there are, they know that they will come to no harm. All of this you can tolerate quite easily. To you it seems simply that they are rather young in their outlook, and you find yourself adopting a parental role with them. You indulge their enthusiasm with an avuncular twinkle in your eye, and they play up to it.

What is less easy for you to tolerate is their knowledge. Sagittarians seem to have been born wise beyond their years, and they already know all that there is to know about everything before you even open a conversation with them. Once you do, they assume that you'd like to know what they know, and they tell you. They are bubbling over with knowledge, and they simply can't keep it all to themselves. This is a bit hard for you to take. You have fairly traditional views on education, and it goes against the grain to be told where you're going wrong by somebody who behaves like a five-year-old with a new toy the whole time. What makes things worse, is they're usually right.

The most incomprehensible thing of all about Sagittarians is their insistence on freedom and movement. They won't let themselves settle down the way you think they should. The very idea of staying in the same job or doing the same thing for years on end the way you do, makes them feel faint, and quite often they will change jobs or even partners, for no other reason than that they have been doing the same thing for the last three years, and it bothers them.

You know how fond you are of a structured and ordered existence, and you see the rules and regulations of a formal lifestyle as a solid framework on which to build. Sagittarians are the opposite. They are frightened of frameworks, because to their eyes every framework looks like a cage. Being trapped is their greatest fear. They are never afraid of anything new, but the thought of never changing from something that they don't like bothers them. You would always prefer an eternity of doing something that you know well, no matter how bad it is, to the possibility of the unknown and untried. You see them as childish, charming, infuriatingly clever and short of staying power. They see you as successful and powerful, but lacking in sparkle and far too hardworking for your own good.

Any friendship between you is likely to be built on a sense of mutual fascination. Most probably, the Sagittarian will take you on as a project, attempting to inject what he sees as necessary gaiety into your life. You'll feel that he needs calming down and directing and will attempt to do that for him. If you succeed, you'll quench the fire in him completely, so it's probably a better idea to allow yourself to be taken along with him on some of his adventures, because as long as you stay close to him you'll come to no harm.

Pick somebody else as a business partner, because Sagittarians are rarely interested in high finance. Money doesn't seem as real to them as it does to you and the work required to make a lot of it simply isn't worth it to them. Marrying a Sagittarian is actually a very smart move from your point of view, provided that you don't stifle them. They are always warm and forward-looking, which is a big bonus in a lifelong relationship, but for them to maintain this outlook, you must be flexible and not try to tie them down too much.

A Sagittarian lover will be everything you could want while he stays interested in you. Sagittarians get bored after a while and start looking around for somebody new. Not better, just new. There's no question of not making the grade, it's just that novelty is a big factor in attracting a Sagittarian.

Capricorn - Capricorn

Forming a relationship with somebody of your own sign is easy on the surface, because you should know what you're getting. There are same-sign combinations that don't work as well as they should, for the simple reason that it's part of the nature of the sign to resent competition, and that can happen here. The only drawback to this relationship is that both of you are striving to get to the top. If the relationship is the most important thing in your lives, then one of you has to lose somewhere and that will cause resentment. There's an easy way round the problem, and it's one that most Capricorn partners employ without even thinking about it.

It's simply not to let the relationship become the most important thing in your life. Most Capricorns are far more interested in their work than they are in their private lives anyway. Rightly so, since public success rather than private happiness is your eventual goal. Besides, you can always pack your private affairs into a separate compartment of your life, and give them some time and attention when you get a spare minute, so they needn't interfere with your career at all.

Your only problem in the past has been to find somebody who understands all this, somebody who will give you support when you need it, somebody who is as keen to succeed as you are, and who will understand when you're too busy to give them any time, even though they may need it. This person will have to be at least as tough as you are, at least as able to endure emotional hardship and at least as able to sacrifice the comforts and pleasures of the present for the rewards of the future. What could be better than another Capricorn? Having another Capricorn as a partner in any sense of the word, means that they understand your motivation, and will automatically make allowances for those times when you're too busy to be sociable, and when other signs would say you were being miserable or rude.

It sounds a good idea on the surface, but it means that the relationship will have a very low emotional content; how could it be otherwise? If you want warmth, love and affection in your life, to compensate for those qualities that you know that you lack, then don't choose another version of yourself to supply them. On the other hand, if you really are dedicated to getting on in life, and you don't feel comfortable with intangible things like sentiment and affection, then this will no doubt suit you. If you do choose this partnership, then you'll both be supporting each other in your struggles, and as the years go by, the relationship will become a sort of achievement factory. Both of you will rise higher and higher in your chosen professions, gaining more and more of that Capricorn product, which is money.

As a light friendship, this pairing has little time to say more than a few words as you pass in the lift at the office, but as a life partnership, either in business or as a marriage, it's much more productive, as we've already seen. The key element is, of course, time. Capricorn does everything best over the long term, and relationships are just the same.

Sexually, the success of the relationship depends on how much time you're prepared to give to this side of it. Sex, power, money and status are interchangeable to you, and it will be very satisfying to you to have a partner who understands this without being told. This could be the only sexual pairing where you can really express your understanding of sex and power, and where you won't put your partner off.

Capricorn - Aquarius

The sign that's one stage further on in the zodiacal cycle from your own is always enticing but elusive. Usually it represents some sort of idea which is beyond your capabilities and that's governed by a planet whose energies are very different from your own. This is a unique case, because you're the only pair in the horoscope that are side by side and both ruled by the same planet, namely Saturn.

You know what you will find in another Saturnine individual, and that familiarity before the event, so to speak, gives you confidence. They will be reserved, unemotional and a bit cool. This is true, but in every other respect, they are vastly different from you. The things that will hit you hardest are that they are very friendly and sociable, which you are not on the whole; and secondly, that they are very firmly opposed to the idea of anybody being in a position of power over anybody else.

This will confuse you. Surely, Saturn will give them some sense of structure. Indeed it does, but in the opposite direction to yours. You're concerned with vertical structures, but Aquarius is concerned with horizontal structures, where everybody is at the same level.

Aquarius is an Air sign, which means that they are working with words and ideas, a realm in which you're not at home. If you watch an Aquarian in action in any social gathering, you'll be able to see how similar he is to you. The only reason you've not seen it before is that you're so much at sea in any sort of personal or emotional situation that you think that all situations are the same. In fact, each group and each party is different, and if you watch the Aquarian, you'll be able to see how he handles people with the same practiced ease that you handle money. He's always at the center of the discussion, but he's never attached to one particular person. The party seems to flow around him, but he's never moved along by it. Although he's very much part of the crowd, he's not of the same stuff as the crowd; he's just a little bit different, separate, distanced almost.

That same distance is there in his eyes if you look. He knows what he's doing the whole time. He's not heartless, and he's not calculating or manipulative, but he doesn't allow himself to be carried away unless he wants it to be that way. It's as though he's ballasted, so that he always floats and always stays upright. In fact, he is ballasted - by Saturn. Once you've seen how cool he is, and how he keeps himself separate and different from all his friends, whilst being a good friend to all of them, you'll be hooked. You'll say to yourself, here is somebody who is as professional in his social life as I am in my business life.

There's more to him than that, actually. He has high principles, humanitarian politics and a determinedly modernist outlook on life, which doesn't fit at all with your cherished ideals of tradition and privilege. You'll fight over these things as your friendship deepens. You may see him as cool and stylish, but he sees you as self-centered, over-conventional and an opponent of progress. It's always much more difficult to think kindly of the sign behind you than the one in front of you, mainly because the sign behind you shows you your own bad side in some respects. For instance, some Aquarians are mercenary enough to trade their principles for hard cash, which is very Capricorn!

Because he's cool, and you're often too busy to give the time to such things, you may not develop a sexual relationship at all. Even if you do, it will be characterized by its cool, post-modernist feeling. Aquarius isn't likely to be quite the business partner of your dreams, though his social skills could undoubtedly be put to good use. Like all the Air signs, he isn't really at home in fixed routines where the product is more important than the people are, because he prefers it the other way round.

As a marriage partner, he's a much better bet. He's cool enough not to make emotional demands upon you, and independent enough to have things to do when you're working late. The question is, though, are you really interested enough in each other to marry in the first place?

Capricorn - Pisces

This is as unlikely a combination as you could ever imagine, and yet it works surprisingly well. You couldn't wish for a less structured and less ambitious person than a Piscean, and yet, they seem to welcome you, and you seem to enjoy their very changeability. How does this come about?

Partly it's because of their extreme sensitivity. You're not very good at expressing yourself, and you only give the slightest hint when you think that you're opening your heart to the world. Pisceans are sensitive enough to pick up the little that you offer, and respond to it in a big enough way for you to gain emotional satisfaction from it. Their response, though genuine, is in no way forceful or enveloping, so it will break over you like a wave on the shore, leaving you unchanged, and that's just how you want it. What you want is somebody who can respond to your needs, but whose response doesn't throw you off-course in any way, or stop you from doing what you see as your work. Pisceans fit the bill. There's a lot of emotion in a Capricorn, but it's slow and deep. The Capricorn animal has the tail of a fish, while Pisces is the sign of the fishes, so Pisces is the only sign through which Capricorn can express emotional energy of this particular kind.

On any other level than the emotional, Pisceans are just the same as you are. To be fair, they are just the same as anybody else in the zodiac, because they are able to take on the qualities of the person they are with at the time through a process of absorption and reflection. This means that while they are involved with you, they are just as ambitious and hard headed as you are. Most of the time, Pisceans are unsure of which direction to take. The fact that you're very sure of where you're going is attractive to them. While they are with you, they can become part of your life and take your firmness of direction upon themselves. It means, of course, that they are then heading in the same direction as you are, but the fact is that they don't care about where they are going, as long as they are going somewhere.

You mustn't expect them to be able to be firm on their own account; what happens is that you take the decisions, and they will mimic you. They probably won't do anything forcefully enough for your taste, so you'll find some of your schemes are starting to come loose at the edges. Only you have the power and the authority necessary to hold things the way you want them. At the same time, if you control their actions too closely, they will be unhappy and try to escape. Piscean fish are very sensitive to any sort of pressure, and it causes them a lot of pain.

Friendship between you is likely to be formed from a basis of mutual emotional sympathy. If you keep it at that level, without trying to control or restrict them, then the friendship should be satisfying to you both. You could do wonders in business with a Piscean if you're in any kind of media business, because they just slip right in.

If you become lovers, then you'll have to make allowances for their changeable moods, and they will have to allow for your lack of imagination (by their standards)! Marriage probably isn't such a good idea for you, though, because they will want more of your time than you're prepared to spare them.

The Approach to Relationships: Aquarius

SYMBOL: WATER-BEARER	♒	ELEMENT: AIR
PLANET: SATURN	♄	QUALITY: FIXED

As an Air sign, like Gemini and Libra, Aquarius' prime energy is mental; ideas, words and speech are what keep these signs going. Aquarius is also a Fixed sign, so here the words and ideas somehow have to be slowed down, kept still. It's the business of Fixed signs to look after what comes their way, caring for it, making it strong and firm, but not adding to it or changing it in any way.

Aquarians care for the world at large, not for themselves. They care for those who have less than the rest, because they sincerely believe that everybody should be equal. They are interested in, and feel comfortable in, any social group; yet they are somehow loners in every group they join - individualists who never quite fit, and are noticeably cool in personal relationships.

Because Aquarius is like a lunar version of Saturn, his energies are always applied for the public good, and in a compassionate manner. Lunar light is a caring light, though not a light in itself - it reflects the light it receives from elsewhere. Thus, Aquarius needs other people around him before he can exercise his social principles, and so he makes sure that he always has plenty of company.

Aquarius - Aries

On the surface, this relationship has a lot to recommend it. Arians are strong and active, and they like to be where the action is; they don't want to stay at home and read a book. They are highly independent and self-motivating and they don't need somebody else to help them get the best out of their life. You may think that because you, too, are of an independent turn of mind and you enjoy the social scene, that you'd be ideally suited. Not so: you are indeed both independent, and the result is that you don't really need each other.

Arians are very active but also very physical. They are at their best when they are actually doing something, and using their muscles to do it. Their particular kind of planetary energy needs to be expressed through the functioning of their bodies. When they are not physically active, they don't know what to do. Not surprisingly, they try to spend as much time as they can in action. Their universe is physical, so they like real problems that they can overcome through hard work and sweat. Yours is the world of ideas - the principles of the matter are more important to you than how they are put into action, and you'll have a great deal of difficulty understanding the Arian's insistence on doing it himself. He likes to be personally involved, because only if he actually does things for himself can he get anything out of the experience. In this respect, he's very different from you, because you don't mind at all if somebody else does the deed.

He's independent, as you are, but more than that, he's individual. He's concerned entirely for and with, his own existence. It isn't that he's selfish; it's simply that other people are outside his comprehension. All of his values come from the feelings that he obtains by doing things, and he can't understand anything that's not in his own direct experience. He can't understand why other people aren't the same, either. Such a sense of being alone and individual, the center of existence, is very alien to you. You're the representative of the ideal of doing things in groups. You see everything as part of a larger society, whose members share the same hopes and ambitions. You like to think of yourself as independent and aloof, but only within the framework of a larger group. Aries doesn't have to recognize the existence of any group, or even of society; he's independent, full stop.

You see him as a tremendously energetic person; full of confidence and eager to do whatever there is to be done. You're slightly in awe of his keenness for getting his hands dirty, as you can't quite bring yourself to get so involved with anything. He seems childishly naive, in some respects, and his opinions seem to be formed instantaneously, without any thought for what other people might say. He seems never to consider what might lie behind some of the things in which he gets involved.

He sees you as lively and sociable, but oddly unwilling to say what you really mean. What he likes about you is that you can always see the reasons behind things, and the helpful way you explain these to him makes him feel that you have his interests at heart. He will do anything he can for somebody as helpful and as friendly as you are, because he's like a child who is eager to please. You like being useful to Arians, because it's part of how you work. In return, they give you their enthusiasm and energy, and the warmth your cold saturnine heart needs.

You may not make the best of lovers, because you just can't muster enough heat to match the Arian's fiery Mars. You have strength, stamina of your own and a cool sense of the erotic and the tantalizing, but Aries isn't subtle enough to appreciate you on that level. He likes it hot, physical, and right now, please.

Marriage is a difficult subject for either of you to think about. It stops the Arian from rushing off and doing things on his own, and it means that you have to commit yourself to one person. You both need movement, so marriage may not suit either of you. Even if you're sure that it's what you want, you may have to wait a very long time before you find an Arian who feels the same way.

As business partners, you should be very successful. You can do the thinking, and he can do the work - between you, you should go a long way.

Aquarius - Taurus

This pairing isn't very easy, at least not in its initial stages, because you're so very different in almost every way. You'd like to be out with your friends, but the Taurean would rather stay at home. You welcome new ideas because they exercise your mind, but the Taurean hates them, because he likes things to be predictably constant. Above all, your definition of wealth is in ideas, but theirs is in possessions.

The thing that will strike you most strongly about Taureans is their insistence on familiarity and security. They like to be in familiar surroundings, doing things the way that they have always done them, so anything that takes them into unfamiliar territory is quite frightening to them. If they can't avoid being away from home, they will try to impose their own routines on their new surroundings. Security is a physical thing to a Taurean; he gets real comfort from his possessions. He's also comforted by what he wears and particularly by what he eats. The idea that mere possessions could improve your opinion of yourself is likely to fascinate you, but you won't really understand it. They seem to be so easily satisfied that you wish they had a broader outlook, one which took in the needs of other people, and which saw beyond the simple acquisition of material security.

From their point of view, they see you as kind and fair but cold and distant. You don't seem to enjoy yourself enough in their opinion. You're as comfortable in the company of your friends as they are in the company of their favorite possessions, and they can appreciate that, but you don't seem to get any real enjoyment from the things you have and they think that's rather sad. Still, as long as you don't interfere with what they have and don't threaten their territory, they won't mind too much.

There's one area in which you have a common interest, and that's music. Not all Taureans are musical, and neither are all Aquarians for that matter, but most of you are. The reasons for this are linked to the planets that govern your signs. Taurus seeks the comfort of a pleasant environment for all of his senses. This includes his hearing, so he will be very fond of tunes he knows well. He's fonder of pure melody than you are, though you probably have a better understanding of rhythm and time. Together, Venus and Saturn produce harmony (in a musical sense); a shared interest in music may well help form a friendship between you.

A friendship between you works best if you let yourself become an addition to his group of friends; that way, you get a wider circle of acquaintance, and he doesn't lose anything with which he was familiar before, which is the best arrangement for both of you.

An affair between you could be better than you might think. You're both strong, and both have stamina. Your emotional coolness will hurt him though, and his passion will surprise you. His possessiveness will bother you, too, because you like freedom and variety. You'll both need to compromise, and you're more flexible than he is though, so it's really up to you, if you think it's worth it. The same problems occur in a marriage. They will want to do things their way or not at all, and you'll have to be very persistent if you are to get them to make any major changes. Lack of commitment isn't the problem, it's a simple unwillingness to change, and you'll find that quite wearing.

As business partners, you'll be supportive to each other, but the partnership will lack the spirit of enterprise necessary to make new projects successful. The Taurean is wary of anything new, and you won't allow yourself the depth of involvement that's a precursor to success.

Aquarius - Gemini

This is a very comfortable and entertaining relationship for you. You're both Air signs, and that means that you're both more concerned with words and ideas than with actions, and neither of you like getting bogged down in the emotional side of things. Gemini is very dry indeed emotionally, because he's almost without deep feelings at all. As far as you're concerned, this isn't a problem, and anyway you're both so busy talking to each other and laughing at each other's jokes that the subject hardly ever crops up.

When it does, you'll notice something about the Gemini that you find a little distasteful. He is unprincipled. Alternatively, as he would no doubt put it, he's flexible in his thinking. To him, an idea is something to play with. He likes to turn it around in his mind, see if he can get it to mean something else, and see if he can make new things from it. Geminis love to experiment in this way with words. Ideas are almost sacred things to you, to be strengthened rather than dismantled, and to be used for the guidance of humankind rather than for the amusement of an individual. Ah, well, that's the difference between the Mutable Air sign and the Fixed Air sign. It would probably do you good to be able to take your beliefs less dogmatically, and to be able to play with them in the Gemini's fashion.

For his part, Gemini sees you as just a little bit dull. Don't be upset: he just likes people to be lively and quick-witted, with an eye for a bargain and a bit of a game on the side. Your big talent is of being friendly to everybody, and being the driving force behind any group you care to join, but that isn't important to him. He can talk to anybody he likes and be friendly too, if it suits him. All the Air signs can, so it's not an impressive thing, in his view. Groups of people, and particularly the beliefs and opinions they all share, don't matter to him. Geminis prefer to work on an individual basis and have little time for fixed opinions. He's willing to listen to what you have to say though, particularly if he hasn't heard it before. His appetite for novelty is even greater than yours is. He uses you as a source of new ideas, which he then plays with and disassembles to see if there's anything else interesting contained in them. This is a one-way process; so don't expect him to contribute anything in return. If he did, would you listen? If you listened, would you trust what he had to say?

The friendship between you is based largely on the fact that you both enjoy talking. You enjoy talking to each other and you enjoy talking to other people too, which means that you can keep up the social circulation that you both need without threatening the relationship between you. Obviously, this is a good thing. The other good thing about this pairing is that neither of you expects or offers any sort of deep emotional attachment. You're "just good friends", literally! The disadvantage of this is that you don't support each other much, but then neither of you expects it, so that isn't so bad.

As lovers, you're quite well matched as neither of you is intense, and you share a sense of humor. Gemini may be too lightweight for Aquarius, because in the final analysis, he would probably rather play games than get serious about anything.

In marriage, as in business, the big question is whether you'd ever get anything done. You like each other well enough, and you can keep each other amused forever, but can you get down to things and get the job done?

Aquarius - Cancer

This is a difficult relationship from your point of view. Almost everything about a Cancerian is exactly opposed to your own point of view, and you'll find it very difficult to get to know them intimately enough for you to understand why they feel the way they do. This is a great pity in many ways, as both of you would like and care for the other very much, since caring is what you both do best, albeit in very different ways.

You're comfortable in a crowd of people, especially if they are your friends. People expect to bump into you socially, and they know that if they go to a party the chances are that you'll be there, chattering away to all and sundry. You also know that you have a private, interior personality, which is known only to you, and never communicated to anyone else at all, not ever. The public face is friendly and helpful, but the private person may not be. Whatever he is, he has a very serious view of himself, and he likes his own company and his own thoughts best. When his own thoughts look likely to take up too much of his time, the private person puts on a public face, and goes out with his friends or he does something that helps others. He does anything to turn his attention away from himself.

Can you imagine a person whose interior is all that they have? Can you imagine a person as private as you are inside, but who has no public personality to hide behind, and whose sense of insecurity makes them shy and nervous when they have to deal with more than a few people at once? Cancer is like that. You're similar in many respects. Both of you need other people to bring out the best in you, to allow you to communicate your planetary energies fully. You like to think that you can be of use to society as a whole. Cancer likes to think that he can be of use to his immediate family and friends. You work on a much larger scale in time as well as space, because you're often thinking about the far future when you adopt a course of action, but you're both trying to do the same thing, which is to benefit other people and to be appreciated for that.

Cancer's urge is to protect and nourish, whereas yours is more impersonal, and this is the difference between the emotional response and the logical response. Aquarians have a distrust of emotional responses. They are random things, and they can appear to distort the truth. You're always concerned that things should be fair and true, without bias of any kind and you'll suppress your own emotional responses to eliminate any possible bias in your own judgments.

Cancer is all emotion and no logic. Emotional security is all that interests him. He will do anything to protect himself and his family against what he sees as a hostile world, and he values the affection they give in return. You'll see them as defensive, shy worriers, while they see you as friendly but impersonal. A friendship between you will take some time to get going, as you'd first have to gain their confidence, and then you'd have to trust them with your internal emotions. It may not be possible for you to do this. If you manage it, you can be sure that Cancer will look after you with a devotion you could not have imagined. What you can offer them is an example of caring on a bigger scale, because if they can understand it, they will take it as seriously as you do. It may not be possible for them to widen their viewpoint sufficiently for you, but they will appreciate the ideals behind your opinions. They are likely to see you as being too cold emotionally.

As business partners, you could do very well indeed. Each of you supplies what the other lacks. In addition, being business partners rather than having an emotional bond keeps things on the unemotional basis.

As lovers, you'd be completely unable to reply to Cancer's emotional demands, and quite unused to the depth they require. You'd feel lost and trapped, which would be a very uncomfortable situation for you, and one perhaps best avoided. In time, if you learned how to trust and respond to each other, you might consider marriage. It wouldn't be easy, as you prefer being on your own, and they need to cling, so you'd both have to make major adjustments.

Aquarius - Leo

This is the sign of the zodiac you find it easiest to dislike, and the feeling is entirely mutual, but provided that neither of you take yourselves too seriously you can be quite good friends, which is something that isn't unknown with signs opposite each other.

The reason for your antipathy is related to your principles of equality, because Leos have an inbuilt feeling of superiority. It seems to them that they are better than the rest of us, as they consider themselves to be grander, larger than life and altogether more important than other people. As a result, they often have extravagant and flamboyant lifestyles and they surround themselves with lots of friends and admirers. It often seems as though Leo's life is one long party, and that his social life is similar to that of a king and his court. In your view, everybody should be the same. When you see the Leo being the center of attention, you want to give somebody else a turn. You want to see him made to look silly or somehow humbled, and to stop him being so self-important. Note that you don't want a chance to wear the crown yourself; you just don't want him to, either.

What you haven't seen is that although you may not need the Leo to put some light into your life, other people do. His energy and warmth are given out for free. He's an essential part of any group of people, and he is its center. A great many people like being around Leos, and to bring him down to the same level as the rest of us would not only harm him, it would deprive us of the good he does.

If nothing else, Leo is personal. He's very fond of simply being himself. You, of course, are impersonal. What you do or what you represent, is far more important to you than who you are. You see him as selfish and opinionated, without much care for the future or for that of anyone else, while he sees you as another face in the crowd, but one whose high principles mean that he has forgotten how to enjoy himself. You'll see, I hope, that you're both wrong. You're trying to define the other person's existence in terms of what has value for you, but not what has value for him.

If you're prepared to let him be at the center of things, and take the leading role, then things will be better, because he will be in his natural place. Your place is around him and by him, but not at the center. You can still enjoy the company of the rest of your friends. Indeed, the group will be brighter for having the Leo at its center. All you have to do is accept his version of himself and not try to limit him. You're both very sociable people and have plenty to contribute to any group in your own ways. If you spend your time at war, nobody will benefit.

Whether or not you succeed as lovers depends on whether you let yourself accept what he has to offer. Leos are genuinely warm and generous people. You're unused to such open affection, and may not allow yourself to be warmed by him. If you do, you may feel that you have to offer something in return. Not so, because Leos are content if you enjoy what they offer. All you have to do is tell him how much you enjoy it.

As business partners you should let Leo be seen as the boss. He may not be the boss, but he must be seen that way. He does do things in an expansive way, but he's no fool: Leos are much better organized than most people expect, and they are very capable of looking after a number of things at once. He will appreciate, in private at any rate, your cool appraisals of the situations you face.

As a marriage partner, you could do a lot worse. Leo will have to be lord in his own home, but he will provide a feeling of well-being and warmth that you could never produce on your own.

Aquarius - Virgo

This is a difficult one, but at least there are no emotional problems here. Virgo usually keeps his feelings to himself unless he's very angry, and then it will be due to some rule being broken, rather than an outburst of feelings. You feel at home with his kind of mentality. You're both reasonable people, and you both have fondness for reasoned scientific thought. Virgo likes to know what the correct way of doing anything is supposed to be, and you like to do things for the right reasons, so there are plenty of similarities there.

Virgo is wonderfully practical in your eyes. You're better at handling ideas than the practicalities of their application, but Virgo is one step on from you, as he's the type of person who understands the machines that do the work. To you, this interest and knowledge about things at their most basic level is as fascinating and as remote as molecular biology. You're full of interest and admiration, but you know that you could never do this sort of thing for yourself.

In Virgo, you see your own idealism translated to the material world. Virgos think things through first. They decide what to do, and then do it in the best way possible, making the best use of the tools and time that they have available. Nothing is done haphazardly, and everything is to the highest possible standard, no matter what it costs in effort. Virgoans are not lazy and they are not selfish either, so they seem to exist to do things for other people, and in the best possible way.

You like all this. You like his ability to see into things, as it matches your own. The problems start when you realize that looking into things is the end of the matter as far as he's concerned. His close-up view of the details of things never takes in the whole picture. What really matters to you, the universal application of ideas, and this has little interest for him. Ideas aren't practical things, as far as he's concerned, and his view of things doesn't really lend itself to considering more than one person at a time. The problem is one of incompatibility, but with an interesting twist. You have similar approaches to things, but you work in different worlds and on different scales, so there's almost no common ground.

A friendship between you isn't impossible, by any means. You're capable of being friendly to anyone, because you're an Air sign, and although he's an Earth sign, he's Mutable, which speeds him up to somewhere near your pace. In addition, he's ruled by Mercury, the planet of words, and while he isn't a talking machine, he's chatty enough. You seem to want to talk to each other, your aims and methods interest each other and your analytical approaches do too.

Though you're suited to each other, you're not really suited to being lovers. Both of you are cool emotionally, and neither of you can generate the heat and passion necessary for an affair to be self-sustaining. It just isn't that important to you. It isn't really the right situation for your talents. Aquarius prefers to be appreciated by the world rather than by one person, while Virgo's often critical comments can destroy a relationship before it has had time to establish itself.

This partnership is a good one from a business point of view, though. You each provide what the other lacks. Add your talent for seeing the larger situation to the Virgo's capacity for hard work and you have a very productive combination. A marriage between you would be as productive as a business partnership, but you might have some trouble generating enough emotional warmth, so you could grow apart from each other after a while.

Aquarius - Libra

This is probably the easiest of your relationships. Libra is interested in the same sort of thing as you are, which is talking to others, and he goes about it in a similar sort of way. He's as friendly and as outgoing as you are, and as much at home in a social situation. If anything, you're too much like one another!

What first attracts you to a Libran is his lightness and pleasantness. He seems to have a knack of putting you at your ease and of saying things that you want to hear. What he says isn't necessarily new or different, but he seems to say it in a way that you find agreeable, and you're left with the impression that this is a very nice person to know. He's genuinely interested in being your friend, but he never makes any demands on you, and this is exactly the sort of thing you want.

What you're reacting to here is an energy that's similar to your own. The great thing about it, as far as you're concerned, is that the Libran is light, bright, and flexible, and he's never bogged down with the dark waters of emotional demands and expectations. It's essentially a surface thing, and doesn't touch the inner layers of the person at all. Some people would consider this to be a major drawback, and they would want the relationship to come from the core of the person rather than the surface, but it suits you well, and it suits the Libran too. A relationship between you is bright, friendly and full of new ideas. Neither of you give yourselves completely to the other, but that doesn't matter at all. The relationship wouldn't be able to stand the extra weight if you did, and neither of you would want the responsibility of the other one's inner self anyway.

What you have that the Libran doesn't have is the ability to work on the grand scale. As you get to know a Libran, and watch him in company, you'll see that he's dedicated to forming personal relationships on a one-to-one level. He has many individual friends and he treats each one separately as though he were the only other person in the world. You have lots of friends, but you see them as a group and have fun with them together, and you prefer to see them together rather than in individual, one-to-one relationships, which are sometimes more intense than you would like.

What he has is charm, and this is a particular kind of charm that you lack. This doesn't mean that you're tongue-tied and clumsy, but Libra's charm is so strong that it becomes a physical force, which shows itself as grace and style. He doesn't seem to be able to make a clumsy move. He always looks attractive whatever he wears, and his sense of color and style is perfect. Librans can make any place nicer just by being there. You can't do that, and if you tried, it would come out as a better way of life instead of a more enjoyable one. They're not the same thing.

If your friendship develops into an affair, you need have no fear. It will be every bit as enjoyable as your original relationship. Most affairs have a heavy emotional ingredient and you're rightly wary of that, but Libra is different. For him, an affair is a thing of Romance with a capital "R". It becomes a game where roles are played and enjoyed in place of real feelings and commitment, and you can enjoy that as much as he does. Sexually you're both playful and not too demanding, so you're a good match for each other.

In business, you're not quite such a good pairing, unless you're in some kind of public relations or personnel business. You'd both rather sit and talk to people than get on with the serious business of working, and since neither of you are Earth signs you both lack the ability to convert work into money. Marriage would be a good thing from your point of view. Your Libran will make sure you have an attractive life and a beautiful home, but he needs your sense of organization to stop him being lazy.

Aquarius - Scorpio

You may be attracted to a Scorpio, and that's nothing to be worried about, because everybody is attracted to Scorpios. If you decide to form some sort of a relationship with a Scorpio though, you'd be well advised to think about what you're taking on. They work in a very different way from you. They see everything in terms of emotions, and they will rearrange the rules of the game to suit themselves, which is something you would never do. Finally, they will never release you, so this may turn out to be more than you want.

It would be a reasonable thing to assume that, since you're both Fixed signs, you're similar. You both like to finish what you start, but there the similarity ends. For your part, you like to understand and be involved in a common interest that draws different people together as friends and associates. The Scorpio wants to understand and control the desires and concerns that make different people into friends and associates. Try it this way. If all of society was in a forest, and all the people were trees, then the Aquarian would only see the topmost leaves waving as the wind blew over them, while the Scorpio would want to control the underground and everything that the roots of the trees drank from.

In your view, people act the way they do because they all have a shared belief. They act for the best of motives, so things will be better in the end for all of us. In the Scorpio view, people act the way they do because they all have desires and fears. If the Scorpio can know what these are, he can control the situation. Your view is upwards and outwards, while his is inwards and downwards. He's at least as penetrating and analytical as you are, but he's looking for different things. Universal principles and humanitarian ideas don't interest him. He works to provide extra information for himself. He's envious of your understanding of society as a whole, as he has to spend too much time with individuals. He would like to develop your talent for seeing the larger scene. He could do with some of your social skills too, or so he thinks. He has a reputation for being secretive or for being irresistibly sexy, and he would actually like to be anonymously pleasant on the surface whilst remaining secretly powerful underneath. Your social skills don't actually work that way, but that's how he sees you.

You see him as magnetically attractive and very powerful. He seems to have the same sort of mental control that you have and the same cold logic. He also seems to have the physical power that you lack, but it's held in check and controlled, in the way you're sure that you would do if you had that power. This is only your viewpoint however, because he isn't really like that. He doesn't have your cold logic at all; he has a hot, irrational temper, held down and controlled by cold logic and he dare not let it go. It's a much more explosive situation than yours. He can't allow himself the luxury of being kind to others in the way you can, because he needs all his energy to look after himself.

A friendship between you is bound to be something of a battle. It will only take you a few minutes to realize that Scorpios are interested primarily in themselves, and that they will happily use whatever you have to offer them for their own profit, without offering anything in return. You need the exchange of ideas and friendship, and this isn't it. As soon as you can get away from the scorpion's claws, you'll be off. The best way to do it is to be even cooler than usual, because Scorpio reacts to your emotional heat.

You're most unsuited as lovers, unless you're specifically trying to experience passion, possessiveness, jealousy, obsession and all the other high emotions that usually have so little meaning to you. Scorpios take sex very seriously – much too seriously to talk about it.

The major obstacle to your business success is that Scorpio can only trust you if he controls you. You're above that sort of thing, and the suggestion that you might be unprincipled annoys you. In any case, you'd rather not be in business with him than be controlled by him.

Marriage would be another battleground. Eventually, you might understand him and make allowances for him, and in return, you'd have a partner whose drive and sensuality will really fire your imagination. You'd stay with each other. Fixed signs do stay put, but he will always be suspicious of anything new or different. Can you live with that?

Aquarius - Sagittarius

This relationship forms very easily. It must have seemed up to now that there's no other sign of zodiac where the mind is interested in ideas for their own sake in the way that yours is. You must also have been disappointed to find that almost everybody else is concerned primarily with themselves and their own welfare, and in the odd occasion where this is not so (Libra), attention seems to be focused on two or three people at the most. Sagittarius can change all that. Sagittarians are so confident in themselves and their ability to cope with anything life can throw at them, that they give almost none of their attention to their own well-being. Instead, they direct their energy upwards and outwards and dedicate themselves entirely to the quest for, and the spreading of, knowledge. Sagittarians are interested in the truth that lies behind everything.

Here at last is the partner with whom you can swap ideas and experiences all day long! It's true, and it's even better than you had dared hope. Sagittarius thinks in a different way from you, but a way that's complementary to your own. You can even take a positive interest in the difference in your approaches!

The difference is a simple one. You work from the outside inwards, defining a general principle in a logical manner, and applying it to everybody equally. The approach is very scientific. Sagittarius works from the inside outwards, from an unshakeable belief in what must be right. You'll be tempted to label this sort of knowledge as "intuitive", but you'd be wrong. Sagittarians are inspired, they look for knowledge in everything and they find it. This process is endlessly absorbing to you. You could sit and watch it for hours. Sagittarians like to have somebody to talk to and to share their discoveries with them, but that person has to be open to big ideas, and they have to be able to think clearly. You're exactly the right person for the job.

Friendship between you is almost instantaneous. You have so much that you want to tell each other! They are more emotional than you are, but because the dominant emotion is happy enthusiasm, you enjoy them being that way. They see you as a bit on the reserved side, but they are determined to make you laugh if they can: they feel sure that you're capable of it! As lovers, you'll probably laugh a lot. Sagittarians have a silly and boisterous side to them, but it's so obvious they don't take things seriously that you don't feel trapped by becoming involved. They also like to stay fancy-free if they can, and as you like to be independent too, you're unlikely to complain.

In business, you could be unstoppable. Sagittarius has the drive you sometimes lack, and you have the overall sense of organization that gets lost in his enthusiasm. You make a great team. The same holds true for marriage. The only question there is whether you can each sacrifice your independence to the extent of actually getting married! If you do, you won't regret it, but it will be a difficult thing for either of you to do. You may well decide that you're happy enough with each other as you are, and not bother.

Aquarius - Capricorn

The sign that's behind you in the zodiacal sequence usually represents all the things that you've left behind, so to speak. People from that sign are living examples of the sort of qualities you'd like to think that you've outgrown.

Capricorns take their station in life very seriously. They work very hard and for a very long time, denying themselves all the comforts that the other signs find so enjoyable, but keeping their sights fixed on the position they want to be in, which is at the top of the tree. When they have made it to the top, they want the world to see where they are, and to be impressed by it. At any stage in their career, they want you to notice how much better off they are than you, and to own things that show you their status: their fine house, the car in the drive, and so on. They never give anything away, and every ounce of their energy is devoted to furthering their career, creating a life of lasting quality and material comfort for themselves and their families.

You're strongly opposed to almost everything the Capricorn represents, and particularly for the reasons that he does it. You know that you could do all of that if you tried, because all you have to do is use your Saturnine energy the way he does, but you also know that if you did, you'd be slipping backwards. The only thing that you agree with in his methods is the fact that he's prepared to work long hours for what he really believes in, and you're like that too.

Everything the Capricorn wants out of life has a price tag on it. His goals are all material, so he doesn't give himself a lot of time to ponder ideas and principles. This isn't surprising; he's an Earth sign, after all. All the things you want out of life are without price, and most of them are not physical at all, because they are qualities and beliefs, like friendship, truth and justice.

He can see your talent for analysis and your ability to lead, and to motivate large numbers of people. He's sure that he could make a lot of money with that sort of ability, and he can't see why you don't. He can see that you have a large number of friends, but he can't see why you don't use them as business contacts. You're going to have a lot of trouble trying to explain yourself to him. He isn't very receptive to ideas, because he prefers practical examples. He's no good at catching nuances from your speech either, or at being imaginative. Most difficult of all perhaps, is his highly traditional point of view. The things that you consider logical, effective and innovative are unthinkable to him. You're only going to be friends if one of you crosses over to the other's territory (that is, if you're relapsing into material comfort, or if he's being unusually progressive), or if you're working together for the same organization, such as a political party. Without shared goals, you'll fight. All business partnerships between you will have to be that way, too. You'll both be able to work long and hard if you have a common target, but if that isn't the case, you'll criticize him for his mercenary motives and his lack of imagination, and he will feel resentful.

Marriage, because it often has shared goals, isn't a bad idea. Both of you prefer to work for a long period of time and neither of you expects instant results. Your personal relationship could be a bit cold and dry, though - two Saturn people don't generate much heat. As lovers, you prefer things lighter and more playful than Capricorn, but he's stronger than you are. He has a more developed sense of humor, too, even if it's something of an acquired taste. You like things cool and offbeat, though, so once you're used to each other, it would probably work very well.

Aquarius - Aquarius

Forming a relationship with somebody from your own sign is both a good and bad thing. You know more or less what you're getting, which is a good thing, but you're not getting anything fundamentally different from yourself, which means that you don't have to stretch your capabilities to accommodate them, so you don't make as much progress as you might.

In this case, the union is by no means as bad as it might be. In fact, it's one of the best of the same-sign pairings. The odd thing about it is that the relationship is rather slow to get going, but it improves as time goes on. If it survives the initial stages and turns into something with a long-term element in it, such as a marriage, then it may turn out to be the most satisfying relationship there is. Your traditional ruling planet is Saturn, and he's the lord of Time, which means that another Saturnine person can provide support and companionship at the level you want it, which is in a non-intense form and for the length of time that you want it.

Your relationship will be very friendly and sociable, which is hardly surprising, as both of you are virtually professional at socializing, and if you can't function on a social level then you can't function anywhere. You could go long a long way on just that level, as you needn't offer or demand each other's trust or affection, so you could keep things light and friendly, chatting away whenever you saw each other, going to cinema together or things like that.

When you deepen the relationship, you'll find that you have more mutual understanding than you had perhaps supposed. Each of you will need some time away from the other, some time when you can be alone with yourself and your thoughts. You need some changes of scene and company, and you don't like to stay in the company of any one person for too long. Who else could ever understand that but another Aquarian? Anyone from any of the other eleven signs would take your need for a few days alone as a signal to end the relationship, but you don't have to explain your motives to another Aquarian, and you understand the same behavior in them.

You make some strange demands on a close relationship. The friend must be similar to you, but different. You must both enjoy the company of others and be part of the crowd, but at the same time, you must feel that you're both separate and different from the crowd. Your partner must be close to you if you're to take the relationship seriously, but he mustn't be attached to you. He must let you go your own way, and alone if that's what you want, from time to time. Only another Aquarian can cope with that.

Friendship is no problem, but what about an affair? It's likely to be very enjoyable for both of you. If you let your imaginations go to work, you can have a wonderful time. There's a hint of it in the Aquarian soul, which could be persuaded, under these circumstances, to blossom into a pale and delicate romance. There's also a dry sort of electricity in you, the same power that makes you so zealous in support of your egalitarian ideals. If this power can be expressed sexually, then the two of you could make a crackling, sparkling, free form relationship, something very different from the sort of stuff the rest of the zodiac gets up to. What you have to guard against is taking your relationship too seriously: then Saturn makes your loving dull and earnest, and you lose all the fun from it.

In business, you become an extension of each other, but that doesn't mean that you're any more successful than you were separately. You'll still need somebody practical and somebody creative to help the business along – in other words, someone other than another Aquarian. In a marriage, you'll get better as time goes on. Your differences and your efforts to remain different from and independent of each other will keep you from becoming dull and inflexible. That way, the essential Aquarian spirit, which needs to stay mentally active, keeps going and keeps you going, too.

Aquarius - Pisces

The relationship you have with the sign that follows yours is always rather strange. You want so much to be part of their world, to progress to their stage in the cycle, but somehow it always seems to be unattainable. They know you very well, as they have already been where you are, so to speak, and they know that they can sink back into you when things get tough.

Pisces seems impossible for you to understand. You pride yourself on being able to handle ideas, and being an Air sign ought to give you a certain adaptability, but Pisceans are something else altogether. Whenever you try to pin them down, they slip away. Whenever you think that you understand what they mean, you find they meant something else. There doesn't seem to be anything constant about them, and your attempts to define the principle on which they work get you nowhere. The truth of the matter is that they don't work on any principle at all; they take on the behavior of what surrounds them. These people react emotionally to everything and everybody they meet and form a pattern of behavior from those responses.

To be so open to external influence is staggering to you, because you're the complete opposite. Though you take in all that you see and hear, very little of it has any real effect on you. You analyze it, examine it and remain unaffected by it for the most part. Pisceans are not nearly so controlled. They positively enjoy being swept away by an intensity of feeling or experience, and they live life in Technicolor, digital stereo sound and probably a few other processes yet to be invented.

It's difficult for the two of you to form a relationship that satisfies you both at once. If things are light and cool enough for you, then they are unlikely to be intense enough for the Piscean. A shared social life could be the answer, because Pisceans get as much enjoyment from their friends as you do, though in a different way. Another good idea is probably to share an interest in music, as that's something you both enjoy and that can serve as a starting point.

A deep relationship between you is bound to have its problems. Remember that the Piscean will pick up and reflect whatever you project, but if you want to be on your own for a while, the Piscean will feel completely isolated and abandoned, because he will have absorbed your emotional state. You'll need to be careful. Episodes like this will enable you to see why he's so difficult to pin down. If he absorbs the emotions of wherever he is, then he must have some means of distancing himself from those he doesn't want near him. It's his self-regulation mechanism, in the same way as being cool and logical is yours.

As lovers, you could have a wonderful time – or not! He will be able to recognize and reflect the slightest emotion from you, so it all depends on how much you want to put into it. The softer and more romantic you are, the warmer the response you'll produce in the Piscean. Sexually, Pisceans are capable of making any fantasy into reality - how imaginative are you between the two of you?

If you marry, the Piscean would keep things from becoming too static. They may be emotional, but they're not obsessive, so any rows would soon be over.

In business, you'd be better than you might think. Let the Piscean absorb some of your logical approach; In return, pay attention to the way he absorbs the feeling of what's going on. When he says that the time is right for a product or a service, it usually is.

The Approach to Relationships: Pisces

SYMBOL: THE FISHES	♓	ELEMENT:	WATER
PLANET: JUPITER	♃	QUALITY:	MUTABLE

Pisces is the most inward-looking of all the signs, and will receive, absorb and use any energy at all; you'll be quite unable to prevent yourself from doing it. You are sensitive to absolutely anything, and to things that other people ignore completely. Even the atmosphere generated by the furnishings in a room can be a powerful force by your standards; so are the emotions and intentions of other people, as are the colors they wear, or the weather today. Like a photograph, a Piscean will faithfully absorb and represent anything he is exposed to, and he will then come to resemble that thing so closely that he is indistinguishable from the original.

You are imaginative, sensitive and caring, but it may not be at all clear to you where you are supposed to be going. To some of you, it may not matter; if everything is in your imagination and you don't like what you're feeling now, you know that you only have to wait for a few minutes for another experience to come along: perhaps that one will be more enjoyable. You are so *passive*, you see; you wait to be moved by the circumstance rather than make active moves yourself. The purpose of your existence, though, is to move round the zodiac, and that means towards Aries: somehow, you have to define yourself and separate yourself from all the roles that you play.

Pisces - Aries

This is one of the most difficult relationships for you to form, although it's probably a little easier for you than it is for the Arian. It represents, in many ways, the unattainable ideal as far as you're concerned, in that all the things that you'd like to be, the Arian already is. By being nearby, you can have a taste of what it's like to be further round the zodiac than you are.

Aries is definite. He may not be much else, but he's certainly definite. He knows where he's going, and he knows how he's going to do things; what's more, he actually goes out and does them, without wasting any more time in thinking about them. His whole existence is centered on effective action, he's useless unless he's actually doing something, and he knows it. Consequently, he keeps himself as busy as he possibly can, and that way he stays happy. Being in action the whole time means that he's seldom at rest, and that he never has time to think. What's more, he never has time to consider the subtle qualities of things, and for that reason much of what you have to offer is lost on him. He simply isn't sensitive to the meaning of things the way you are. As far as he's concerned, what you see is what you get, and the physical qualities of anything are all that matter.

From your point of view, he's everything you find appealing, and everything you're trying to avoid, all in the same package. He's simple and straightforward in his approach to life, so much so that he seems naive at times. His physical strength and power are enormous, and yet you know that he wouldn't use them against you on purpose, because he has no malice in him. He's incapable of being devious or cruel, and you feel safe in his company. His emotions may be strong, but they are easy for you to understand, and he isn't trying to trap you. You're reassured by that thought.

One of the unexpected ways in which you suit each other is that you don't crowd each other's space. When an Arian has something to do, he concentrates on doing it, which means that he ignores other people. If the truth were told, he likes his own company best, because he doesn't like wasting time talking to people when he could be active. If you're in the way when he's busy, you'll sense it, and melt away in the usual Piscean manner. He won't mind in the least. In fact, he will rather appreciate it. On those occasions when you want to slip off and do something without him, he can usually find something else to do, so he won't be bothered.

You can see that your preference for mobility and his preference for getting on with the job are compatible, though not in the way that one would immediately think.

He sees Pisces as something almost akin to a fairy creature; a fascinating being that vanishes when he tries to pin it down. He never understands the range of the your imagination or emotional sensitivity, but he remains endlessly fascinated by it. He can see that you have none of his physical capabilities, and simply can't meet a problem head on and deal with it, so he feels that he ought to do this sort of thing for you. It's a good arrangement, though you'll have to do something in return.

What you will have to do will become apparent quite early on in the friendship. Arians have no sense of time, because to them, everything happens in an eternal present. Consequently, on the few occasions when they fail at something, they are terribly upset. Like toddlers, they can't imagine how they fell over, and how the pavement bit their knee, and how they are ever going to recover. Your job is to comfort them; it's something you're very good at, especially as they only need it for a few minutes, and you can melt away again afterwards.

You could succeed in business together, but probably only in the media, where your imagination would be useful. He has enough drive for both of you, but he needs directing over the long term, and you may not have the firmness of purpose for that.

You won't be able to complain about the intensity of the experience if you become lovers. Arians are all strength and drive, and you'll love it, provided that you can respond strongly enough in return.

As marriage partners, you could make a lot of progress in the early years, but after that it looks less promising. You'd eventually find him too simple and straightforward, unless he could somehow adapt to your way of thinking.

Pisces - Taurus

This is a very easy relationship to form, and a most relaxing one to be in, for both of you. It moves extremely slowly though, and there are no sudden moves. A friendship between you would have rhythms that would be noticeable over years rather than weeks, so if you want something snappy and rapidly changing, this isn't it.

What you will notice first about a Taurean is how steady they are. They are always going to do things their way and in their own time, and they don't let anything put them off. This can be very reassuring. It can also be very exasperating, because when you lose your temper with them, you won't have the slightest effect. You could beat your tiny fists on their chest with rage all day, and they wouldn't take any notice. Taurus is Fixed Earth, remember, and your Mutable Water just runs off it like the rain from the hills. Yes, I admit that the rain eventually erodes the hills, but it does take several lifetimes.

What you have in common with Taurus is an appreciation of the emotional qualities of material. This sounds impenetrable, I know, but there are some things that make you feel good just to be with them. Some houses are like this and some rooms. Favorite old pullovers are like this and so is a bowl of soup on a cold day. Pisceans appreciate the mood that these things generate, and feel reassured by it, while Taureans get to the same result from the opposite direction. They appreciate the substances in themselves, and feel reassured by their warmth, familiarity and rightness.

You'll realize at once that there are many things you could do together which you can both enjoy in your own ways. You'd probably enjoy going to the opera to enjoy the lavish sets, the sumptuous surroundings and the familiarity of a plot that your partner already knows, while you enjoy the fantasy and the drama of it all. Staying at home and entertaining is another example. Taureans are famous cooks, and they have an almost magical affinity with food. From your point of view, there are the evocative smells of the kitchen, the almost invisible feeling of satisfaction radiating from a Taurean as he does the cooking and the chatter of everybody at table. Both of you can enjoy the atmosphere of an event, and that forms a strong bond between you.

The problems arise when Taurus refuses to change or try something new. No matter how much you enjoy something, you do get bored with it after a while and you long for something else. Taureans simply don't; what's more, they won't change under any circumstances. You can find your way out by slipping away as you always do. Unfortunately, Taureans are very possessive, and they will be forced to act rather than to give you up. When this happens, the outcome is very upsetting for everybody concerned.

You appreciate their stability, reliability and appreciation of your sensitivity. They appreciate your softness and imagination, your recognition of the importance of the emotional side of things, and though it sounds rather harsh, the fact that you're no threat to their security.

If you like your quiet life together, it can go on for years, with friendship slipping easily into marriage. You stop them becoming dull by providing variety, while they stop you from floating away by providing an anchor. This can be very useful if the two or you are business partners, and is of course a sure recipe for a stable marriage. Only as lovers will your differences show. He will appreciate your sense of romance, but you're likely to be bowled over by the strength of his passion. Taureans have deep and powerful passions, but they take a while to get going.

Pisces - Gemini

This one probably isn't such a good idea. It's like a knife in the water. It glitters and flashes with a wicked attractiveness, but it's sharp and deceptive to the touch. Gemini is Mutable, as you are, and his greatest assets, like yours, are his mind and his imagination, but the similarities end there.

A Gemini analyses his surroundings, in a way that you don't. To him, every new thing is a puzzle, something that he can apply his mind to and solve. He takes situations and people apart, probing here and there, seeing what there is to see, looking at them from all possible angles; he examines them. When he has understood something, he plays with it if he can, to see if it does anything different or if it can be approached in another way. To you this process seems horribly clinical. He seems to lose completely the essence of the experience by dissecting it. You don't work like that; you let experiences wash over you, feeling their qualities as you absorb them. The major difference in your approach is that you're quite willing to be changed by the experience, and even to become part of it, while he's determined that he won't be affected by it. He's trying to understand things from an intellectual viewpoint, and as far as possible to leave emotional responses out of it. Geminis don't have the same facility with their emotions that you do, and they tend not to enjoy them.

Because he stands apart from the things that he deals with, and doesn't feel personally involved in the way that you do, he can be rather cruel. Anything is reasonable to him, if it helps him understand what is going on. The result of this is a curiously amoral viewpoint, which shows itself from time to time in his actions and, more frequently, in what he says. Geminis have a lot to say for themselves. They are the great talkers of the zodiac, and everything they experience is converted into words and re-broadcasts, in a similar process to the way you convert everything you experience into images which are stored inside your memory for creative re-cycling later. His experiences are for public consumption, whereas yours are kept for personal use.

If you remember the similarities that you share, you'll be able to handle him very well, and you may even be able to enjoy his ideas. What you won't enjoy though, is the way that he sometimes changes the truth of things. All he's doing is playing with the words, changing the order or making adjustments to the story from time to time. It amuses him to do so, just as it amuses you to fetch images from your imagination and replay them when you're bored. The only difference is that his games are played out as speech, and many people don't realize that they are games. He attaches no emotional weight to what he says, and he doesn't expect anyone else to either.

A friendship between you can be very bright and bubbly on the surface. After all, if you mix air and water, you can usually make bubbles. He will love analyzing your imaginative ideas and you'll probably enjoy absorbing his observations. If you're in a business where communication is involved, you could do very well indeed. It probably isn't a good idea to be your own bosses though, because you're both too changeable.

Being lovers will have its problems. Geminis have no sense of romance, because to their way of thinking, it's all sentimental nonsense; nor are they happy with the emotional demands of an intimate relationship. They are not particularly physical either, so you'd be much better off staying as friends. Marriage will be difficult. He will dismiss your impressionability as woolly- headedness, and you'll come to dislike his sharp intellect. Besides, neither of you likes too much stability.

Pisces - Cancer

Here, you find yourself in the company of somebody else whose view of life has the emotional side of things at the top. Cancer is a Cardinal sign though, and you're not, so you'll find to your surprise that these people are determined to have things their way, and you'll have no alternative but to do as they tell you.

It won't take you very long to feel familiar with the Cancerian point of view. They are careful, self-preserving individuals, and they make sure that any threats to their security are adequately dealt with in advance wherever possible. Cancerians work on the principle of defense rather than avoidance, though they have been known to dodge the issue at times;

their attitude is certainly one that you understand. They are very protective of those they care for. If you're part of a Cancerian's circle, you know that they are doing everything they can to shield you from harm, and to give you any emotional reassurance you may need on the inside.

Cancerians generate emotional energy. Scorpios collect it and Pisceans absorb and reflect it, but Cancerians actually generate it. Theirs is the original maternal instinct. The fact that they have an apparently endless source of inner strength is something you find quite wonderful, and you admire them very much. It seems so much better a thing to be than what you are at the moment; they seem to be able to do without effort all the things you have to work at.

It may help you to get your relationship into perspective if you consider that the two of you are separated by the scale on which you work. To be sure, the Cancerian cares deeply for others, because Cancer works on the level of a parent to a child when dealing with someone on an individual basis. Pisces is a much more widely dispersed form of the same energy. Pisces can care for everybody, and not just your immediate friends and relatives. What is concentrated in one place can't be everywhere at once, and vice versa.

A friendship between you will be very easily formed, and it's one in which you will instinctively know each other's likes and dislikes. Once you know each other a little better, you'll find that you allow the Cancerian to take the lead. Doing things in the way that works for him will work, but the odd thing is that he won't lead you anywhere new or interesting, so you'll soon become bored and wander off. You don't have the same kind of need for security, and you know that you can vanish when things get difficult, but he can't. You don't mind seeking out new experiences just to see what they're like, but you're sure to worry your Cancerian. You may be timid in comparison with some people, but against a Cancerian, you're positively rash.

Being lovers is likely to be a very rewarding experience for you both. Cancerians are stronger physically than you might imagine, but their true interest lies in the emotional relationship behind the sexual one. They are as sensitive to details as you are, but they have a stronger passion, which you will enjoy. The only trouble is that they are possessive. In marriage, you could be happy but you have to adjust to the fact that he isn't adventurous, while you want more that just sitting around. You both love children though, so this could be the glue that holds you together.

You may not get very far in business, because you may stand still and make no progress.

Pisces - Leo

Here you meet somebody who is different from you in every way, but who seems to have a great affinity with you. Leos don't have your love of variety, they are completely insensitive to the feelings of others at times, and yet you can't help liking them. The most useful way of comparing the two of you is by looking at actors and the way they perform. It's not a bad analogy, because you both feel very much at home in the theatre, and you may well meet your Leo in a theatrical setting. If a Piscean actor works through reflection, then the Leo works through projection.

You're well aware that you absorb and represent what people want you to be. When your audience looks at you, they see in you what they want to see, and you're happy to reflect their expectations back at them. Leos don't work that way at all. They project themselves through the role they are playing, so that their own energy shines out from behind the costume. Nobody in the audience is in the slightest doubt who it is that they are watching. They know that they are seeing the actor rather than the character, but they don't mind. Leos are the stars of the show, and the audience would rather see them being themselves than see them in character.

From your point of view, being close to a Leo can be a very good idea. They radiate warmth and fun, so wherever they are is the place to be. If you can absorb this from them (and that isn't hard for somebody like you) then you can have as good a time as they do. The clever part comes in being not quite as Leonine as they are, because there's only room for one of them in their world and they resent competition, but you're more sensitive than enough to spot that situation in its early stages, and melt back into the background for a while.

Together you'll have a very good time indeed. Everybody loves a Leo, and Leos have many friends. For somebody like you, who likes dramatic and interesting people who have plenty of variety, Leo's social circle should provide you with more than enough emotional energy for your needs. There are odd occasions when a Leo feels unloved and unsure of himself, and he's difficult to comfort then, but your ability to be there when you're needed, and not when you're not, is most likely to give the Leo what he needs.

He sees you as somebody who seems to sparkle all the more brightly as he puts more energy into you, and he likes to see that. He also sees you as an imaginative source of new ideas, which he can put into practice. He doesn't feel that he's stealing your ideas, because he knows that you probably don't have the capacity to make your dreams real in the way that he does, and he's right. It's a mutually beneficial arrangement. Your imagination is tied to his ability to organize and make things happen. Without your ideas, it must be said, he would run out of things to do.

Friendship between you looks like the attraction of opposites, and on the surface, it probably is. To begin with, you'll play roles with each other, preferring to stay behind your masks while you get to know each other better. Even when you've been together a long time, there will be little routines that you'll perform with each other for fun. At a deeper level, you'll realize that you're both really useful to each other over the long term, too, and that you really need each other to get the best from yourselves.

The only problem you will have as lovers is whether you can afford it all. Once Leo has shown you how to turn your fantasies into extravagant realities, it's difficult to stop.

As business partners, provided that the business itself isn't too dull, you'll be wonderful together. Similarly, marriage is a good idea too, as long as you don't let it become all work and no play. Keep things bright and the marriage can last forever.

Pisces - Virgo

You probably expect things to be difficult with a person who represents the opposite sign to your own, and you won't be disappointed. What is likely to annoy you more than anything else about him is his ability to pin you down and hurt you. The fact that he doesn't really mean to hurt you only makes it worse.

Virgo is a Mutable sign, just like yours is, and that means that he's at least as quick on the uptake as you, and he doesn't mind if things keep changing. He's an Earth sign though, and that gives him patience and endurance in a way that your Water sign doesn't. In addition, he deals with the real world, so feelings are very low on his list of priorities. His mind is sharp and penetrating, but it has a disconcerting dryness to it. Emotion and sentiment aren't there at all, and you'll find it difficult to come to terms with that. The overall feeling, as far as you're concerned, is one of precision. You're interested only in how your car feels, and whether a different one would make you feel any better. Virgos are interested in how their car works and whether they can do anything to make it any more efficient. In the same way, you eat the food that you enjoy, but Virgos eat the food that does them good.

Virgo understands everything in a very precise way. He will be able to say exactly what it is that you're doing and why. He will also be able to tell you how to do it better. This is a very painful process for you, because you like to please yourself and not to be pigeonholed. Your vagueness and constant mobility are both your greatest defense and your greatest pride, but Virgo can pin you down and tell you what you're doing. Speared fish tend to writhe a bit and you're no exception. The reason the Virgo does it though, is that he wants to help. Can you believe this? Not if you think about it. He's Mutable, as you are. His way of reacting to outside influences is to break them down and analyze them until he understands what makes them the way they are. Then he tries to make a better world by putting things back together in a better order. He tries to improve things where he can, for everybody's benefit. You see him as shortsighted, over-critical and unfeeling.

What you should see him as, is somebody who is as familiar with the workings of material things as you are with the workings of emotion and sentiment, but whose special interest leads him to examine smaller and smaller details, while yours leads you to deal with larger and more universal feelings and ideas. His energies are focused and concentrated while you're unfocused and diffuse. You're simply at opposite ends of the zodiac and that's all there is to it.

He sees you as disordered, vague, and something of a victim of circumstance. He can just about believe that such a person as you, completely unfamiliar with the details of the real world, can exist, but he's sure that you need his help. What he should see, and probably can't or won't, is that the world of the imagination is just as real as any other, and that being receptive opens up huge realms of experience which are otherwise inaccessible. His security comes from knowing what's going on, so he threatens your mobility and you threaten his view of the world.

As business partners, you'll need a calmer third person to work with you.

Friendship will only grow if you each trust the other not to invade your own world. As lovers, you'll find Virgo's range of response rather limited, while his unintentional criticisms may hurt you at vulnerable moments. Marriage may be too difficult, but there again, if the marriage is part of an extended family, with others there to act as a bridge for you, it may be possible.

Pisces - Libra

This relationship works best on an artistic level, as art, design and music are interests that you both share. As a relationship, this may be too soft. Both of you are known for your affability, for your willingness to fit in with other people's wishes and preferences. The trouble is that neither of you like making decisions, and if you're both looking for a lead from the other, then you may not find it anywhere.

You'll get a better idea of what is actually happening if you look at what the Libran is trying to do. He's not the kind of person who absorbs energy from others; that's your territory. What he's trying to do is to promote agreement and balance. He wants to find points of contact and points of agreement between himself and anybody else. He wants to link himself to you as a balanced partner, perfectly matching or counterbalancing all the quirks in your character with all of the quirks in his. The problem is that he can only do this on a one-to-one basis, but he feels a need to do it with everybody he knows. What he ends up with is a series of intimate friends, all of whom are convinced that they are uniquely special to him.

From your point of view, there's a good side and a bad side to this. The good side is that he usually has a varied and active social life because he needs to stay in circulation. Libra is an Air sign, and they need to keep moving. You're a fish who likes to swim in running water, so the two of you will enjoy being in the company of others as much as you enjoy being together.

The bad side is that you may feel tied by his idea of relationship. Librans aren't jealous, but relationships are the only things that really matter to them, and they can't function unless they have somebody by their side. While you may be quite happy and flattered to play that role for a while, there will come a time when you feel like slipping away for a bit. Without a partner, they are lost. How can you be the partner they need, who must counterbalance what they have to offer, when you can only absorb and reflect what you receive? The fact is that they need somebody firm and active to take the decisions for them, and preferably somebody with some sort of talent in the real world. Your world of moods and impressions is no place for a Libran, as he can only relate to one thing at a time.

Friendship between you is best if it centers on a shared interest. He would dearly love to add your sensitivity to his own artistic tastes, while your rather uncontrolled emotional whirl could benefit from some of his balance and order. Libran order isn't restricting in any way; it simply makes things nicer and puts them into a better relationship to each other. You could probably do with some of that. There's much that you can give each other and a lot that you can take. What you have to do is give and take freely, but with both of you standing up, unsupported. The moment you start to lean on one another, you'll fall over.

Should you fall in love, which is all too easy for you both, the affair may well resemble something from a Mills and Boon romance. Remember that such a relationship is a sort of ideal for a Libran, and he will enjoy the relationship far more than he enjoys the person with whom he shares it. You're similar. Your imagination goes into overdrive when you're given a chance to surround yourself with the paraphernalia of romantic love. In a way then, neither of you are really in love with the other person, which is possibly just as well.

In a long-term relationship, either in business or as a married couple, you both have problems with decision-making. At the end of the day, the Libran will probably be the one who makes the decisions, as his is a Cardinal sign, which is more decisive than your Mutable one, but it will take him time to make up his mind.

Pisces - Scorpio

This is the sort of thing you've been promising yourself. Like a diet of chocolate cake, it will do you no good and you know it, but you don't care a bit. Scorpio is a Water sign like yours is, but with the kind of force and intensity you can only dream about. It will chew you up and spit you out. You know that you can escape in your usual way, but you also know that he can probably find you, and you're not at all sure that you want to escape anyway. Scorpio is a very dangerous drug, but if addiction is the price of ecstasy, then you're prepared to pay.

Scorpio seems to have all that you've ever wanted. He's so sure of what he wants, for a start. When he has decided on something, he will go straight for it. It may take him a while to get it, because there will inevitably be people in the way, but he will get it in the end, and he won't take as long over it as many others would have done. Like you, he's sensitive to the feelings of those around him, and he lives in a world where hopes and wishes are much more important than bricks and mortar. He's not afloat or adrift in this world in the way that you are though, because he knows exactly where he's going, and he doesn't allow himself to be influenced by what's around him. His confidence in himself and his sense of purpose are much too sure for that. He's a predator in your home waters.

You want to bask in the power he puts out. He's so emotionally powerful that being near him is like getting a mild electric shock, and he makes you tingle. You deeply desire intense experience, and it doesn't matter much whether the experience is good or bad, as long as it's intense, so you'll find this person's company simply irresistible. Most people think that Scorpios are very sexy, and in a way, they are, because the energy of Mars is the only sort they have to play with. In real life, Scorpios do everything with the intensity that other people reserve for sex. You don't really care. It's simply the most intense energy you've ever experienced, and you want to be near the source of it.

What could he ever want from you? He has most of your sensitivity and he's far more effective and controlled, so as far as you can see, you have nothing that he could possibly want. However, he wants two things. One is superficial and another is from very deep down in your soul. He wants to be invisible and he wants your confidence in him. The first part is relatively easy to understand. Scorpio needs to know all that he can about everybody who is around him, and for that reason he has developed the habit of digging deeply into people's past history so that he has all the information he needs. Most people don't see this coming, but he feels that he's being dangerously obvious. Being able to disguise himself by fading into the background is something he would love to be able to do, but with his sense of identity and purposefulness still intact. The second part, about wanting your confidence, is more difficult. Scorpio is so powerful, so secretive and so keen on protecting himself that he doesn't trust himself, and that's the truth. You have the confidence to cast yourself upon the waters and see what comes along, but he dare not do that.

Therefore, he thinks that your habit of doing so is truly wondrous. Perhaps, over a very long time, you could teach him how to relax, to trust and not to worry.

Friendship, an affair, a marriage or going into business with a Scorpio all boil down to the same thing from your point of view. You're so helplessly drunk on his sheer magnetism that you're of almost no practical use to him anyway. Ask yourself this: do you really want a relationship that leaves you as limp as a wet rag from the intensity of it the entire time? Do you have the strength and endurance to cope with it?

Pisces - Sagittarius

This is a lot better than you'd think. Not only are both your signs Mutable, but you also share a ruling planet, which is Jupiter. Not many pairings work in this way. What you have in common is your optimism, your imagination and your sense of fantasy. Both of you have the genuine ability to greet the future with enthusiasm. You're both certain that it will be interesting and worthwhile. None of the other signs can do this. Partly, it comes from your belief that no serious harm will come, and partly because you both get bored easily, and therefore, welcome anything by way of a change or novelty.

Sagittarius doesn't live in a dream world in the same way that you do. He's in the real world, making huge progress and bounding along from one adventure to the next. His humor and optimism never let him down, and he gets out of trouble repeatedly by an almost uncanny blend of sheer talent and the most sublime good luck. He has imagination, and he has knowledge, because his mental capacities are the most highly developed of all of the Fire signs. He can think logically and clearly, but what characterizes his thoughts is that his heart is also in them. In other words, he believes in what he says, and it's the emotion behind the thought that makes him so attractive to you.

He doesn't have your sensitivity, and he would rather live in the real world than your world of moods and feelings, but he knows that your world exists and he's curious to find out more. His interest helps you warm to him. He's sure enough of his own position not to feel the need to challenge you or frighten you away. In addition, his enthusiasm and genuine good humor are there for you to absorb and enjoy. He doesn't cling, because he values his freedom, and assumes that you do the same. He's loyal and trustworthy though, because he's already so secure that there's no advantage for him in being dishonest. Besides, his principles are higher than that.

You see him as a sort of Labrador retriever: friendly, bouncy, loyal and always ready for a new adventure, and he seems so sure that it will be fun. When you look at the real world and the people in it, it always seems to you that they are having such a dull time. The Sagittarian is the only one who seems to have struck the right balance between responsibility and enjoyment, and who hasn't let the search for material security closes the doors of his imagination.

He sees you as representing the finer things in life and its subtler values, too. Whenever daily life gets too dull for him, a few minutes with you will re-awaken his imagination and let him see the meanings behind the things he does. This in turn re-awakens his intellect, his knowledge and his wisdom. He needs you as a sort of pure source, to which he returns from time to time for refreshment.

You wouldn't want to become each other, but you like and admire each other a great deal, so for this reason any friendship between you will be close and loyal. You might not want to become lovers, but if you do, you'll find that his bounciness extends to all areas of his life, often at the expense of subtlety. A marriage might work, because both of you have the humor and the imagination to see past the immediate problems to a brighter future ahead.

There are better business partnerships than this one, because you'd both sooner change directions than stick at something if it didn't work at the first attempt, but it's not at all bad.

Pisces - Capricorn

On the surface, there can be no more unlikely pairing than the soft and sensitive Piscean and the hardheaded, taciturn Capricorn. Yet, this is a useful and satisfying pairing. It's based on alliance and help rather than power and passion, but it's unaffected by being gentle, and it's deeper than it looks.

Capricorns are not the world's great communicators. They have a fairly fixed view of the world, and they work long hours to do what they see as their duty to those both above and below them in the order of things. They are well-regulated people who keep their feelings to themselves for the most part, and use any spare energy that they may have for self-improvement.

They are not dumb, but they take a while to get talking, and they are not very expressive. You're the ideal person to listen to them. They express their feelings as strongly as they can, but it takes someone as sensitive as you are to realize that they are in fact shouting. Capricorns are very grateful for the attention that you give them, and particularly for the way that you get the message the first time, so that they don't have to go through the agony of trying to express themselves twice. They don't like being told what to do, and they don't like people who pull them away from tasks. Luckily, you don't do either of those things. Your energies are too slight to move the Earth of Capricorn, and anyway you don't have enough push to change the direction of a Cardinal sign. Nor do you stay where you're not wanted, so when they are busy, you fade out of sight.

Like elephants, Capricorns never forget. If there's anything that you'd like them to do, they will do it for you, because you've been kind enough to listen to them. Therefore, they feel that they are in your debt. As it happens, there's a great deal that they can do for you, and they only have to move a muscle to do it, because they have only to be themselves. It's simply this: your own life can get a bit hectic from time to time, and you often allow yourself to get swept away by something that takes your fancy. It's very reassuring to have some kind of constant, something unchanging to which you can relate, and to which you can compare your experiences, a sort of anchor and yardstick in one. It's best for you if a person rather than a situation can supply the constancy, and in a Capricorn, you have exactly that. Capricorn will enjoy listening to your experiences. They will sound outlandish to him, and he will be very thankful that he doesn't live in your world, but he will enjoy hearing them nonetheless. You keep him up to date. The earth doesn't feel quite so dry and dull when the flowing water of Pisces has washed over it.

Friendship between you is a quiet and fond affair, often conducted over long periods of time. Neither of you needs frequency of contact to intensify the experience. It isn't going to get any more exciting, and anyway that isn't the point here. Besides, you both have plenty of other things to do, and if the other one were around more, he'd only be in the way.

As a lover, you might like his slow and traditional approach, but there again you might not. He will be constant, but that isn't always important to you, as you might be faithful to him or you might not, if you let yourself be swept away by newer and stronger passions. Marriage could be a good idea and it might be better than most people would imagine.

Everything with a Capricorn gets better over the long term, and you could benefit from his steadiness, provided that he doesn't expect you to be like him all the time.

Capricorn as a business partner is always a good idea, because business is his home ground. He will probably do more for you than you for him in this respect, so the best thing for you to do would be to reflect his energies and do things the way he does them. Given time, he will be very successful, so if you'd like to share in his success in return for being his companion and confidant, then stay with him.

Pisces - Aquarius

The relationship between yourself and the sign that's behind you in the zodiacal sequence is always difficult. The people of the preceding sign always seem to be particularly hostile to your way of life, and yet they can be a great support to you if you let them.

Aquarians are too cool for you. They are analytical, as you are, but while you might speak to him about your passion for Art with a capital "A", he will speak to you of the spirit of the times, the pleasing optical effect of regular and proportional shapes, and of the expressionist movement. What you consider achingly personal is highly impersonal to him and it can be explained and analyzed away. He won't allow you to believe that what you feel is in any way individual and unique, because that would prove that collective thought and universal opinions are not possible, and he couldn't live with that. He will encourage you to think and to express your thoughts, because he's an Air sign, but he doesn't hold with the business of feeling, which to you is the most important part of expression, and more important than thinking.

Perhaps it's because he can see the meanings that lie beyond our normal actions that the Aquarian upsets you so. He can appreciate your world, but he's so cool emotionally that he casts a very long shadow over your world of feelings, so it will be difficult for you to see him properly. You can get very angry with him. The thing that really makes you mad is how, for all his wide ranging interests and his willingness to get involved with political or humanitarian, he never really seems to get involved, or at least not by your standards. If his arguments or his beliefs carried him away, or if he cared enough for something to give his all to it just once, you'd forgive him. What you need is for his confounded know-it-all smartness to be completely submerged in the passion of the event, but you know it won't happen.

Do you know why you want this change? Because you fear that you just might be like he is. You have this nagging doubt in the back of your mind that you might be as cool and unmoved as he is, watching life's experiences float by you like so many video films. You're not like that though, as you're much, much more involved in life, because you're concerned to experience things as intensely as possible. You want to become each new thing as it passes, and you worry that you might not be using yourself as well as you might. That's what you don't like about Aquarians. They are what you see if you look over your own shoulder, showing you the sign before yours, and therefore, where you came from.

If you don't let him worry you, and you don't get angry, the two of you can have a very pleasant time. Aquarians love to socialize. In fact, they are at their very best in company, more so even than the rest of the Air signs. They are bright conversationalists too, so things need never be dull. Just don't look for the personal intensity of experience that's so important to you. They're not you. There are worse people to go into business with, but you won't enjoy their way of working.

It's probably not a good idea to become lovers. They are much less successful on a one-to-one basis, and they don't have the emotional range that you find so desirable. Marriage is possible but not necessarily a good thing, unless you're both prepared to try to see things from the other's point of view. You could do each other a lot of good, but you may not choose to see it that way.

Pisces - Pisces

A partnership with somebody from your own sign emphasizes the mutual talents and shortcomings of both. In the case of two Pisceans, it's almost impossible to say which way it will turn out; you can take your pick from hundreds of roles, and play any one of them.

Pisces, perhaps more than the other signs, works on more than one level at once. At the very least, there's an outward appearance and an inner meaning, and often there are quite a number of other things in between as well. Consequently, the union between two Pisceans can take almost any form. At the very highest level, it may be an almost psychic rapport between two musicians or dancers, who seem to know what the other is about to do. It may be a long and caring friendship, where each intuitively knows what the other would or wouldn't like, without having to ask. Then again, it may be two people from widely different lives, who trust each other and enjoy getting very drunk in each other's company.

You won't be able to give each other encouragement, but you'd be able to give each other discouragement, in that you'll be able to suggest escape routes to each other, so that you can avoid being decisive or definite about things. You can have no secrets from each other. Each of you is perceptive enough to be able to read the other quite easily. After a few exercises in one-upmanship, you should come to trust one another, simply because you have no alternative, and then you'll see that you have more to offer each other by being constructive and helpful. Eventually, you'll begin to use your relationship as somewhere to offload emotional rubbish that you pick up as you go along. You'll have a great deal of fun working through each other's experiences. It's a bit like living in a scrap yard, and after a while you get quite good at spotting the useable items from the junk.

You can stop each other from getting lonely. Only another Piscean can appreciate things on the sort of levels of meaning that are important to you, and therefore only another Piscean can help if you want to talk about those levels of experience, or to offload them onto somebody else. This isn't the sort of relationship you get into because you want it to go somewhere; this is the one you choose precisely because you know that it won't. This is the sloppy armchair of friendships. It's no good for your back and it doesn't look very smart, but you can come home, kick off your shoes and fall into it with a sigh. You know who your friends are.

For exactly those reasons, it makes a very poor business partnership. Neither of you is assertive enough to make your mark in the commercial world; you need somebody other than another Piscean to work with you.

As lovers, you're likely to encourage each other's worst habits. It will be a very private relationship, because you know that no outsider will be able to appreciate what is going on. At its highest level, it will be sublime and almost spiritual. At its lower levels, you'll simply indulge each other's sloppiness.

If you choose this pairing for marriage, it's because you definitely want it to be a retreat from the world, and somewhere you can stop acting for a while. Perhaps you have a strenuous public life, so while this is not an ambitious or progressive marriage, it could be just what you're looking for, and one place where you don't have to be invisible or to pretend.

A Last Word...

You can use this book to check your compatibility with your partner, or you can choose to look more deeply into the relationships that exist between the sun signs. If you decide to look further, go back to the first chapter (Zodiac Relationships), and look at the situation between your sign and those that are one, two, three, four, five or six signs away from yours.

The list below shows the zodiacal order in which the Sun signs appear. If yours is towards the end of the list, go down the list and then back to the top again, to check separation analysis between two signs. For example, if you are an Aquarian, go forward through Pisces and then work your way though Aries, Taurus, Gemini and so on.

THE SIGNS OF THE ZODIAC
Aries
Taurus
Gemini
Cancer
Leo
Virgo
Libra
Scorpio
Sagittarius
Capricorn
Aquarius
Pisces

Don't forget that there are facets of the sun sign preceding yours that you have shaken off or that you are bored with, while the sign following yours incorporates energies, talents, abilities and an outlook that you envy and may wish to emulate. For instance, a shy Virgo might envy the

Libran's happy knack of chatting to everyone he meets, while a courageous, pioneering Aries might look down on his sensitive and mystical Piscean predecessor.

I hope you find my book useful. I wish you the best of luck with all your friendships and relationships, and I hope this book increases your interest in astrology.

Bernard Fitzwalter

Index

Zambezi Publishing Ltd

We hope you have enjoyed reading this book. The Zambezi range of books includes titles by top level, internationally acknowledged authors on fresh, thought-provoking viewpoints in your favourite subjects. A common thread with all our books is the easy accessibility of content; we have no sleep-inducing tomes, just down-to-earth, easily digestible, credible books.

~~~~~

Please visit our website (www.zampub.com) to browse our full range of Mind, Body & Spirit, Lifestyle and Business titles, and to discover what might spark your interest next...

~~~~~

Please note:-

Our books are available from good bookshops throughout the UK, but nowadays, no bookshop can hope to carry in stock more than a fraction of the books published each year (over 200,000 new titles were published in the UK last year!). However, most UK bookshops can order and supply our titles swiftly, in no more than a few days (within the UK).

You can also find our books on amazon.co.uk, other UK internet bookshops, and on amazon.com; in the USA, sometimes under different titles and ISBNs. Look for the author's name.

Our website (www.zampub.com) also carries and sells our whole range, direct to you. If you prefer not to use the Internet for book purchases, you are welcome to contact us direct (our address is at the front of this book, and on our website) for pricing and payment methods.

Lightning Source UK Ltd.
Milton Keynes UK
24 March 2010

151771UK00002B/48/P